INTERNATIONAL SECURITY
AND PEACEBUILDING

INTERNATIONAL SECURITY AND PEACEBUILDING

Africa, the Middle East, and Europe

Edited by Abu Bakarr Bah

Indiana University Press

Bloomington & Indianapolis

This book is a publication of

Indiana University Press
Office of Scholarly Publishing
Herman B Wells Library 350
1320 East 10th Street
Bloomington, Indiana 47405 USA

iupress.indiana.edu

The paper used in this publication meets the minimum requirements of the American National Standard for Information Sciences— Permanence of Paper for Printed Library Materials, ANSI Z39.48–1992.

Manufactured in the United States of America

Library of Congress Cataloging-in-Publication Data

Names: Bah, Abu Bakarr, editor.
Title: International security and peacebuilding : Africa, the
   Middle East, and Europe / edited by Abu Bakarr Bah.
Description: Bloomington : Indiana University Press, 2017. |
   Includes bibliographical references and index.
Identifiers: LCCN 2016024833 (print) | LCCN 2016044068 (ebook) |
   ISBN 9780253023766 (cloth : alk. paper) | ISBN 9780253023841
   (pbk. : alk. paper) | ISBN 9780253023902 (ebook)
Subjects: LCSH: Security, International—Case studies. |
   Peace-building—Case studies. | Responsibility to
   protect (International law)—Case studies.
Classification: LCC JZ5588 .I5774 2017 (print) |
   LCC JZ5588 (ebook) | DDC 327.1/72—dc23
LC record available at https://lccn.loc.gov/2016024833

1 2 3 4 5   22 21 20 19 18 17

Contents

INTERNATIONAL SECURITY
AND PEACEBUILDING

Introduction

The Conundrums of Global Liberal Governance

Abu Bakarr Bah

THE END OF the Cold War was supposed to usher in a new era of real peace based on flourishing democracies and free market economies around the word. When Francis Fukuyama proclaimed the end of history, the idea was that democracy and free market economy had been proven to be better than all other systems in advancing freedom, prosperity, and peace.[1] While multiparty democracy and free market economy have spread to more countries, insecurity has also increased in many corners of the word.[2] Since the end of the Cold War, new forms of insecurity have emerged. Mary Kaldor refers to post–Cold War wars as new wars.[3] As Kaldor writes, new wars

> are wars that take place in the context of the disintegration of states (typically authoritarian states under the impact of globalization); wars that are fought by networks of state and non-state actors, often without uniforms . . . as in the case of the Croatian militia in Bosnia Herzegovina; wars where battles are rare and where most violence is directed against civilians as a consequence of counter-insurgency tactics or ethnic cleansing; wars where taxation is falling and war finance consists of loot and pillage, illegal trading and other war-generated revenue; wars where the distinctions between combatant and non-combatant, legitimate violence and criminality are all breaking down; wars that exacerbate the disintegration of the state. . . . Above all, these wars construct new sectarian identities (religious, ethnic or tribal) that undermine the sense of a shared political community.[4]

New wars, including terrorism warfare, have now become the key threat to international and regional security. New wars have plagued countries in Eastern Europe, the Middle East, South Asia, and Africa and sent refugees and fear to all other parts of the world, including Western Europe and the United States of America. At the same time, countries neighboring places where new wars are waged continue to receive huge influxes of refugees.

A critical question in addressing contemporary security challenges is whether the orthodox notion of new wars is applicable to wars related to the War on

Terror. This question is important as we seek to examine a wide range of international and regional security problems ranging from civil wars in Africa, typically centered on violent struggles to take over the government based on ethnic or regional interests, to the ethnonationalist wars in the former Yugoslavia, and the wars related to the War on Terror campaigns in Afghanistan and Iraq. Clearly, the post–Cold War civil wars in most parts of Africa (e.g., Sierra Leone, Liberia, Democratic Republic of Congo, and Côte d'Ivoire) and the former Yugoslavia aptly fit the orthodox notion of new wars. The more challenging question is whether the terrorism warfare waged in places such as Afghanistan, Iraq, and Nigeria is fundamentally different from the wars that have typically been referred to as new wars. In this book, we extend the notion of new wars to include the terrorism warfare that erupted in response to the United States invasion of Afghanistan and Iraq after the 9/11 terrorist attack. To make this extension, however, two important differences must be noted. First is the use of suicide and car bombings, which were not a common feature of the wars in former Yugoslavia and most parts of Africa. Suicide and car bombings, are common features of the terrorism warfare in Afghanistan and Iraq. The use of suicide and car bombings as modes of violence is most common in wars involving Islamist groups, such as in Iraq, Afghanistan, Nigeria, Somalia, and Libya. However, we see this difference as largely a matter of choice and availability of means. What is more important is that both terrorism warfare and orthodox new wars deliberately target civilians as a way to wage war. The second difference relates to the origins and evolution of the wars. Clearly, the terrorism warfare in Afghanistan and Iraq is largely the result of the United States' invasion of those countries in response to the 9/11 terrorist attack. In contrast, the orthodox new wars in the former Yugoslavia and African countries are rooted in domestic political, social, and economic grievances. However, the wars in Afghanistan and Iraq have significantly evolved from their original character as resistance to United States invasion to sectarian wars. In both countries, the wars are now significantly driven by domestic grievances. As Deniz Gökalp shows in her chapter on Iraq, the current violence in Iraq is largely about sectarian struggles for power among Sunnis, Shi'i, and Kurds after the disintegration of the Iraqi state. In Afghanistan too, the war is largely a sectarian struggle for power that pits various ethnic groups against one another and Islamists against secularists.[5] The degeneration of the wars in Afghanistan and Iraq from resistance to United States invasion to largely sectarian wars over power is what makes those wars similar to the orthodox new wars we have seen in former Yugoslavia and most parts of Africa. For us, the notion of new wars is a useful concept for understanding the variety of cases of wars waged by nonstate actors in which the state has disintegrated and the distinction between "legitimate violence and criminality are all breaking down" and "new sectarian identities (religious, ethnic or tribal) that undermine the sense of a shared political community" are firmly entrenched.[6] Whether combatants use bombs or light weapons or they began the fight as resistance to foreign invasion or due to domestic grievances, the reality is that they are all producing generalized violence that is devoid of any meaningful social justice cause and undermining human security in ways that necessitate robust international intervention.

New wars have been not only recognized as major threats to security, but also attributed to lack of democracy and poverty.[7] Insecurity has increasingly been tied to lack of democratic governance and economic and social development. As such, democracy and free market economy, promoted through noncoercive and coercive means, combined with international development aid have become the key means for maintaining security in the poor and unstable countries of the world. This security-democracy-development matrix is embodied in what Mark Duffield has dubbed global liberal governance.[8] Global liberal governance has become a problematic solution to new wars. In a post–Cold War context, global liberal governance is a Western ideological and policy mechanism for maintaining security and development around the world in accordance with the interests of Western governments, NGOs, military establishments, and private companies. Global liberal governance primarily rests on policies of robust international intervention (including the use of military force) and postwar reconstruction in countries experiencing new wars as embodied in the doctrine of responsibility to protect (R2P), which developed through the United Nations (UN) in the aftermath of the genocides in Bosnia-Herzegovina and Rwanda, and the War on Terror.[9] In principle, global liberal governance should be a benign way of promoting Western security interests and securing the human security needs of people in poor and fragile non-Western countries. However, the realities of new wars and global liberal governance raise critical questions about international interventions and state building under the banners of R2P and the War on Terror: Whose interests are promoted through international interventions and state building? What are the moral and practical challenges of promoting peace and security through international intervention? How successful are international interventions and state building in promoting democracy, peace, and development? All of these questions point to moral ambiguities and practical challenges in the application of R2P and the War on Terror under the guise of state building, which are the hallmarks of global liberal governance.

Roughly three decades after the outbreak of the first catastrophic post–Cold War new wars in former Yugoslavia and Rwanda, the questions raised above are even more pressing as global liberal governance continues to be pursued as the remedy to human insecurity in countries such as Iraq, Syria, Yemen, Afghanistan, Libya, Sudan, Somalia, Democratic Republic of Congo (DRC), and Mali. This edited book interrogates the issues raised in the above questions through theoretical, historical, and empirical studies of international interventions in Afghanistan, Iraq, Bosnia-Herzegovina, and various African countries. The chapters contribute to the discourses on security, human security, peacebuilding, and international state building by interrogating the moral and practical challenges of military humanitarianism and international state-building ventures geared toward enhancing security through global liberal governance. The chapters expand on some of the issues discussed at two sessions on humanitarian intervention and international state building at the 2014 International Sociological Association conference in Yokohama, Japan.[10]

As with all studies, this book is selective in its geographical discussion of cases. The book consists of three chapters on Africa and one chapter each on Afghanistan, Bosnia-Herzegovina, and Iraq. It also contains one chapter that draws generally from across all regions. Clearly, there are more cases on Africa and none from Latin America. The focus on Africa and to a lesser extent on Eastern Europe, Middle East, and South Asia is driven by the preponderance of cases of new wars and corresponding international interventions based on R2P and the War on Terror in those regions. This book is not just about insecurity and new wars. Rather, it is more about the exertion of global liberal governance through explicit claims to R2P and the proclaimed justifications of the War on Terror. As such, the chapters in this book deal only with new-wars cases where there has been robust international intervention under the banners of R2P and/or the War on Terror.

Since the emergence of what have been dubbed new wars in the post–Cold War era, global liberal governance under the banners of R2P and/or the War on Terror has been applied in countries such as former Yugoslavia, Afghanistan, Iraq, Libya, Sierra Leone, Liberia, Côte d'Ivoire, and Mali. In all of these cases, international intervention has been based on strong United Nations Security Council mandate (typically under Chapter VII of the UN Charter) or the firm commitment of the United States to state building under the ambit of its War on Terror. By focusing on contemporary new wars that have led to robust international intervention, this book excludes the Cold War–related conflicts in Latin America and the ongoing conflict in Colombia and other forms of major violence in countries such as Mexico, El Salvador, Guatemala, Honduras, and Nicaragua.[11] Currently, the only United Nations (UN) peacekeeping mission in the Americas is the UN Stabilization Mission in Haiti (MINUSTAH). MINUSTAH was established in 2004 to deal with the conflict that followed the exile of President Jean-Bertrand Aristide. However, since the 2010 earthquake in Haiti, the mission has largely shifted to supporting the recovery and reconstruction effort. Apart from Haiti, there are no international humanitarian interventions currently in the Americas. In fact, the last UN mission in the region, apart from Haiti, was the UN Verification Mission in Guatemala, which ended in 1997.[12] While Latin America has had brutal civil wars (e.g., Colombia, Nicaragua,

El Salvador, Mexico), those civil wars fall outside the scope of this book because they are Cold War–era conflicts that occurred before the emergence of the doctrine of R2P or the War on Terror.

The Middle East and the wider Muslim world has also been experiencing new wars, most notably in Afghanistan, Pakistan, Iraq, Syria, Yemen, and Libya. However, only Afghanistan, Iraq, and Libya have so far experienced robust international intervention under R2P and the War on Terror. Each of these three countries is covered in this book. Though the War on Terror has been clandestinely waged in Pakistan, Syria, and Yemen, R2P-based intervention or international state building has not been robustly applied to those countries. So far, the interventions in Pakistan, Syria, and Yemen are mostly covert counterinsurgency operations, rather than overt operations to restore order and rebuild the state.[13] The only UN peacekeeping missions in the Middle East and Muslim world are missions that relate to the Arab-Israeli conflict and boundary issues, which are weak UN observer missions that are outside the realm of R2P or international state building.[14] Thus, the Middle East and the Muslim world actually provide very limited cases of robust international intervention, beyond the ones discussed in this book.

The limited application of R2P in new wars is also evident in Europe. Though there have been new wars in Eastern Europe, R2P has not been applied there, except for former Yugoslavia. In particular, the wars in Georgia, Chechnya, and Ukraine have not received any meaningful international humanitarian interventions, largely due to Russian military power.[15] The only international interventions in those areas are clandestine or overt Russian military operations in pursuit of its own national interests. As with the Middle East and the Muslim world, there are very limited cases of R2P-based intervention in Europe beyond the case of former Yugoslavia discussed in this book.

In contrast to the other regions, Africa has experienced substantial international interventions since the end of the Cold War (e.g., Sierra Leone, Liberia, Côte d'Ivoire, DRC, Libya, and Mali). In 2015, for example, nine out of the sixteen UN peacekeeping missions were in Africa.[16] With the exception of the UN Mission for the Referendum in Western Sahara (MINURSO), all the missions in Africa have very strong UN mandates to protect civilians based on R2P principles. Currently, Africa is the only region with such strong UN missions. Moreover, Africa is the only region that has developed a regional R2P doctrine.[17] Through its doctrine of nonindifference, the African Union (AU) has developed a mechanism for robust international intervention in African new wars. The combination of insecurity in Africa and the AU's willingness to apply R2P in partnership with the UN, European Union (EU), and North Atlantic Treaty Organization (NATO) has made Africa a prime region for studying R2P and global liberal governance in the post–Cold War era. As Abu Bah notes in chapter 6, the AU has become a partner in the application of global liberal governance in Africa. However, as Dauda Abubakar argues in his discussion of Libya and Sudan in chapter 2, that partnership is firmly subjugated to Western interests.

The works in this book not only provide rich analyses of the applications of global liberal governances, but also provide insightful comparisons within and across regions. Collectively, the chapters show the similarities and differences in the factors that lead to global liberal governance, its application, and its effects. Such similarities and differences are evident within African cases and among regions. The application of global liberal governance to new wars is a phenomenon that naturally lends itself to comparative analysis because of the diversity of regions and contexts within which R2P and the War on Terror have been exerted. In an edited book, such comparisons flow from the very selection of cases and the contents of specific chapters. The comparisons within and across chapters not only deepen our understanding of global liberal governance, but also point to lessons about the potentials and limitations of global liberal governance in fostering security and building peace.

Military Humanitarianism and International State Building

International interventions in new wars have both humanitarian and military dimensions. This military humanitarianism is rooted in the doctrine of R2P and the proclaimed justifications of the War on Terror. Since the end of the Cold War, there has been an increase in military humanitarianism, in both its R2P and War on Terror variants. Military humanitarianism has become a major vehicle for the exertion of global liberal governance.[18]

In principle, the War on Terror is geared toward enhancing the national security of the United States and its allies through legitimate self-defense means. Moreover, the United States, especially under the administration of George W. Bush, has presented the War on Terror as a fight for human freedom and dignity and an effort to build democratic states that can be models for peace and progress in the Middle East. Under the Bush doctrine in particular, the War on Terror has had a far-reaching scope that includes preemption.[19] The War on Terror has been varyingly presented as an appropriate self-defense strategy, a benevolent mission to protect vulnerable people against jihadists at home and abroad, and a civilizing mission to promote democracy and human development. Often, it is presented as a stark choice between good and evil.[20] However, the context of the War on Terror varies significantly. For example, the War on Terror waged in Afghanistan was a direct response to the 9/11 terrorist attack on the United States. Moreover, the overwhelming evidence pointed to Al-Qaeda, which was based in Afghanistan with the consent of the Taliban government of Afghanistan, as the mastermind of the terrorist attack.[21] In that sense, the invasion of Afghanistan can be viewed as a reasonable case of self-defense and retaliation for an act of aggression by a terrorist nonstate actor.[22] In contrast, the United States' invasion of Iraq occurred in the context of debates about Iraqi violations of UN resolutions on weapons of mass destruction. Even more problematic is that US claims about Iraqi violations of UN resolutions and possessions of weapons of mass destruction were not sufficiently valid. As such the extension of the War on Terror to Iraq has always been seen as aggressive assertion of dubious national interests.[23] Ironically, the War on Terror has produced terrorism in places were terrorism was not present. In the case of Iraq, War on Terror–induced terrorism has become a justification for waging the War on Terror in Iraq and more recently in Syria. The terrorism warfare that emerged in Iraq in the aftermath of the United States invasion has now erupted in neighboring Syria. Depending on the context, the War on Terror can be viewed as an acceptable self-defense and an effort to protect civilians or a mere case of aggression. One of the central problems of the War on Terror has been the blurring of the line between self-defense and aggression.

Despite the seeming humanitarian connections between R2P and the War on Terror, the former is distinct. R2P is "the idea that sovereign states have a responsibility to protect their own citizens from avoidable catastrophe—from mass murder and rape, from starvation—but that when they are unwilling or unable to do so, that responsibility must be borne by the broader community of states."[24] Unlike the War on Terror, R2P, in principle, is centered on the human security needs of the people at the country where R2P is applied, instead of the interests of the states applying R2P. Moreover, R2P emerged out of series of concrete international deliberations on the meaning of sovereignty and the relation between sovereignty and international peace and security as outlined in Chapters I, VI, VII, and VIII of the UN Charter.

R2P principles can be traced back to the establishment of the Red Cross in 1864 and later UN resolution 260 of 1948 (i.e., Convention on the Prevention and Punishment of the Crime of Genocide). However, those developments do not fully capture the current notion of R2P, which took clear policy meaning after the genocides in former Yugoslavia and Rwanda. The R2P debate goes back to the use of the term "Sovereignty as Responsibility" by UN officials in the 1990s.[25] The basic idea was that the persistence of crimes against humanity, war crimes, genocide, ethnic cleansing, and the like requires a fundamental rethinking of the Westphalian notion of sovereignty as the autonomy of self-interested states in global affairs. They argued that sovereignty should necessarily entail responsibility on the part of governments to protect their citizens. Key elements of this argument were articulated in former UN secretary-general Boutros Boutros-Ghali's 1992 report, "An Agenda for Peace, Preventive Diplomacy, Peacemaking and Peace-keeping" and former UN secretary-general Kofi Annan's 1999 paper, "Two Concepts of Sovereignty."[26] This line of thinking about the relation between state sovereignty and the responsibility of states to protect their citizens was expanded on by the International Commission on Intervention and State Sovereignty (ICISS) and the Commission on Human Security (CHS), which respectively produced their reports in 2001 and 2003.[27] In its report, ICISS states that "the responsibility to protect acknowledges that the primary responsibility in this regard rests with the state concerned, and that it is only if the state is unable or unwilling to fulfill this responsibility, or is itself the perpetrator, that it becomes the responsibility of the international community to act in its place. In many cases, the state will seek to acquit its responsibility in full and active partnership with representatives of the international community. Thus the 'responsibility to protect' is more of a linking concept that bridges the divide between intervention and sovereignty."[28] The 2001 report of the ICISS was discussed at the September 2005 World Summit held at the UN headquarters in New York. In October 2005, the UN General Assembly adopted the 2005 World Summit Outcome, which provided further legal basis for R2P.[29]

R2P has domestic and global dimensions of sovereignty, which expands sovereignty from state sovereignty to popular sovereignty centered on human security. This dual aspect of sovereignty is well articulated in the 2005 World Summit Outcome. In the first place, "each individual State has the responsibility to protect its populations from genocide, war crimes, ethnic cleansing and crimes against humanity. This responsibility entails the prevention of such crimes, including their incitement, through appropriate and necessary means." The international community is called on to appropriately "encourage and help States to exercise this responsibility and support the United Nations in establishing an early warning capability."[30] Globally, the 2005 World Summit Outcome states, "The international community, through the United Nations, also has the responsibility to use appropriate diplomatic, humanitarian and other peaceful means, in accordance with Chapters VI and VIII of the Charter, to help to protect populations from genocide, war crimes, ethnic cleansing and crimes against humanity." It called on states to "take collective action, in a timely and decisive manner, through the Security Council, in accordance with the Charter, including Chapter VII, on a case-by-case basis and in cooperation with relevant regional organizations as appropriate, should peaceful means be inadequate and national authorities are manifestly failing to protect their populations from genocide, war crimes, ethnic cleansing and crimes against humanity."[31]

Similar debates have occurred in the scholarly works on security and international intervention. Proponents of R2P principles anchor international intervention, including the use of force, in the moral imperative to rectify wrongs and protect the innocent under natural law.[32] They distinguish state security from human security and decouple the security interests of the state and its power elite from the human rights and safety of the citizenry. Despite the strong support for the promotion of human security through international interventions, military humanitarianism has been questioned as reinforcement of the vestiges of colonialism and a skewed way of legitimatizing domination in the name of humanitarianism.[33] At best, Mark Duffield sees military humanitarianism as simply part of an emerging system of global liberal governance dominated by the northern strategic networks and complexes (i.e., Western governments, NGOs, military establishments, and private companies).[34] Even more problematic, Laurence McFalls characterizes military humanitarianism as a form of iatrogenic violence—social disruption and political violence produced by the very intervention aimed to prevent violence. This iatrogenic violence, which typifies military humanitarianism, casts doubts on the wisdom of military humanitarianism even in cases where the humanitarian imperatives have been strong and the operations deemed successful.[35] This iatrogenic violence is best exemplified in Gökalp's chapter on Iraq and Abubakar's chapter on Libya. One of the key concerns of the scholarly critiques of military humanitarianism is the misuse of legitimate international principles, such as R2P, for the political and economic interests of military powers. Rebecca Gulowski's chapter examines how R2P can be misused, while successfully being framed as benevolent, morally justified, and legal action, and thereby create a distorted form of legitimacy rooted in distorted communication.[36] In the end, genuine human security problems and legitimate self-defense situations are mixed with hidden and dubious national security agendas in ways that cast generalized doubts about the utility of military humanitarianism as a justified path to international security and peacebuilding.

While R2P and the War on Terror are different in terms of origin and strategic objectives, the two are increasingly been merged under global liberal governance, especially in terrorism warfare. Libya is a case where R2P and the War on Terror was merged into a single NATO military humanitarianism mission. As Abubakar notes in chapter 2, however, that mission was very problematic because it vividly exposed the mixed-motives problem of Western powers and the misuse of R2P. Afghanistan and Iraq also show how professed War on Terror missions have been sustained beyond their immediate vengeance and regime change goals by transforming the wars into security-cum-humanitarian missions. As Gökalp shows in chapter 7, the application of the War on Terror to Iraq produced a veritable human security crisis, which has been used to give the War on Terror R2P qualities. Evidently, the use of military force in the War on Terror has generally been presented by the United States and its allies as missions to protect civilians (abroad and at home) from the terrorism of radical Islamists groups, such as Al-Qaeda and Islamic State in Syria and the Levant (ISIL). Moreover, military missions are accompanied by state-building programs. In this sense, the War on Terror is presented as primarily humanitarian along the lines of the principles embedded in R2P.

Both the R2P and War on Terror variants of military humanitarianism see international state building as a critical part of promoting human security and ensuring regional and international security. In essence, global liberal governance sees military humanitarianism as a first step toward security, which must be boosted with democratic governance and social and economic development. In its most benevolent form, international state building is an elaborate postwar reconstruction effort to transform a war-torn country into a functional democracy on the path to economic growth, human development, and sustainable peace.[37] As the ICISS states, "The responsibility to protect implies the responsibility not just to prevent and react, but to follow through and rebuild. This means that if military intervention action is taken—because of a breakdown or abdication of a state's own capacity and authority in discharging its 'responsibility to protect'—there should be a genuine commitment to helping to build a durable peace, and promoting good governance and sustainable development. Conditions of public safety and order have to be reconstituted by international agents acting in partnership with local authorities, with the goal of progressively transferring to them authority and responsibility to rebuild."[38] In the case of Bosnia-Herzegovina, postwar reconstruction was to solidify peace and smoothen ethnic animosities.[39] Similar commitments to international state building have been made under the War on Terror, most notably in Afghanistan and Iraq. In both countries, the United States, especially under the Bush admiration, pursued an ambitious state-building strategy as a way to defeat terrorism and create good allies in those countries.[40] As Gökalp notes in her chapter on Iraq, United States sought to engineer democracy and economic liberalization in Iraq. In both Iraq and Afghanistan, political and economic liberalism dovetail with efforts to rebuild infrastructure, such as schools, roads, and hospitals.

International state building is predicated on restoration of peace through negotiated settlement or military defeat of the antidemocratic forces in the conflict.[41] In practice, postwar reconstruction is a fluid process that is often plagued by lingering insecurity, lack of sufficient funds, and divergences between the priorities of local and external actors.[42] While military humanitarianism is the pacification phase of global liberal governance, international state building is supposed to be the more humane and lasting side of global liberal governance. In many ways, international state building is the nonmilitary aspect of peacebuilding in new war situations. Under global liberal governance, state building should create the political, social, and economic conditions for sustainable peace and provide social legitimacy for military humanitarianism. In essence, international state building is supposed to yield concrete improvements in the security, political, economic, and social conditions of countries subjected to international intervention that would validate the human security, democracy, and development claims of global liberal governance. In cases where international state building fails, especially in its initial and immediate phase, global liberal governance increasingly becomes dubious and creates new conditions for violence. Like the iatrogenic violence of military humanitarianism, the failures of international state building pose moral and practical challenges for promoting security through global liberal governance.

The success of international state building is very much tied to the success of the military humanitarianism. In cases where R2P is misused or the War on Terror unjustifiably waged, military humanitarianism faces local resistance, which equally undermines international state building.[43] In those kinds of situations, global liberal governance tends to fail—militarily, economically, and/or socially. Perhaps one critical issue that is often overlooked in sweeping analyses of global liberal governance is the context in which military humanitarianism and international state building occurs. Iraq, Afghanistan, and Libya all show that when the national security and economic interests of the intervening powers are deeply rooted in the country where global liberal governance is applied, global liberal governance produces morally intolerable iatrogenic violence leading to violent local resistance to military humanitarianism and international state building.

Notwithstanding the problems associated with global liberal governance, there is real need for appropriate and sufficient responses to new wars. Terrorism-related new wars should be addressed through proportionate and thoughtful security and diplomatic measures, while orthodox new wars are approached through genuine application of R2P. Indeed, R2P emerged as a specific response to the failures of traditional peacekeeping approaches based on unrealistic expectations of neutrality. As Unsal Sigri, M. Abdulkadir Varoglu, and Ufuk Basar note in their chapter on EU peacekeeping in Bosnia-Herzegovina, the first- and second-generation UN peacekeeping missions were inadequate for the new wars that emerged after the Cold War, which led to the third-generation peacekeeping missions based on R2P principles. Indeed, it is difficult to make the case that the world would have been a better place without R2P. Clearly, third-generation peacekeeping missions have enhanced human security and promoted regional peace in countries such as Sierra Leone, Liberia, Côte d'Ivoire, Burundi, and Bosnia-Herzegovina.[44] Arguably, a timely application of R2P would have averted the genocides in Rwanda and Bosnia. Similar arguments can be made for robust peace mediation combined with robust peacekeeping based on R2P. As Amy Niang notes, robust peace mediation by President Blaise Compaoré of Burkina Faso worked better than orthodox peace mediation in Côte d'Ivoire, even with Compaoré's notorious record on African conflicts and obvious support for the rebel movement in the Ivoirian civil war. Despite the lack of real postwar reconciliation, military humanitarianism has ended the Ivoirian civil war. Even more important, robust peace mediation under the Ouagadougou Peace Accord led to the resolution of the citizenship dispute, which was the central issue in the civil war.[45] A key feature of Compaoré's successful peace mediation in Côte d'Ivoire was his ability to exert personal sovereignty in the process in a way that is akin to the international appropriation of sovereignty under R2P.

A critical question in gauging the benefits of global liberal governance is the extent to which military humanitarianism and international state building are supported or resisted by the people where international intervention occurs. In cases where international intervention is driven primarily by genuine humanitarian reasons and the political and economic interests of intervening powers are moderate, global liberal governance is more likely to be accepted and contribute to the enhancement of human security and regional peace. As Gulowski points out in chapter 2, the key issue in R2P is legitimacy. Too often, intervening powers seek to gain legitimacy at home through a deliberate discourse of humanitarianism and security. Another aspect of the legitimacy question is how people in countries undergoing new wars feel about international intervention. In Bosnia-Herzegovina and many African countries, international intervention under the ambit of R2P has been welcomed and seen as a necessary means for protecting vulnerable people from militants and oppressive security forces. In Sierra Leone, Liberia, and Côte d'Ivoire, robust Economic Community of West African States and UN interventions under Chapter VII of the UN Charter became necessary to restore human security.[46] In Sierra Leone and Liberia, there was overwhelming support for UN intervention. Even in Côte d'Ivoire, a significant portion of the population supported international intervention. In all three countries, peace has been restored, postwar reconstruction is progressing, and democracy is developing. The problems typically associated with military humanitarianism in these kinds of cases are logistical issues, abuses committed by individual peacekeepers, inefficiency, and failures to reach peace agreement or properly implement agreements.[47] While these kinds of problems do impede the success of peacekeeping missions, they do not typically amount to wholesale rejection of international intervention. As Sigri et al. actually note in their chapter on Bosnia-Herzegovina, many of these micro-level problems can be resolved. Niang's chapter on Côte d'Ivoire provides rich nuances on the political economy of peace mediation and the challenges associated with the election-driven approaches to peacebuilding. Her chapter captures the contradictions in international peace mediation and the need for creative and localized approaches to peacebuilding, which may fall outside of the ambit of Western approaches to global liberal governance. Despite the contradictions, international intervention was critical in ending the civil war in Côte d'Ivoire. Similar arguments about the benefits of R2P can be made based on the experiences of the former Yugoslavia. In these kinds of successful applications of R2P, international interventions are interwoven with efforts to negotiate a comprehensive peace agreement that would lead to multiparty elections. Because the core grievances in these kinds of cases are virtually domestic, democracy combined with generous postwar reconstruction support tend to provide a useful base for long-term peacebuilding.[48]

The real challenges for global liberal governance are the cases where military humanitarianism and international state building are resisted by a significant portion of the people in the country where global liberal governance is applied. Typically, these are cases where international intervention is primarily driven by the interests of the intervening powers. War on Terror–related new wars typically fall into this category as most evident in Afghanistan, Iraq, and Libya. In these kinds of cases, military humanitarianism and international state building become very difficult even when the wars devolve into primarily domestic matters. As Gökalp shows in her chapter on Iraq, even when occupation formally ends and the vast majority of foreign forces withdraw, international state building continues to be resisted because it is associated with the vested political and economic interests of the occupying powers. A similar situation exists in Afghanistan, where the Taliban continues to see international state building as simply part of the occupation. Such skepticism about the humanitarian claims of the War on Terror is intensified by apparent contradictions between professed values of international missions and practices on the ground. In their chapter on Afghanistan, Michelle Schut and Eva van Baarle examine the responses of Dutch military personnel in Afghanistan when faced with moral dilemmas, such as sexual violation of children, most notably the dancing boys (*bacha bazi*). In particular, they note that Dutch military personnel refuse to intervene due to either improper training on how to deal with such human rights violations or strategic decisions to not undermine the good relations they have with their Afghan collaborators. Such failures are likely to increase accusations of double standards and expediency in the application of human rights principles. Even more problematic is the economic aspect of international state building. As Gökalp argues in the case of Iraq, for example, international state building is largely seen as brute capitalist exploitation.

Themes and Scope

The chapters in this book address a wide range of challenges associated with military humanitarianism and international state building in Afghanistan, Bosnia-Herzegovina, Iraq, Côte d'Ivoire, Libya, Sudan, and Africa as a whole. Collectively, the works provide theoretical and empirical critiques of the application of global liberal governance through R2P and the War on Terror. More importantly, the chapters examine specific forms of dilemmas and challenges that are associated with international security and peacebuilding under global liberal governance. Three prominent themes crosscut all the chapters. First is the moral dilemma and legitimacy issues associated with military humanitarianism.

The second theme relates to practical micro-level challenges and moral dilemmas in international peacebuilding and state building that actors (e.g., peacekeepers, military person, and peace mediators) typically face on the ground. The third theme deals with the effects of and reactions to global liberal governance, most notably in the forms of co-optation and resistance.

The first theme, relating to moral dilemmas and legitimacy, is most evident in the two chapters written by Gulowski and Abubakar. Gulowski's chapter examines the discursive nature of R2P and the conflicting narratives about legitimized use of force. Based on a largely philosophical approach, she frames international interventions in terms of what she refers to as the "order of violence." Using insights from the international interventions in places such as Sierra Leone and former Yugoslavia, various international norms on humanitarian intervention, and the "Just War" discourse, she argues that the use of violence under R2P is largely legitimized through deliberate narratives aimed at convincing Western audiences that military intervention is desired and based solely on humanitarian principles. However, Gulowski points that these narratives are often disingenuous or, to use the language of Jürgen Habermas, they are systematically distorted to mask more cynical security and political interests.[49] For Gulowski, one of the key conundrums in the application of R2P is the near monopoly by Western powers in framing the normative texts and narratives about when force can be legitimately used outside of a self-defense situation. Her chapter examines these conundrums through a careful analysis of the relevant provisions of the UN Charter, the 2001 report of the International Commission on Intervention and State Sovereignty, the 2005 World Summit Outcome, and various UN Security Council resolutions. In the end, Gulowski concludes that R2P is a label that is affixed to a wide range of security crisis situations to provide social legitimacy, even when the underlying motivations for international intervention are not all that noble.

Abubakar's chapter continues the critique of military humanitarianism by examining the levels and contexts of NATO, UN, and AU interventions (or lack of intervention) in Libya and Darfur. He points to the inconsistencies in the application of R2P by Western powers in African conflicts, which raise questions about the motivations behind the doctrine of R2P. Abubakar's chapter carefully examines the security and humanitarian crises that developed in Libya under the late Muammar Gaddafi and in Darfur due to the actions of the Sudanese government and the different levels of international intervention in those two countries. If R2P is a truly benevolent humanitarian policy, Abubakar suggests that robust UN intervention, supported by Western powers, would have occurred in Darfur to save the masses from (near) genocide perpetuated by the government of Sudan and its allied Janjaweed militia. However, this did not happen because Western powers had minimal interests in Sudan, while non-Western powers were bent on protecting oil and arms economic interests in Sudan. In contrast, Libya generated a swift and robust NATO intervention, which was carried out in the name of R2P. By analyzing the geopolitical context of the NATO intervention in Libya, Abubakar argues that Western powers were more motivated by the opportunity for regime change against a stubborn enemy accused of terrorism than by the humanitarian problem itself. In particular, he points to the way NATO intervention exceeded the UN mandate and ignored the recommendations of the AU. In the end, Abubakar's chapter points to a double failure of R2P due to the mixed-motives problem. R2P failed to protect deserving people in Sudan because Western powers were not willing to apply it, while in Libya it was abused by NATO and eventually produced colossal iatrogenic violence, which created anarchy in Libya.

The second theme relates to micro-level dilemmas and practical challenges in international peacebuilding and state building, most notably on issues of judgement, skills, and resources. While the first theme examines the motives for military humanitarianism and provides a cynical assessment of the application of global liberal governance, the micro-level dilemmas and challenges point to some of the factors that impede peacebuilding and state building under global liberal governance. In their chapter on the dancing boys phenomenon in Afghanistan, Schut and van Baarle examine the way Dutch military personnel handle morally difficult situations based on ethnographic research. The practice of dancing boys, which is common in Afghanistan, entails some kind of patronage and sexual relation between young boys and privileged men. While the dancing boys phenomenon may not seem like a security issue, it raises important questions about international interventions and state building. State building in Afghanistan is about exerting global liberal governance, which would require the promotion of human security, democracy, and human development. Viewed from the Western perspective of the intervening forces in Afghanistan, sexual acts against children are a violation of their human rights and are morally wrong. Since the intervention has been presented by the United States and its allies, including the Netherlands, as an effort to promote human security and democracy, it is difficult for their personnel to avoid taking action in cases that clearly violate human rights. After all, the international troops in Afghanistan are performing some kind of policing and security functions in the country. The critical question is why international military personnel are not taking police action against persons committing sexual acts against children in violation of human rights. The chapter provides detailed accounts of situations where Dutch military personnel have been aware of sexual acts against children but failed to take any action. The key issue in the chapter is how Dutch military personnel deal with these morally challenging situations. In most cases, they ignore the problem or simply rationalize it as an accepted cultural practice, even though Islam prohibits any sexual relation outside of marriage between a man and a woman. Schut and van Baarle argue that Dutch military personnel avoid taking action because they typically do not want to offend their Afghan colleagues or local leaders, who are the main perpetrators of sexual acts against the dancing boys. In addition, they note that Dutch military personnel are unprepared to properly handle these kinds of problematic situations because the Dutch military establishment has not provided proper training or guidelines on how to deal with them even though the Dutch military command and NATO are fully aware of the dancing boys phenomenon. At any rate, the Dutch military personnel all agree that sexual acts against the dancing boys are wrong. As in the macro critiques of military humanitarianism, state building in Afghanistan is complicated by the contradiction between the stated values of Western interveners and their unwillingness to take appropriate police actions when their security and political interests can be jeopardized.

In their chapter on the operations of the European Union Forces in Bosnia-Herzegovina (EUFOR), Sigri et al. address a range of logistical and organizational challenges faced by peacekeepers. As they note, peacekeepers on the ground face a range of problems that can hamper the success of a peacekeeping mission. Such problems include lack of sufficient resources, intercultural communication among various national units in the force, disconnections between peacekeepers and local populations, and stress from the warlike situation under which peacekeepers serve. Based on their personal experiences as peacekeepers under EUFOR and survey research, the authors identified a range of managerial skills that peacekeepers may develop during their deployment to overcome the challenges that they face on the ground. Building on experiential learning theories, they argue that the peacekeeping experience provides opportunities for military personnel to develop their managerial skills. More importantly, they point out how peacekeepers' soft skills can go a long way in compensating for the institutional weaknesses of peacekeeping missions and thereby contribute to the overall success of the mission. Though the chapter does not examine the conditions and intentions that lead to international intervention, it does point to several problems that often hamper the success of military humanitarianism and international state building. Thus, even when R2P is undertaken for purely humanitarian reasons, a critical issue is how to effectively implement it on the ground without causing more problems between the intervention forces and staff and the local people. Part of the answer, the authors suggest, lies in the possession of soft interpersonal and managerial skills that are grounded in benevolence, multiculturalism, and transparency. The chapter provides a bright spot on the application of global liberal governance by examining a fairly appropriate and successful case of the application of R2P and by pointing to how implementation challenges are resolved.

Niang examines the peace mediation role of President Compaoré of Burkina Faso in the civil war in Côte d'Ivoire. While the chapter may seem like a critique of the activities of one particular person (i.e., Compaoré), it actually provides a very rich analysis of a specific mode of robust peace mediation based on personal sovereignty that defies the pre-R2P notion of neutrality in peace mediation. In addition, Niang provides an insightful critique of the political economy of new wars, election-driven approaches to conflict resolution, and more broadly global liberal governance. Niang frames the chapter in terms of what she refers to as personalized mediation based on a complex network of collaborators associated with Compaoré (i.e., the Compaoré system). Niang argues that peace mediation as evident in the Ivoirian crisis is far from being a neutral and a sincere act aimed at alleviating humanitarian suffering. Rather, peace mediation is part of geopolitics and the political economy of new wars. As she points out, Compaoré is a recognized mastermind and beneficiary of the civil war in Côte d'Ivoire. Yet, he managed to broker a fairly successful peace agreement (i.e., Ouagadougou Accord of 2007) in a conflict, where many others had failed to broker a meaningful peace agreement, and transformed himself into a peacemaker and an African statesman. This paradox of war-maker and peace-maker, which Compaoré embodied, is at the heart of Niang's analysis of peacebuilding. Moreover, she presents an angle on conflict resolution that deviates from the excessive emphasis on multiparty election as the only path to peace so ingrained in the Western approach to global liberal governance. By analyzing the activities of the controversial, but formidable, Compaoré in the Ivoirian crisis, Niang delivers a rich analysis and critique of the nature, motivation, and impacts of personalized mediation as a specific mode of peacebuilding, which is quite different from global liberal governance. Like R2P, this robust mode of peace mediation rests on the appropriation of sovereignty by an outside international agent.

The final theme deals with the effects of global liberal governance and the reactions it generates, most notably in the forms of cooptation and resistance. Military humanitarianism and international state building have largely been Western applications of global liberal governance on non-Western poor and weak countries. However, global liberal governance is an evolving phenomenon in which the subject countries are also seeking to be actors. Subject countries respond to global liberal governance in various forms ranging from cooptation to outright resistance. Bah's chapter on African agency examines the ideological and political context within which the AU developed mechanisms to promote peace, democracy, and good governance in Africa. In particular, he points to the shift from the Organization of African Unity's policy of noninterference in the internal affairs of states to the AU's doctrine of nonindifference to issues of human security and governance in Africa, which is akin to the doctrine of R2P. Bah argues that the shift toward nonindifference and the establishment of the African Peace and Security Architecture (APSA), which includes a standby military force, is a stratagem by African leaders to appropriate the application of global governance in Africa and thereby thwart the neoimperialistic tendencies of Western global liberal governance. Based on the implementation of the doctrine of nonindifference through APSA, African leaders are exerting an African breed of global liberal governance, which does little to promote peace and democracy in African countries, but goes a long way in mitigating the application of global liberal governance in Africa by Western powers.

Gökalp's chapter on the United States invasion and state-building adventure in Iraq vividly illustrates the cynical motives behind global liberal governance, its failure to enhance human security, democracy or human development, and the local resistance it has generated in the form of terrorism warfare. Based on her field experiences and interviews in Iraq, she examines the problematic American invasion of Iraq and the subsequent effort to build democracy and promote free market economy in Iraq. As evident in the global news, military humanitarianism and international state building in Iraq have been a failure so far. Gökalp adds to what we already know from the news by providing a rich analysis of the history of colonial state making in the region and the social problems that have emerged in Iraq since the American invasion. One key point in her chapter is how cosmopolitan Iraq, especially Bagdad, which had a fairly good history of ethnic and religious diversity and fairly developed state services and welfare system, has degenerated into a situation of sectarian war in the form of terrorism warfare and increasing poverty under the weight of global liberal governance. Gökalp delivers a rich and passionate critique of global liberal governance by showing the adverse social effects of what she refers to as a misguided war on terror and a neoliberal state-building venture in Iraq. She adds richness to our understanding of military humanitarianism in Iraq by juxtaposing the effects of the intervention on Iraqi Kurdistan with the rest of Iraq. Gökalp's critique of the United States invasion is by no means an argument in favor of the dictatorial Ba'ath party regime led by Saddam Husain. Like the chapters by Gulowski and Abubakar, Gökalp's critique is about the misuse of military humanitarianism by Western powers to promote more cynical political and economic interests. Gökalp's chapter also points to a more assertive, albeit problematic, resistance to global liberal governance in Iraq. In a way, she sees the various insurgencies in Iraq as an armed grassroots resistance to the American invasion and the ill-conceived state building. Unfortunately, that resistance is constantly hijacked by various groups waging terrorism warfare, which leads to further incentives for Western application of global liberal governance on Iraq. As with the Ba'ath party regime, Gökalp does not argue in favor of the insurgents in Iraq. Rather, she sees the terrorism warfare in Iraq as an unfortunate byproduct of the application of global liberal governance.

Conclusions

In sum, what all the chapters provide is a critical analysis of the macro and micro challenges of military humanitarianism and international state building. The challenges are rooted in the disconnections between the human security values of R2P and the War on Terror and the security, political, and economic interests of powerful countries that are exerting global liberal governance under the banners of benevolence and (preemptive) self-defense. In practice, events on the ground provide a wide range of challenges that actors have to resolve. In some cases external actors have to improvise to compensate for the deficits of international missions, and in other cases local leaders have to adapt, coopt, or fight in order to moderate global liberal governance. In cases such as Iraq, the challenges are too formidable even for the most powerful countries, which partially explains the colossal failure of a global liberal governance that is driven by cynical security, political, and economic interests.

One of the things that clearly emerges from this book is the problematic application of R2P and the overreach of the War on Terror. All the cases recognize the need to protect civilians from the brutality of armed militia, oppressive governments, and terrorist networks. R2P, as articulated in the relevant international policy documents, would have been a fair balance between the responsibility to vulnerable people and the political specifics of countries and regions. Moreover, R2P was conceived as a doctrine that applies to all people under grave human security threats in any part of the world. If R2P is limited to issues and cases where there are the broadest international consensus and significant local support and is applied consistently and indiscriminately in all deserving cases, R2P could maintain its moral justifications and generate more support. However, the chapters in this book clearly show that R2P has been misused and applied selectively. R2P can still be a useful tool for dealing with present and future new wars if it is not misused and applied too unevenly. Like R2P, the War on Terror has also faced growing cynicism, which makes it even more difficult to deal with current and future cases of terrorism warfare. The 9/11 terrorist attack on the United States was clearly a gross attack on human security that cannot be condoned. Not surprisingly, the invasion of Afghanistan to destroy Al-Qaeda was widely supported and viewed as a justified case of the application of global liberal governance. However, the extension of the War on Terror to Iraq, under false claims of weapons of mass destruction and widespread condemnation of unilateral military action, has undermined the genuine claims of the War on Terror. While the War on Terror was morally defensible in Afghanistan, it lost credibility in Iraq. This credibility problem, which again emerged in Libya, has made it even more difficult to generate sufficient international support to deal with the ongoing terrorism warfare in places such as Iraq, Syria, Yemen, and Libya. In the end, any misapplication of military humanitarianism generates iatrogenic morality and resistances to global liberal governance, which further undermine human security.

Notes

1. Fukuyama, *The End of History and the Last Man*; Huntington, *The Third Wave*.

2. Cederman and Gleditsch, "Conquest and Regime Change," 603–629; Reno, *Warlord Politics and African States*; Clark, *Waging Modern War*; Fukuyama, *Nation-building*; Napoleoni, *Insurgent Iraq*; Jones, "The Rise of Afghanistan's Insurgency," 7–40.

3. Kaldor, *New and Old Wars*.

4. Kaldor, "Old Wars, Cold Wars, New Wars, and the War on Terror," 492.

5. Jones, *The Rise of Afghanistan's Insurgency*; Shahrani, "War, Factionalism, and the State in Afghanistan," 715–722.

6. Kaldor, "Old Wars, Cold Wars, New Wars, and the War on Terror," 492.

7. Commission on Human Security, *Human Security Now*; UN, *Report of the World Commission on Environment and Development*.

8. Duffield, *Global Governance and the New Wars*.

9. ICISS, *The Responsibility to Protect*; Annan, "Two Concepts of Sovereignty," 49–50; Cohen and Deng, *Masses in Flight*.

10. Some of the chapters are based on papers presented at: (1) session on *International Humanitarian Intervention and State-Building*. Research Committee on Armed Forces and Conflict Resolution, RC01, XVIII International Sociological Association, World Congress of Sociology, Yokohama, Japan (13–19 July 2014), chaired by Abu Bah, and (2) session on *New Humanitarianism and International State-Building*. Working Group on Historical and Comparative Sociology, WG02, XVIII International Sociological Association, World Congress of Sociology, Yokohama, Japan, (13–19 July 2014), chaired by Abu Bah.

11. Centeno, *Blood and Debt*; Katz, *Riot, Rebellion, and Revolution*.

12. UN, *Peacekeeping*, "Past Peacekeeping Operations."

13. The situation in Syria is likely to change toward more robust international intervention following the ISIL terrorist attacks on the Russian plane in Egypt and in Paris in October and November 2015, respectively.

14. The missions are: UN Mission for the Referendum in Western Sahara (MINURSO), UN Interim Force in Lebanon (UNIFIL), UN Military Observer Group in India and Pakistan (UNMOGIP), and UN Truce Supervision Organization (UNTSO). Similar past missions include: UN Supervision Mission in Syria (UNSMIS), UN Yemen Observation Mission (UNYOM), UN Iraq-Kuwait Observation Mission (UNIKOM), UN Emergency Force (UNEF), and United Nations Good Offices Mission in Afghanistan and Pakistan (UNGOMAP).

15. Toft, *The Geography of Ethnic Violence*; Asmus, *A Little War That Shook the World*; Kudelia, "Choosing Violence in Irregular Wars," 149–181.

16. UN, *Peacekeeping*, "Current Peacekeeping Operations."

17. Tieku and Hakak, "A Curious Case of Hybrid Paternalism," 129–156.

18. Bah, "The Contours of New Humanitarianism," 2–26; Commission on Human Security, *Human Security Now*; ICISS, *The Responsibility to Protect*; Duffield, *Global Governance and the New Wars*.

19. Monten, "The Roots of the Bush Doctrine," 112–156; Obama, *National Security Strategy of the United States*.

20. Singer, *The President of Good and Evil*.

21. Kean and Hamilton, *The 9/11 Report*.

22. Greenwood, "International Law and the Pre-emptive Use of Force" 7; Franck, "Terrorism and the Right of Self-defense," 839–843; Rosand, "Security Council Resolution 1373, The

Counter-terrorism Committee, and the Fight against Terrorism," 333–341; UN Resolution 1373 (2001), adopted by the Security Council at its 4385th meeting, on 28 September 2001.

23. Glazier, "Ignorance Is Not Bliss"; Agnew, "American Hegemony into American Empire?," 871–885; Gordon and Trainor, *Cobra II*; Taft and Buchwald, "Preemption, Iraq, and International Law," 557–563.

24. ICISS, *The Responsibility to Protect*, 7.

25. Deng et al., *Sovereignty as Responsibility*; Barnett, "Humanitarianism Transformed," 723–41.

26. Boutros-Ghali, Report of the Secretary-General: "An Agenda for Peace"; Annan, "Two Concepts of Sovereignty."

27. ICISS, *The Responsibility to Protect*; Commission on Human Security, *Human Security Now.*

28. ICISS, *The Responsibility to Protect*, 17.

29. UN, "2005 World Summit Outcome."

30. Ibid., 30.

31. Ibid.

32. Nardin, "The Moral Basis of Humanitarian Intervention," 57–70; Weiss, *Humanitarian Intervention*; Cohen, *Masses in Flight*; Bah, "The Contours of New Humanitarianism."

33. Ayoob, "Third World Perspective on Humanitarian Intervention and International Administration," 99–118; Crawford, *Argument and Change in World Politics*.

34. Duffield, *Global Governance and the New Wars*, 2.

35. McFalls, "Benevolent Dictatorship: Sovereign Authority and Humanitarian War"; Hoffman, "The Civilian Target in Sierra Leone and Liberia," 26; Sheridan, "Iraq Death Toll Reaches 500,000."

36. Habermas, "On Systematically Distorted Communication," 205–218.

37. Ghani and Lockhart, *Fixing Failed States*; Bah, "People-Centered Liberalism"; Fukuyama, *State-Building.*

38. ICISS, *The Responsibility to Protect*, 39.

39. Pugh, "Postwar Political Economy in Bosnia and Herzegovina," 467–482; Caplan, *International Governance of War-Torn Territories.*

40. Paris and Sisk, *The Dilemmas of Statebuilding*; Fukuyama, Nation-Building; Rashid, *Descent into Chaos.*

41. Bah, "The Contours of New Humanitarianism."

42. Autesserre, *Peaceland*; Duffield, *Development, Security and Unending War.*

43. MacGinty, *International Peacebuilding and Local Resistance.*

44. Bah, "The Contours of New Humanitarianism"; Francis, Faal, Ramsbotham, and Kabia, *Dangers of Co-Deployment*; Paul, *War and Conflict in Africa*; Belloni, *State Building and International Intervention in Bosnia*; Burg and Shoup, *The War in Bosnia-Herzegovina*; Chandler, "Democratization in Bosnia," 78–102.

45. Bah, "Democracy and Civil War," 597–615.

46. Adebajo, *Building Peace in West Africa*; Bah, "The Contours of New Humanitarianism"; Bellamy and Williams, "The New Politics of Protection?" 825–850.

47. Olonisakin and Aning, "Humanitarian intervention and Human Rights," 16–39; Adekeye, Building Peace in West Africa; Kabia, *Humanitarian Intervention and Conflict Resolution in West Africa.*

48. Coles, *Democratic Designs*; Paris and Sisk, *The Dilemmas of Statebuilding*; Emmanuel, "Peace Incentives," 1–32; Bah, "Democracy and Civil War"; Bah, "People-Centered Liberalism."

49. Habermas, "On Systematically Distorted Communication."

References

Adebajo, Adekeye. *Building Peace in West Africa: Liberia, Sierra Leone, and Guinea-Bissau.* Boulder, CO: Lynne Rienner, 2002.

Agnew, John. "American Hegemony into American Empire? Lessons from the Invasion of Iraq." *Antipode* 35, no. 5 (2003): 871–885.

Angel Centeno, Miguel. *Blood and Debt: War and the Nation-State in Latin America.* University Park: Penn State Press, 2003.

Annan, Kofi. "Two Concepts of Sovereignty." *Economist*, September 16, 1999. http://www .economist.com/node/324795.

Asmus, Ronald. *A Little War That Shook the World: Georgia, Russia, and the Future of the West.* London: Macmillan, 2010.

Autesserre, Séverine. *Peaceland: Conflict Resolution and the Everyday Politics of International Intervention.* Cambridge: Cambridge University Press, 2014.

Ayoob, Mohammed. "Third World Perspective on Humanitarian Intervention and International Administration." *Global Governance* 10 (2004): 99–118.

Bah, Abu Bakarr. "The Contours of New Humanitarianism: War and Peacebuilding in Sierra Leone." *Africa Today* 60, no. 1 (2013): 2–26.

———. "Democracy and Civil War: Citizenship and Peacemaking in Côte d'Ivoire." *African Affairs* 109, no. 437 (2010): 597–615.

———. "People-Centered Liberalism: An Alternative Approach to International State-Building in Sierra Leone and Liberia." *Critical Sociology* (2015): 1–19. doi:10.1177/0896920515583538. http://crs.sagepub.com/content/early/2015/05/04/0896920515583538.full.pdf+html.

Barnett, Michael. "Humanitarianism Transformed." *Perspectives on Politics* 3 (2005): 723–41.

Bellamy, Alex J., and Paul D. Williams. "The New Politics of Protection? Côte d'Ivoire, Libya and the Responsibility to Protect." *International Affairs* 87, no. 4 (2011): 825–850.

Belloni, Roberto. *State Building and International Intervention in Bosnia.* London: Routledge, 2008.

Boutros-Ghali, Boutros. Report of the Secretary-General: "An Agenda for Peace." United Nations Document A/47/277-S/24111. *Council on Foreign Relations.* http://www.cfr.org/peacekeeping /report-un-secretary-general-agenda-peace/p23439.

Burg, Steven L., and Paul S. Shoup. *The War in Bosnia-Herzegovina: Ethnic Conflict and International Intervention.* Armonk, NY: M. E. Sharpe, 1999.

Caplan, Richard. *International Governance of War-Torn Territories: Rule and Reconstruction.* New York: Oxford University Press, 2005.

Cederman, Lars-Erik, and Kristian Skrede Gleditsch. "Conquest and Regime Change: An Evolutionary Model of the Spread of Democracy and Peace." *International Studies Quarterly* 48, no. 3 (2004): 603–629.

Chandler, David. "Democratization in Bosnia: The Limits of Civil Society Building Strategies." *Democratization* 5, no. 4 (1998): 78–102.

Clark, Wesley K. *Waging Modern War: Bosnia, Kosovo, and the Future of Combat.* New York: PublicAffairs, 2002.

Cohen, Roberta, and Francis Mading Deng. *Masses in Flight: The Global Crisis of Internal Displacement.* Washington, DC: Brookings Institution Press, 2012.

Coles, Kimberley. *Democratic Designs: International Intervention and Electoral Practices in Postwar Bosnia-Herzegovina.* Ann Arbor: University of Michigan Press, 2007.

Commission on Human Security. *Human Security Now.* New York: United Nations, 2003.

Crawford, Neta. *Argument and Change in World Politics: Ethics, Decolonization, and Humanitarian Intervention*. Cambridge: Cambridge University Press, 2002.

Deng, Francis Mading et al. *Sovereignty as Responsibility: Conflict Management in Africa*. Washington, DC: Brookings Institution Press, 1996.

Duffield, Mark. *Global Governance and the New Wars: The Merging of Development and Security*. London: Zed Books, 2001.

———. *Development, Security and Unending War: Governing the World of Peoples*. Cambridge: Polity Press, 2007.

Duffy Toft, Monica. *The Geography of Ethnic Violence: Identity, Interests, and the Indivisibility of Territory*. Princeton, NJ: Princeton University Press, 2005.

Emmanuel, Nikolas. "Peace Incentives: Economic Aid and Peace Processes in Africa." *African Conflict and Peacebuilding Review* 5, no. 2 (2015): 1–32.

Francis, David J., Mohamed Faal, Alex Ramsbotham, and John Kabia. *Dangers of Co-Deployment: UN Cooperative Peacekeeping in Africa*. Aldershot, UK: Ashgate, 2004.

Franck, Thomas M. "Terrorism and the Right of Self-Defense." *American Journal of International Law* (2001): 839–843.

Fukuyama, Francis. *The End of History and the Last Man*. New York: Simon and Schuster, 2006.

———, ed. *Nation-Building: Beyond Afghanistan and Iraq*. Baltimore, MD: Johns Hopkins University Press, 2008.

———. *State-Building: Governance and World Order in the 21st Century*. Ithaca, NY: Cornell University Press, 2004.

Ghani, Ashraf, and Clare Lockhart. *Fixing Failed States: A Framework for Rebuilding a Fractured World*. Oxford: Oxford University Press, 2009.

Glazier, David. "Ignorance Is Not Bliss: The Law of Belligerent Occupation and the US Invasion of Iraq." *Rutgers Law Review* 58 (2005): 121.

Gordon, Michael R., and Bernard E. Trainor. *Cobra II: The Inside Story of the Invasion and Occupation of Iraq*. New York: Vintage, 2006.

Greenwood, Christopher. "International law and the Pre-emptive Use of Force: Afghanistan, Al-Qaida, and Iraq." *San Diego International Law Journal* 4 (2003): 7.

Habermas, Jürgen. "On Systematically Distorted Communication." *Inquiry* 13, no. 1–4 (1970): 205–218.

Hoffman, Danny. "The Civilian Target in Sierra Leone and Liberia: Political Power, Military Strategy, and Humanitarian Intervention." *African Affairs* 103, no. 211 (2004): 26.

Huntington, Samuel P. *The Third Wave: Democratization in the Late Twentieth Century*. Norman: University of Oklahoma Press, 1993.

ICISS. *The Responsibility to Protect: Report of the International Commission on Intervention and State Sovereignty*. Ottawa: International Development Research Centre, 2001.

Jones, Seth G. "The Rise of Afghanistan's Insurgency: State Failure and Jihad." *International Security* 32, no. 4 (2008): 7–40.

Kabia, John M. *Humanitarian Intervention and Conflict Resolution in West Africa: From ECOMOG to ECOMIL*. Surrey, UK: Ashgate, 2013.

Kaldor, Mary. *New and Old Wars: Organised Violence in a Global Era*. Cambridge: Polity, 1999.

———. "Old Wars, Cold Wars, New Wars, and the War on Terror." *International Politics* 42, no. 4 (2005): 491–498, 492.

Katz, Friedrich, ed. *Riot, Rebellion, and Revolution: Rural Social Conflict in Mexico*. Princeton, NJ: Princeton University Press, 2014.

Kean, Thomas H., and Lee H. Hamilton. *The 9/11 Report: The National Commission on Terrorist Attacks upon the United States*. London: St. Martin's Press, 2004.

Kudelia, Serhiy. "Choosing Violence in Irregular Wars: The Case of Anti-Soviet Insurgency in Western Ukraine." *East European Politics and Societies* 27, no. 1 (2013): 149–181.

MacGinty, Roger. *International Peacebuilding and Local Resistance: Hybrid Forms of Peace*. New York: Palgrave Macmillan, 2011.

McFalls, Laurence. "Benevolent Dictatorship: Sovereign Authority and Humanitarian War." In *Contemporary State of Emergency: The Politics of Military and Humanitarian Intervention*, edited by Didier Fassin and Mariella Pandolfi. Brooklyn: Zone Books, 2010.

Monten, Jonathan. "The Roots of the Bush Doctrine: Power, Nationalism, and Democracy Promotion in US Strategy." *International Security* 29, no. 4 (2005): 112–156.

Napoleoni, Loretta. *Insurgent Iraq: Al Zarqawi and the New Generation*. New York: Seven Stories Press, 2011.

Nardin, Terry. "The Moral Basis of Humanitarian Intervention." *Ethics and International Affairs* 16 (2002): 57–70.

Obama, Barack. *National Security Strategy of the United States*. Collingdale, PA: DIANE, 2010.

Olonisakin, Funmi, and Emmanuel Kwesi Aning. "Humanitarian Intervention and Human Rights: The Contradictions in ECOMOG." *International Journal of Human Rights* 3, no. 1 (1999): 16–39.

Paris, Roland, and Timothy D. Sisk, ed. *The Dilemmas of Statebuilding: Confronting the Contradictions of Postwar Peace Operations*. London: Routledge, 2009.

Paul, William D. *War and Conflict in Africa*. Cambridge: Polity Press, 2011.

Pugh, Michael. "Postwar Political Economy in Bosnia and Herzegovina: The Spoils of Peace." *Global Governance* 8, no. 4 (2002): 467–482.

Rashid, Ahmed. *Descent into Chaos: The US and the Failure of Nation Building in Pakistan, Afghanistan, and Central Asia*. New York: Penguin, 2008.

Reno, William. *Warlord Politics and African States*. Boulder, CO: Lynne Rienner, 1999).

Rosand, Eric. "Security Council Resolution 1373, The Counter-terrorism Committee, and the Fight against Terrorism." *American Journal of International Law* 97, no. 2 (2003): 333–341.

Shahrani, Nazif M. "War, Factionalism, and the State in Afghanistan." *American Anthropologist* 104, no. 3 (2002): 715–722.

Sheridan, Kerry. "Iraq Death Toll Reaches 500,000 Since Start Of U.S.-Led Invasion, New Study Says." *Agence France Presse*, 10/15/2013. http://www.huffingtonpost.com/2013/10/15/iraq -death-toll_n_4102855.html.

Singer, Peter. *The President of Good and Evil: The Ethics of George W Bush*. London: Text, 2010.

Taft, William H., and Todd F. Buchwald. "Preemption, Iraq, and International Law." *American Journal of International Law* 97, no. 3 (2003): 557–563.

Tieku, Thomas Kwasi, and Tanzeel F. Hakak. "A Curious Case of Hybrid Paternalism: Conceptualizing the Relationship between the UN and AU on Peace and Security." *African Conflict and Peacebuilding Review* 4, no. 2 (2014): 129–156.

UN. *Peacekeeping*. "Current Peacekeeping Operations." http://www.un.org/en/peacekeeping /operations/current.shtml.

———. *Peacekeeping*. "Past Peacekeeping Operations." http://www.un.org/en/peacekeeping /operations/past.shtml.

———. *Report of the World Commission on Environment and Development: Our Common Future*. New York: United Nations, 1987.

————. "2005 World Summit Outcome." Resolution adopted by the General Assembly 60/1. 2005, Sixtieth session Agenda items 46 and 120, October 24, 2005.

Weiss, Thomas. *Humanitarian Intervention: Ideas in Action*. Cambridge: Polity Press, 2007.

1   Negotiating Narratives

R2P and the Conundrum of the Monopoly of Legitimized Use of Force

Rebecca Gulowski

VIOLENCE IS CONDEMNED as the dark side of humanity. Containing violence is deemed one of the most important achievements of our modern times. Limiting violence, particularly the state monopoly over the legitimate use of force, by democratic means is considered a successful and ongoing task of the evolving process of civilization and modernity.[1] However, the path to modernization has often been marked by conflicts and wars. The twentieth century witnessed two world wars and nuclear armament worldwide as well as an increasing occurrence of intrastate conflicts. This reality conflicts with the idea of containing international violence through international law, most notably the Charter of the United Nations (UN). The fundamental principles of the prohibition of violence and nonintervention in the affairs of states and the provision for limited intervention in exceptional cases, as respectively outlined in the UN Charter, were particularly challenged by the violent conflicts in Iraq (1991), Somalia (1992–1995), Rwanda (1994), and Bosnia-Herzegovina (1995). However, there have been increasing international interventions. As Alex Bellamy stated, "By the mid-1990s, therefore, there was widespread recognition of the legitimacy of humanitarian intervention sanctioned by the Security Council."[2] When the violence moved closer to Western Europe with the 1999 Kosovo conflict in former Yugoslavia, the legitimization of international intervention shifted. Until the Kosovo conflict, interventions were primarily justified under international law. In the case of Iraq in 1991, for example, the intervention could not be explicitly justified on the grounds of protecting a persecuted minority. Based on UN Security Council resolution 688 (S/RES/0688 [1991]), the UN actually intervened in the affairs of Iraq. The UN determined that the conflict in Iraq constituted a threat to international peace and security under Chapter VII of the UN Charter, thus circumventing the nonintervention rule. In contrast, the mission in Kosovo took place without a mandate from the UN Security Council. The justification was based not on the UN Charter, but on the moral claims of protecting and helping persecuted and threatened ethnic and religious minorities.[3] Under these conditions it is particularly remarkable that the Kosovo conflict was the first mission that the German Bundeswehr had participated in since World War II. In Germany, the pressure to legitimize German participation for the public was enormous. For most of Western Europe, the Kosovo conflict was an important juncture in post–Cold War international intervention.

Since the first decade of the twenty-first century, which has been characterized by narratives of insecurities and uncertainties, the international security principles of the UN have been significantly challenged. In addition to terrorism, weapons of mass destruction, and radical Islamism, aggressive-interventionist and unilateral foreign policies have been adopted and made part of the narrative of uncertainty. At the same time, the discourse of a new humanitarianism has been constituted by the narratives of international intervention, responsibility to protect (R2P), development, and human security. As Abu Bakarr Bah notes, new humanitarianism "is a radical outgrowth of extant post–Cold War humanitarian intervention policies for dealing with the security challenges of new wars."[4] These new policies with their specific patterns of narratives have been confronted by the prevailing principles of international relations. Thus, the principles as well as the narratives have been put up for renegotiating, in order to be integrated in a reasonable way into the discourse.[5] This renegotiation has led to a discursive bifurcation of insecurities and threat on the one hand and humanitarian motifs on the other.

Similarly, orthodox theories of modernization, which focus on the inherent connectivity between violence and the modern state, have become less persuasive.[6] These perspectives isolate instances of violence—such as the Holocaust, atrocities, and genocides—as historical singularities and irregularities of modernity.[7] By focusing on universal laws (such as increasing modernization leads to a decrease in violence), they programmatically ignore specific historical constellations and antecedent conditions of violence as if there were no connection between historical processes and the use of violence. However, the empirical observations of the last decades indicate that "all in all, the overall non-violent character of modern civilization is an illusion. More exactly, it is an integral part of its self-apology and self-apotheosis; in short, of its legitimizing myth."[8] In reality, any kind of order—even a modern, democratic one—is created by violence. The link between order and violence is inextricable.[9] Therefore, explaining the development of a new global order following the 1990s, which was characterized by critical junctures and cleavages in the context of post–Cold War international relations, entails explaining the order of violence that is also on the move. What can be observed is that the order of violence is determined by negotiation between the good and the evil, the legal and the illegal, and the legitimate and the illegitimate. It is a question of the distribution of power for which the attribution of meaning prevails. As Mahmood Mamdani points out, "Counter-insurgency and inter-state violence is after all what states do. It is genocide that is violence run amok, amoral, evil. The former is normal violence, only the latter is bad violence."[10] By renegotiating this order, new trajectories of using violence as well as new inequalities emerge.

Between Good and Evil: The Order of Violence in New Humanitarianism

Based on the sequencing of historical developments, George Kubler argues that "the important clue is that any solution points to the existence of some problem to which there have been other solutions, and that other solutions to this same problem will most likely be invented to follow the one now in view."[11] The core of the post–Cold War conundrum lies in the order of violence, which entails maintaining the stability and the destruction of the system of international order based on notions of the good and the evil. The Latin terms *potentia/potestas* and *vis/violentia* can be etymologically distinguished to describe this aspect of good and evil.[12] The question of what is considered good violence (potestas) or evil violence (violentia) is answered by attributing meanings to social actions during negotiations, which are determined by the distribution of power.

In this sense, one of the most important historical events for international order was the founding of the UN following two world wars. The dramatic experience of violence during the world wars demanded political entities that can prevent conflicts of similar scale. The UN can be regarded as the solution to the historical problem of untrammeled force. With the UN and the establishment of its principles of peace and use of violence, the relationship between violentia and potestas was clearly sharpened. The use of violence between states and the use of military force as a political means were condemned in international relations. At the domestic level, potestas was defined as state monopoly over the use of force. Conversely, violentia denotes situations where states use military force against other states, which makes them perpetrators. The only permitted violence was either self-defense or international intervention authorized by the UN Security Council under Chapter VII of the UN Charter. Under this system of international order, state sovereignty is of utmost importance.

Since the founding of the UN in 1945, however, the international system has changed profoundly. The demands on the UN have changed as the discrepancy between the previous authority of the UN Security Council and the current spate of conflicts has become apparent.[13] The complete inability to act during serious crimes against humanity, such as those committed in Srebrenica and Rwanda, can be understood as the unintended consequence of actions that took place within the limits of state sovereignty. These cases have challenged the international community to resolve the dilemma between preserving national sovereignty and the necessity to intervene in severe humanitarian crimes. The UN Security Council has extended its corresponding responsibilities and focused its attention on the disregard of minority and human rights, the disruption of state order, and the violent suppression of democracy. In the course of these developments, the boundaries of new humanitarianism are negotiated, thereby redefining international interventions, security, human rights, sovereignty, and human development.[14] At the same time, apprehensions about the misuse of the tenets of international security and R2P (e.g., the 2003 US invasion of Iraq) in order to enforce political power interests and the fear of being a silent and passive witness to atrocities have grown.

Although the order of violence is still determined by the categories of good and evil, they are increasingly losing their categorical clarity. The interpretive framework of the order of violence has expanded, while the relationship between the use of force and its legitimization has been maintained. Consequently, while the parameters of international interventions are expanding, every government is under increased pressure to legitimize every deployment of troops at both the national and international levels. James Gow and Milena Michalski argue that "destructive brute force, to a considerable extent, might be able to secure victory in warfare through combat—and indeed, might lead to the control of territory and the physical subjugation of the people on that territory, but success in the modern world is only possible with legitimacy."[15] This indicates that victory in warfare and the power of states are determined by the order of violence. Apart from the control of territory and the physical subjugation of people, it is legitimacy that frames violence and force as potestas to establish an intended good order. Thus, legitimacy—more precisely, the legitimacy of using force—decides the binary between good violence and evil violence as well as the images of the protagonists and antagonists in the post–Cold War international security system.

Legal Violence and Legitimate Violence: Two Sides of the Same Coin

At first glance, common sense may be challenged by the distinction between legal and legitimate violence. However, the notion of legitimacy unfolds two entangled dimensions of justification: legal and social motifs. An act of violence can be clearly deemed either legal or illegal by the UN Security Council and the International Criminal Court (ICC) under international law. However, that legal judgment may not necessarily overlap with social judgment of that act of violence, which can be viewed as either violentia or potestas. Though legal and legitimate violence need not lead to the same conclusion, they are nonetheless inextricably intertwined. For example, the Independent International Commission on Kosovo stated that the "NATO military intervention was illegal but legitimate.

It was illegal because it did not receive prior approval from the United Nations Security Council."[16] However, the commission considers that the "intervention was justified because all diplomatic avenues had been exhausted and because the intervention had the effect of liberating the majority population of Kosovo from a long period of oppression under Serbian rule." It also states that "there is no basis in the available evidence for charging specific individuals with criminal violations of the Laws of the War during the NATO campaign."

Legal and legitimate violence are mutually dependent. This is particularly reflected in the notions of international intervention and R2P. Both terms refer to the reasoning of international law and at the same time are discussed in terms of humanitarian motifs and public support. As such, military force is always bounded by public acceptance.[17] The concept of legitimization applied here goes beyond a one-sided justification of the use of military force. Legitimization is a mutual process of legitimization and legitimacy. *Legitimacy* refers to the process of public acceptance, or nonacceptance, and the "ethical recognition, which in turn results from a negotiation of sense-making institutions on the morality of security politics," whereas *legitimization* entails disseminating concrete ideas to the public to answer why something is justified.[18]

The international response to the civil war in Sierra Leone showed this kind of relation between legal and legitimate. In 1991, the Revolutionary United Front (RUF) took up arms to remove the government in Sierra Leone, resulting in a decade of violence and atrocities. More than 75,000 people died and around half of the population of 4.5 million was displaced. After a coup by the Armed Forces Revolutionary Council (AFRC) in March 1997 against an elected government, a civil disobedience movement emerged, with the international community also strongly condemning the coup.[19] The international community "took a clear political and military stance against the RUF."[20] Against this background, the UN Security Council passed resolution 1270 of October 22, 1999, mandating the establishment of a UN Mission in Sierra Leone (UNAMSIL). UNAMSIL troops acted explicitly under Chapter VII of the UN Charter, so "that in the discharge of its mandate UNAMSIL may take the necessary action to ensure the security and freedom of movement of its personnel and, within its capabilities and areas of deployment, to afford protection to civilians under imminent threat of physical violence, taking into account the responsibilities of the Government of Sierra Leone and ECOMOG" (S/RES/1270: 3). However, UNAMSIL was not very successful in implementing its tasks. The RUF attacked UNAMSIL troops, and several hundreds of UN personnel were taken hostage. This led to an additional, but unilateral, intervention by Britain.[21]

UNAMSIL intervention was legal given the fact that Sierra Leone had become a failed state and in effect lost its sovereignty since the legitimate government was not able to protect its people against violence. The nonintervention rule was circumvented by invoking Chapter VII of the UN Charter: "action with respect to threats to the peace, breaches of the peace, and acts of aggression." The unilateral British intervention was not based on the applicable legislation of the UN Charter. However, the legitimization for both interventions was that the people of Sierra Leone and the UN personnel needed help to protect themselves from a major and concrete threat. The legitimacy of both interventions was the prevailing humanitarian morality, which should be ensured to prevent violence and crimes against humanity. Assuming that legitimacy results from a negotiation process, legitimization refers particularly to communication, most notably to the use of signs and other symbolic forms to which meanings are attributed. The case of Sierra Leone shows that the social dimension of the legitimacy of the interventions was at least just as important as the judicial dimension. Mary Kaldor points out that "civil society groups inside Sierra Leone were strongly supportive of effective outside intervention, whether or not it was authorized by the United Nations."[22] Haja Zainab Hawa Bangura, a Sierra Leonean politician and social activist, wrote in an email communication with Kaldor in 2001 that "the only language the RUF understands is violence. For there to be peace, the military capability of the RUF has to be reduced. This can be only done by force."[23] Kaldor concludes that in the case of Sierra Leone, civil society made a significant contribution to the interpretation of the legitimacy of interventions. Beyond the legal dimension, it is the process of legitimization through communication that is decisive for the determination of the order of violence and power. Thus, power can be exercised by monopolizing the right to give meaning to certain norms. Legitimization generates power if it is convincing under the current circumstances. In Sierra Leone, the unilateral British intervention gained legitimacy because of the failure of UNAMSIL and the previous UN missions in Sierra Leone. The narrative of the importance of effectiveness of an intervention, with or without a robust mandate from the UN Security Council, was very compatible with the prevailing discourse on international intervention and R2P.

As Sierra Leone shows, discursive changes are associated with historical changes and can be regarded as a reflection of political and social change.[24] Moreover, the structure of power is determined by interactions between established constellations of power (e.g., UN, NATO, Britain, Nigeria, United States, civil societies, and NGOs) and current discourse events (i.e., concrete cases of violations of human rights, genocide, and mass starvation) that are renegotiated. By reconstructing legitimization processes, essential conclusions regarding the regularities and rules of military intervention in the twenty-first century can be drawn.

The cases discussed in this chapter provide insights into the processes of negotiating narratives in the discourse on the legitimized use of military force. The epistemological interest relies on the questions about which discursive regularities and rules the negotiation process is based on. The basic assumption that language is the only way to experience the world and that discursive constructions build a frame of reference of possible action illustrates the pivotal importance of linguistic representations.[25] Terms or concepts such as *terrorism, war,* or *R2P* are linguistic representations, although "the distinction between war, counterinsurgency, and genocide is blurred in practice."[26] However, the distinction in language causes profound differences for the consequences of action as well as its legality and legitimacy. The extent to which civil wars are constructed as a threat to international security in times of national sovereignty crisis hinges on the question of discursive compatibility and, thus, directly affects the possibility of using military force. As such, "decisions made at a particular point in time delimit future options" and initialize new ones.[27] The legitimacy of military operations is, therefore, a key in discursive negotiations. The argumentative structure must be directly connected to social and political narratives because it affects the most essential aspect of being human, namely, making the decisions of life and death.

Legitimization of Military Force

Questions concerning the meanings attributed to military force extend the discussion of the extent to which military intervention conforms to international law. In this context, a historical change in the legitimization of armed forces can be identified on a phenomenological level. During the late nineteenth century and the first half of the twentieth century, the role of Western European militaries changed profoundly. Within Europe, the primarily defensive positioning of the military for the deterrence and self-defense of a state and its society shifted with World War I and World War II toward an offensive positioning. As a result of these changing roles, the armed forces have forfeited legitimacy. The redundancy of both roles became visible toward the end of the twentieth century. The relevance of the military decreased because of the radical changes in the international system in the aftermath of the Cold War.[28] For a short period after the end of the Cold War, it was assumed that the containment of violence would be institutionalized in ways that comply with UN standards and international law. In accordance with this interpretation, human rights, understood in a phenomenological instead of a positivistic sense, gained increasing relevance in the international order. In many European countries, the military seemed to lose its central position within states. Against this backdrop, a tendency toward demilitarization and a turnover to conflict resolution through nonmilitary means were noticed, which Martin Shaw described as a "post-military society."[29] The societal relevance of the military has continued to decline because of the incompatibility between military values, which orient themselves toward the collective lifestyles as well as high commitment, and the socially relevant values of autonomy and self-determination.[30] Since the end of the Cold War, governments have been pressured to justify military operations. The legitimization of the use of force has faced the challenge of coping with both tendencies of demilitarization within society as well as the utopia of democratic peace on an international level that led to changing narratives that are more compatible with the nascent arguments of a post-military society.

The reasons for military deployments are becoming increasingly more abstract with regard to their contents and references to global risks and threats.[31] At the same time, the deployment of troops must also be legitimized domestically. Similarly, military operations require the agreement of the citizens. According to Gow and Michalski, "the key to successful strategy then shifts from destroying an enemy's assets to undermining the narratives, which give appeal to that enemy and mobilize support for it."[32] In terms of the use of force, excluding self-defense, governments endeavor to establish narratives that can justify military operations at home and abroad, including the country that is the object of intervention. Success, therefore, depends on the victory of a military as well as on its political persuasiveness.[33] Moreover, the narratives have to identify the perpetrators and the victims that need help. Such strategic narratives are aimed at the values interests and the prejudices of respective societies.[34] The narratives can be considered strategic because they do not arise spontaneously, but are developed intentionally through the purposeful strengthening of prevailing ideas and tendencies. Successful narratives draw on specific occurrences, while the others are detached from them. It is recognizable that emotions, metaphors, and partly dubious historical analogies are integrated into the narratives alongside primarily evident or analytical explanations. Narratives create a functioning history through which situations are interpreted. Such narratives raise the awareness of conflicting parties and the subject of conflicts. Most importantly, they simplify the complexity of the conflict and create a dichotomy between victims and perpetrators, friends and enemies, and good and bad.

What is striking about the legitimization of the military during the 1990s is the emergence of pacifistic narratives. Gerhard Kümmel argues that the military was specifically rebranded by assigning it noble tasks such as constructing human development infrastructure, protecting civilians, facilitating humanitarian aid distribution, and responding to natural disasters. Beyond the employment of troops in the context of natural disasters or human development projects, the legitimization of military force has been realigned. This includes the deployment of military forces for humanitarian interventions under the aegis of North Atlantic Treaty Organization (NATO) or participation in UN peace enforcement missions.[35] This brings forth the question of whether countries that demilitarize domestically, but remilitarize with respect to their foreign policies by entering into coalitions with other nations or serving in a UN mission, are only changing the emphasis of their action.

International Intervention and the Responsibility to Protect: Linked Solutions

The doctrine of R2P consists of three main pillars, which emerge out of the international humanitarian intervention discourse of the 1990s. These pillars are: (1) the responsibility to prevent, (2) the responsibility to react, and (3) the responsibility to rebuild. Protection means an early recognition of risks, a willingness to act as well as to shoulder the consequences of the intervention. Furthermore, intervention must be based on the right intention, be used as the last resort, be proportional, and have a reasonable prospect of success.[36] In terms of temporal dimension, processing, and narrative, R2P is compatible with the extant notions of international humanitarian intervention. R2P raises questions that cannot be answered by legal reasoning alone, most notably: Why does R2P emerge in an institutionalized form given the fact that legalized military deployment had been conceptually defined as humanitarian intervention under Chapter VII of the UN Charter? Why has the resort to R2P increased? In light of existing possibilities for international intervention under the UN Charter, why was a new ground of justification needed to react to systematic violation of human rights given the fact that violent conflicts, warfare, and atrocities have been taking place throughout history?

If one understands history as a process, humanitarian catastrophes and violent conflicts can be regarded as critical junctures. A critical juncture is a response to "cleavages (or crises) that emerges out of the antecedent conditions" and enables contingent alternatives that set a specific trajectory of development.[37] Ronald Aminzade argues that "the concept of trajectories, or a path, of change refers to the sequential order of events. . . . Path dependency refers to the notion that for any given trajectory, past choices and temporally remote events can help to explain subsequent path of development and contemporary outcomes."[38] Based on this, the processuality of narratives can explain why R2P emerged. The narratives in which R2P is embedded point to what kind of trajectory of the order of violence in the international system has emerged by focusing on a period of time after and during a fundamental change in the relationship between the notion of state and humanitarianism.[39] This process of change is not characterized by its temporality (i.e., the old versus the new) alone. Rather, the distinction between old and new wars causes a problem of categories and comparison between traditional and contemporary notions of warfare. Influential studies contrast today's intrastate wars with interstate wars before 1990, instead of systemizing the processes leading to the current (civil) wars.[40]

The interpretation of conflicts and their associated foreign policy practice (e.g., British intervention in Sierra Leone, UN missions, NATO missions) lead to a stabilization along given and emerging trajectories of the order of violence in the international system. The stability along the given trajectories is sustained by shared norms, as accepted collective ideas, which become mandatory "understandings of how people should act morally in their relations with each other."[41] Longstanding ideas of morality and ethics are often preserved by narrations referencing historical events and collective memories where decisions were already made and meanings attributed through ideologies. A similar development can currently be observed in the field of humanitarianism, which is revealed through the establishment of humanitarian justification and the revival of the Just War theory.[42] The trajectory of the order of violence in the international system has changed and is increasingly characterized by tolerance for military interventions under the aegis of a specific humanitarian ideology, which refers to the *intentio recta* (right intention) and *causa iusta* (just cause). The International Commission on Intervention and State Sovereignty (ICISS) explicitly points to these ideas and notes that "while there is no universally accepted single list, in the Commission's judgment all the relevant decision making criteria can be succinctly summarized under the following six headings: right authority, just cause, right intention, last resort, proportional means and reasonable prospects."[43] The difference between these ideas under the orthodox Just War theory and their contemporary implementation under R2P is that the ideas of the Just War theory are traditionally based on religion and conscience. Today, these ideas are transformed into a secular concept. The concept of international interventions has a long tradition in the discourse on Just War. R2P must be seen as a sequential figure of thought. R2P, international interventions under Chapter VII of the UN Charter and the idea of a *bellum iustum* (just war) all relate to the same conundrum of finding appropriate solutions to untrammeled force.

The Idea of International Humanitarian Intervention

International humanitarian intervention may generally be considered as an "enforcement of humanitarian objectives through the use of military means."[44] This implies that interventions run contrary to the principles of Article 2 (4) and (7) in Chapter I of the UN Charter, which prohibits violence and intervention inasmuch as each violent and nonviolent intervention aims to alter the structure of the authority of the intervened state. As a result, the legality of international humanitarian intervention is inherently questionable, thus extending the room for a (interpretative) legitimization process. Given the lack of a uniform interpretation of international law, a generally accepted definition of international humanitarian intervention has never evolved. Thus, the debate on intervention has folded around the central problems of "authorization, selectivity, and the absence of a general doctrine."[45]

Basically, the principles of humanitarian intervention predate the twentieth century. As early as the period of the crusades and also in the sixteenth and seventeenth centuries, intervention invoking *iusta causa belli* (the just cause of war) was a tool for implementing confessional ideologies. Under the guise of humanitarian principles, interventions enforced and legitimized power interests.[46] There is no evidence even in the nineteenth century that humanitarian claims took precedence over strategic interests, but as Martha Finnemore argues, they "provide states with new or intensified interests in an area and new reasons to act where none had existed previously."[47] The issues of international interventions, especially since the 1990s, have expanded to various aspects of the international order. Interventions are not only related to humanitarian motives but also to ecological, democratic, antiterrorism, antidrug, and economic motives. The narrative of development has also gained strength in the context of interventions.[48] Generally, humanitarian interventions expressly refer to humanitarian motives.[49] Thus, the focus of humanitarian intervention has shifted toward the motivation and good will of the interveners.

As Immanuel Kant would argue, however, "good will is good not because of what it performs or effects, not by its aptness for the attainment of some proposed end, but simply by virtue of the volition."[50] It is the categorical imperative that "commands a certain conduct immediately, without having as its condition any other purpose to be attained by it. . . . This imperative may be called that of morality."[51] If an action is justified by the fact that it is based on a good will, actors driven by rationality are exempt from an assessment of their morality, which relegates the intention for the intervention into the background. The good will "is good in itself."[52] In this sense, even with a robust mandate of the UN Security Council, the concept of humanitarian intervention is negotiated between the interpretation of the international law and moral responsibility that was set a priori.

However, Bellamy stresses that the problem with a motive-based approach to assessing intervention is that it may lead to the problem of inappropriate means. He shows that according priority to moral motives increases the likelihood of the ends of a mission being undermined. It is particularly revealing to look at concrete actions in order to identify the intentions of an actor and evaluate a humanitarian mission. Bellamy argues that "an actor who proclaims humanitarian goals but chooses indiscriminate weapons or strategic bombardments cannot be said to have a humanitarian *intention*."[53] The Kosovo mission (KFOR) shows that legitimization was mainly based on moral motives. However, these motives were severely challenged by the concrete conduct of the mission. The NATO airstrikes hardly protected the civilian population, and they caused numerous civilian casualties. This cleavage between morality motives and the concrete procedure of the mission led to criticism of the mission, which did not support the establishment of humanitarian interventions as an integral part of customary international law. It can even be assumed that the negative international perception has already rendered the concept of humanitarian intervention useless for legitimizing military force. As a result, humanitarian intervention can be regarded as a linguistic construction of the past and not a construction of the twenty-first century. However, the problems that should be solved with humanitarian interventions still exist.

"Responsibility to Protect" as a Label

Ulrich Hahn points out that the concept of humanitarian intervention was mainly criticized because it was not sufficiently thought out. R2P has added nothing fundamentally different to the debate on humanitarian interventions after KFOR in 1999 and can be understood as merely a new label for the same thing.[54] However, this criticism is untenable because it narrows the discussion of R2P.

The development of R2P is based on a debate on the Kosovo mission at the end of the 1990s and is mainly affected by the incidence of mass atrocities in Rwanda and Srebrenica. Based on these experiences, interventions that could be justified explicitly on the basis of humanitarian motives increasingly became part of the UN.[55] Former UN secretary-general Kofi Annan is considered a pioneer of R2P. In 1998, in his Ditchley Park speech, he emphasized the concept of responsibility in a debate on state sovereignty and human rights. As he stated: "The Charter protects the sovereignty of people. It was never meant as a license for governments to trample on human rights and human dignity. Sovereignty imposes responsibility, not just power."[56] The 2001 ICISS report and the 2005 World Summit Outcome can be regarded as the most important documented primary sources of R2P.[57] Gareth Evans and Ramesh Thakur, representatives of the Canadian government and key figures of the ICISS report, continually supported the principles of R2P after submitting the 2001 report. Equally important, Annan included the issue of R2P on the agenda of the 2005 World Summit at the UN, making it part of the discourse of the international community. Without the support of Annan, R2P as a label would not have been as prominent as it is today.[58]

Following the events in Kosovo and the subsequent debate about the NATO mission, R2P became a dominant theme of the UN and the foreign and security policies of individual states. R2P continues to be a key international security tool, as most evident in the NATO intervention in Libya. UN Security Council resolution 1973 of March 17, 2011, authorized the enforcement of an arms embargo, the protection of civilians by taking all necessary measures, and the imposition of a no-fly zone over Libya. After seven months, the mission toppled the regime of Colonel Muammar Gaddafi, and "many lauded this intervention as evidence of the R2P's influence."[59] Although R2P principles had been applied before 2011 in Sierra Leone, the Libyan mission was considered a "quasi-experiment of the responsibility to protect (R2P) doctrine."[60] Resolution 1973 contained explicit rhetoric of responsibility, which refers almost invariably to violence against civilians.

The ICISS Report: Shifting Sovereignty

The UN is "based on the principle of the sovereign equality of all its members" as stated in Chapter I, Article 2 (1) of the UN Charter. If the UN Security Council determines the existence of any threat to the peace, breach of peace, or act of aggression, it can authorize interventions, including the use of military means in accordance with Chapter VII of the UN Charter, which would circumvent the nonintervention rule. However, Chapter VII does not negate the principle of sovereignty under international law. A critical question in cases where the UN fails to intervene is whether it is due to the principle of sovereignty or other pragmatic considerations. The cases of Rwanda and Srebrenica increasingly show that the principle of sovereignty is not the only reason for the UN's failure to protect civilians. In both cases, UN troops were already present in those countries before the genocides. Aidan Hehir suggests that "the ineffective response of the international community . . . derived from a lack of interest and will on behalf of those with the capacity to intervene rather than any commitment to uphold a tenet of international law that precluded intervention."[61] Against this background, Annan pleaded at the UN General Assembly in 1999 and in 2000 for an analysis on how to respond to gross and systematic violations of human rights.[62] This debate resulted in a year-long investigation by the ICISS and, subsequently, the 2001 ICISS report.

The most obvious difference between the traditional notion of humanitarian intervention and R2P is the rhetoric deployed in the ICISS report and the contrasting terminologies used to describe the two concepts. There was a discursive shift from coercive action to political action in R2P. Thus, the critical starting point of international action is not the crimes of the perpetrators but the suffering of the victims. In this sense, the principle of sovereignty is broken only if the state does not uphold its primary responsibility to protect its citizens.[63] As a consequence of an intervention based on R2P, a state temporarily loses its defining element of sovereignty. The ICISS report extends the understanding of sovereignty as more than just the right of self-defense to include the responsibility for carrying out internal functions and external tasks.[64] The ICISS report states that although each state bears the responsibility of protecting its population as its primary responsibility, this responsibility may be transferred to the international community as a secondary responsibility under certain circumstances where the state is unwilling or unable to protect its people. With R2P, the concept of state sovereignty changes in that the primary responsibility of the state becomes the protection of its citizens. Certainly, the underlying idea that sovereignty feeds on the protection of its population is not new. A state consists of a defined territory, has constitutive people, and holds a monopoly on the legitimate use of force. Sovereignty is the imaginary common thread linking the three elements. Thomas Hobbes argued that the contract between individuals and the state is invalidated if they are threatened by death and if the state fails to fulfill its primary responsibility.[65] In the 1990s, however, the idea of sovereignty got a new impetus due to interconnections between humanitarian intervention and R2P debates. The ICISS report creates two scenarios in which the responsibility for the population of a state can be appropriated by the international community. One scenario is if the state is unable or unwilling to protect its population from genocide, war crimes, ethnic cleansing, or crimes against humanity. The second is if the state is unable or unwilling to protect its population from a hazard that could cause too many deaths. The circumstances of these scenarios may be either urgent or merely anticipated. These new obligations for the intervening actors are clearly formulated and increase the legitimate sphere of international action. In addition to the intervention itself, reconstruction and reconciliation must be supported. This reflects a fundamental orientation toward long-term solutions and the narrative of development and civilization.[66]

2005 World Summit Outcome: Taking a Step Backward

Officially, states have recognized the doctrine of R2P as an international principle by their membership in the UN or their representation at the 2005 World Summit. R2P was enshrined in Articles 138 and 139 of the 2005 World Summit Outcome of the high-level plenary meeting of the General Assembly, which explicitly addressed the question of the responsibility to protect individuals within and outside national borders. However, a comparison of the ICISS report and Articles 138 and 139 of the 2005 World Summit Outcome shows that there are essential differences. It is remarkable that the concrete results and proposals of the ICISS report were not included in the 2005 World Summit Outcome. The heads of states and governments at the General Assembly meeting rejected the request of the ICISS to include precise criteria for when to intervene under R2P. Furthermore, a proposal to formulate rules of conduct in the event of a veto by one or more of the permanent members of the UN Security Council was rejected. Even a discussion on possible coercive measures without the authorization of the UN Security Council was omitted. In the 2005 World Summit Outcome, R2P basically consists of (1) strengthening of the primary responsibility of each state,

(2) an assisting role for the international community, and (3) the demand to respond in a timely and decisively manner.

The first dimension of R2P under the 2005 World Summit Outcome refers to the primary responsibility of the state to protect its own population. In paragraph 138, it is clearly stated that "each individual state has the responsibility to protect its populations from genocide, war crimes, ethnic cleansing and crimes against humanity."[67] The second dimension concerns the international community's assistance to states to fulfill their responsibility to protect. It is postulated that states should encourage other states to protect their citizens. In addition, states should give direct assistance to other states when they start experiencing escalating crises and conflicts, especially in areas where war crimes and serious human rights violations by a government are evident. The practical implementation of the second dimension is often not possible. In such cases, the third dimension becomes important. For the most serious crimes against humanity, R2P demands that the international community respond to the situation in a timely and decisive manner. In addition to the use of diplomatic channels and other peaceful means, R2P provides for the use of force in accordance with Chapter VII of the UN Charter. The third dimension is regarded as particularly effective but also the most controversial dimension.

The responses to the 2005 World Summit Outcome have been subdued, particularly by not providing any answer on what to do if the UN Security Council, which provides the legal basis for the application of R2P, is unable to reach a consensus on an intervention case. Thus, the ability of the UN to act under R2P still remains limited, as the case of Syria shows. Syrian civilians have been suffering under the authoritarian regime of Bashar Hafez al-Assad, but at a meeting of the UN Security Council in early 2012 in New York, China and Russia voted against a resolution authorizing intervention in Syria. In addition, the emphasis on human rights in the ICISS report was lost, thereby leading to disillusionment and questions of legitimation.

Conclusions

Arguably, no profound legal basis for R2P has come from either the ICISS report or the 2005 World Summit Outcome. R2P is indeed supported by the ICISS report and the 2005 World Summit Outcome, but these are considered only as sources of legal guidance and appeals to the moral responsibility of states rather than a legally binding agreement among UN member states.[68] R2P is not about establishing a legally binding force in international law. Rather, it is a norm or a guiding principle that governments can invoke to justify violence. However, if a norm is seen primarily as shared expectations of an appropriate behavior of actors, it may be problematic that R2P prescribes a complex set of different actions and, thus, yields quite different expectations. The crucial point is whether

R2P is a reformed version of orthodox humanitarian intervention or a clear legal justification for international interventions that may conceal power interests. This is evidenced by the high degree of selectivity in interventions. NATO intervention in Libya was robust and presented as application of R2P, but the violent repression of the opposition in Bahrain has barely received attention from the international community.[69] Perhaps, Libya shows that R2P is essentially another attempt at solving the conundrum of the order of violence. Even though the term has lost its popularity in the past years, particularly with the inability to act in the case of Syria, the underlying ideas of R2P are still changing the discourse on the legitimized use of military force by establishing specific expectations within the international community. Libya and Syria seem to suggest that such expectations are mainly aimed at the individual responsibility of each state to protect its people and the demand of the international community to protect people against authoritarian regimes.

It is comprehensible to say that R2P, as it was constituted in the ICISS report and reaffirmed in the 2005 World Summit Outcome, is a rhetoric that "adds nothing substantially new" to the debates on humanitarian interventions.[70] At first glance, the two conflicting lines of argument within the political discourse on R2P and humanitarian interventions may not be surprising. There seems to be a strong view that R2P should replace orthodox humanitarian intervention policies, as the latter failed to protect people in Rwanda and Bosnia-Herzegovina from genocides. In that sense, the international community, notably the Western world, should make R2P a norm that would prevent future humanitarian failures.[71] Under that view, violence would be acceptable if it is a means to protect citizens, and R2P would be regarded as part of international peacebuilding. Alternatively, R2P is criticized on the grounds that no evidence exists to show that previous humanitarian interventions contributed to a sustained improvement in the stability of the concerned countries. In practice, R2P and humanitarian interventions are seen as essentially the same, with R2P viewed as a wolf in sheep's clothing.

However, a typical debate on the virtues and evils of R2P obscures its fundamental issue, namely, the order of violence established by political norms. The postulated conundrum of the legitimized use of military force by major powers was described as the dilemma between sovereignty and humanity when the UN Security Council is unable to act. This can be regarded as the main interpretive pattern in post–Cold War international relations. Given the experience of Kosovo and the discussion on international interventions, the rejection of humanitarian intervention can be recognized at both a political and a discursive level. The ICISS report explicitly referred to Annan's argument by asking, "If humanitarian intervention is, indeed, an unacceptable assault on sovereignty, how should we respond to a Rwanda, to a Srebrenica—to gross and systematic violations of human rights that offend every precept of our common humanity?"[72] To not intervene simply means looking the other way, which can be as reprehensible as being jointly responsible for violations. The only opportunity for action is to intervene, which does not necessarily hinge only on the authorization from the UN Security Council alone, but also is derived from morality. This is all the more astonishing as the 2005 World Summit Outcome omitted a discussion about possible coercive measures without UN Security Council's authorization. As pointed out earlier, the member states were not willing to formulate rules of conduct in the event of a veto in the UN Security Council, which led to the rather vaguely formulated paragraphs 138 and 139 of the 2005 World Summit Outcome. The omission of a concrete implementation mechanism of the R2P doctrine narrows the discourse on interventions by focusing on the moral dimension without any practicable methods of application. However, a specific thematic difference between the "responsibility to protect" versus "humanitarian intervention" and the "responsibility to protect" versus "no responsibility to protect" can be identified. These different binaries establish new actants in the discourse on the legitimization of interventions. For example, the narrative of humanitarian interventions at the end of the 1990s cast states as active agents. This was true for both the intervening state and those states that were unable or unwilling to protect their citizens. Thus, the discourse clearly determined the perpetrators using bad violence and those using legitimized violence—the potestas. This determination yields a specific order of violence, which defines moral order in the international system.

With the establishment of the principles of R2P in the first decade of the twenty-first century, this narrative of two confronted actants, the evil perpetrators versus the legitimate interveners, has changed. The interpretive pattern is composed of speech acts, which focus on terms like "victims" and "helpers." The relation between these actants is complementary. The narrative is not that (amoral) violence must be met with (legitimate) violence through humanitarian intervention, but it is about being an active helper—an intervening state to protect a passive victim needing help. Mamdani characterizes this relationship as trusteeship and wardship. In this process, an entity of the political, military, and humanitarian dimension has emerged seeking to create structures of democracy and terminate a humanitarian emergency entangled in the use of military force.[73] State building, conceived as the responsibility to rebuild, has become an integral component of the legitimization of military force. State building adds a decisive new dimension to R2P, sparking debates in southern countries of neocolonial paternalism.

Legitimization has not only admitted the narratives of democracy and security, but its narratives are increasingly becoming tied to a differentiated solidarity of alliance and ad hoc decision making. The boundaries at which transgression allows the use of force are negotiable. A change is emerging in the discourse on violence in which terms like "support," "assistance," "science," and "evaluation" are emphasized during legitimization, which includes relatively less consideration of moral motives. Narratives are becoming more detailed. Instead of invoking universality, legitimatization supports a paradigm of a (self-)reflexive society, which prefers the ideas of individualism, self-determination, and autonomy. These ideas are pleasant, and the people who do not live in countries subject to intervention are pleased with the legitimization of force as long as it is wrapped in the frame of "well-evaluated" and autonomic paradigm.

The trajectory of the order of violence in the international system has evident asynchronicities. The trajectory refers to former colonial structures and asymmetries by emphasizing the complementary (active and passive) actants of trusteeship and wardships in the international system. At the same time, this is intertwined with the paradigm of individualism and a (self-)reflexive modernity with its principles of autonomy, self-responsibility, and liberalism. This is the crucial point of the initial question—what conundrum arises from analyzing the narratives of humanitarian intervention and R2P that are regarded as solutions to the problems of the post–Cold War era? The narrative structure of humanitarian intervention and R2P in the discourse on the legitimate use of military force refers to the still-existing path dependence of a colonial order with southern wards placed under the trusteeship of the great powers. As Mamdani points out: "the new humanitarian order claims responsibility for the protection of 'vulnerable populations.' That responsibility is said to belong to the 'international community,' to be exercised in practice by the UN, and in particular the Security Council whose permanent members are the great powers."[74] At the same time, the discourse on R2P obscures the fact that the formerly colonial Western powers ignore existing structural "inequalities of power and wealth in the international order" by constructing active agents under the category of helper, invoking moral commitments, but at the same time rejecting any binding commitments.[75] The trajectory of the legitimized use of military force is also asynchronous with its overall picture, revealing the conundrum of the new order of violence.

The order of violence shapes a bifurcated trajectory. On the one hand, the trajectory indicates a still-existing order of asymmetries in power and the social and economic inequalities of former colonialism. The countries in which states intervene are most likely countries of the global south that are continuously constructed as passive wards. On the other hand, Western, (self-)reflexive modernity with its values of individualism and autonomy is emphasized. This conjunction leads to narratives of passive and deficient individuals who should be protected but are faulted for their condition. The current discourse on the legitimized use of military force does not merely attempt to solve the dilemma of humanity and sovereignty. It also tries to solve the problem of sustaining a former (colonial) order of power by washing hands clean from complicity in (re)producing (new) inequalities.

Notes

Acknowledgment: This chapter is primarily based on a collaborative research with my former colleague Verena Stitz. Our working paper, *Negotiating Narratives in the Discourse of the Legitimized Use of Military Force: The Triform Linkage of Action, Institution, and Structure*, was presented at the 55th Annual Convention (March 2014) of the International Studies Association. A version of this chapter was also presented at the 2014 International Sociological Association Conference in Yokohama, Japan. Many thanks to Verena for granting me permission to use some data from our joint research in this chapter.

1. Elias, *The Civilizing Process.*
2. Bellamy, "Motives, Outcome, Intent and the Legitimacy of Humanitarian Intervention," 216–232.
3. Habermas, "Bestialität und Humanität."
4. Bah, "The Contours of New Humanitarianism," 3–26.
5. To renegotiate is used in accordance with symbolic interactionism. Negotiating is more than discussing something in order to reach an agreement. Negotiating means a sequence of interpretive actions in which meanings (defined in terms of actions and their consequences) are attributed and modified through an interpretive process. See Blumer, *Symbolic Interactionism.*
6. Elias, *The Civilizing Process.*
7. Böhme, "Gewalt im 20 Jahrhundert."
8. Baumann, *Modernity and the Holocaust*, 96–97.
9. Sofsky, *Traktat über die Gewalt*, 10.
10. Mamdani, "Responsibility to Protect or Right to Punish?," 129.
11. Kubler, *The Shape of Time*, 33.
12. Imbusch, *Moderne und Gewalt*, 26.
13. Brock, "Frieden durch Recht," 1–12.
14. Bah, "The Contours of New Humanitarianism."
15. Gow and Michalski, *War, Image and Legitimacy*, 203.
16. Independent International Commission on Kosovo (IICK), *Kosovo Report*, 4–5.
17. Reeb, "Öffentlichkeit als Teil des Schlachtfeldes," 200.
18. Ibid., 201.
19. Kaldor, *A Decade of Humanitarian Intervention*, 135.
20. Bah, "The Contours of New Humanitarianism," 10.
21. Kaldor, *A Decade of Humanitarian Intervention*, 135.
22. Ibid., 138.
23. Ibid., 139.
24. Weller, "Zivile Konfliktbearbeitung: Begriffe und Konzeptentwicklungen," 9.
25. Nonhoff, "Konstruktivistisch-Pragmatische Methodik," 96.
26. Mamdani, "Responsibility to Protect or Right to Punish," 129.
27. Aminzade, "Historical Sociology and Time," 462–463.
28. Kümmel, "Militärische Aufträge und die Legitimation der Streitkräfte," 111–118.
29. Shaw, *Post-Military Society.*
30. Kümmel, "Auftrag und Aufgaben des Militärs im Wandel," 57.
31. Kantner, "Der Nationalstaat und das Militär," 43–44.
32. Gow, *War, Image and Legitimacy*, 6.
33. Shaw, *The New Western Way of War*, 92–93; Wilson, *Effectiveness, Legitimacy, and the Use of Force in Modern Wars*, 19–20.
34. Freedman, *The Transformation of Strategic Affairs.*

35. Kümmel, "Militärische Aufträge," 111–118.
36. ICISS, *The Responsibility to Protect,* 7.
37. Collier and Collier, *Shaping the Political Arena,* 29–30.
38. Aminzade, "Historical Sociology and Time," 462.
39. Collier, *Shaping the Political Arena,* 28–29.
40. Kaldor, *New and Old Wars;* Münkler, *Die Neuen Kriege;* Münkler, "Die Neuen Kriege."
41. Mann, *The Sources of Social Power,* 22.
42. Bellamy, "Motives, Outcome, Intent," 216–232; Heinze, *Waging Humanitarian War;* Steinhoff, *On the Ethics of War and Terrorism;* Wheeler, *Saving Strangers.*
43. ICISS, *The Responsibility to Protect,* 23.
44. Münkler and Malowitz, "Humanitäre Interventionen," 7.
45. Pieterse, "Sociology of Humanitarian Intervention," 73.
46. Danish Institute of International Affairs, *Humanitarian Intervention,* 78.
47. Finnemore, "Constructing Norms of Humanitarian Intervention," 168.
48. Schetter, "Von der Entwicklungszusammenarbeit zur humanitären Intervention," 31.
49. Weber, *Der UNO-Einsatz in Somalia.*
50. Kant and Abbott, *Fundamental Principles of the Metaphysics of Morals,* 7.
51. Ibid., 23.
52. Ibid., 7.
53. Bellamy, "Motives, Outcome, Intent," 229.
54. Hahn, "Responsibility to Protect (R2P," 33–35.
55. Hehir, "The Responsibility to Protect in International Political Discourse," 1334.
56. Annan, "Reflections on Intervention," 6.
57. ICISS, *The Responsibility to Protect;* UN, "2005 World Summit Outcome"; Bellamy, *Responsibility to Protect;* Cooper and Kohler, *Responsibility to Protect;* Evans, "Responsibility to Protect"; Thakur, *The United Nations, Peace and Security.*
58. Bellamy, *The Global Effort to End Mass Atrocities,* 95.
59. Hehir, *The Responsibility to Protect,* 12.
60. Bah, "The Contours of New Humanitarianism"; Robert Murray, "Humanitarianism, Responsibility or Realty?," 15.
61. Hehir, *Rhetoric, Reality and the Future of Humanitarian Intervention,* 185.
62. ICISS, *The Responsibility to Protect,* 7.
63. Bellamy, "Responsibility to Protect or Trojan Horse?," 35.
64. ICISS, *The Responsibility to Protect,* 13.
65. Hobbes, *Leviathan.*
66. Ashford, "The Responsibility to Protect," 36–37.
67. UN, "2005 World Summit Outcome," 30.
68. Rausch, *Responsibility to Protect.*
69. Haid, "Persilschein für Interventionen in Bürgerkriegen?," 9–13.
70. Chomsky, "The Skeleton in the Closet," 13.
71. Schetter, "Von der Entwicklungszusammenarbeit zur humanitären Interventionen," 31.
72. ICISS, *The Responsibility to Protect,* 2
73. Mamdani, "Responsibility to Protect or Right to Punish."
74. Ibid., 126.
75. Cunliffe, "Introduction," 4.

References

Aminzade, Ronald. "Historical Sociology and Time." *Sociological Methods and Research* 20, no. 4 (1992): 456–480.

Annan, Kofi. "Reflections on Intervention: 35th Annual Ditchley Foundation Lecture, June 26 1998." In *The Question of Intervention: Statements by the Secretary-General*, 6. New York: United Nations, 1999. 6.

Ashford, Mary-Wynne. "The Responsibility to Protect: A New Notion of State Sovereignty." *Medicine, Conflict and Survival* 19, no. 1 (2007): 35–38.

Bah, Abu Bakarr. "The Contours of New Humanitarianism: War and Peacebuilding in Sierra Leone." *Africa Today* 6, no. 1 (2013): 3–26.

Baumann, Zygmunt. *Modernity and the Holocaust*. Cambridge: Polity Press, 1989.

Bellamy, Alex J. "Motives, Outcome, Intent and the Legitimacy of Humanitarian Intervention." *Journal of Military Ethics* 3, no. 3 (2004): 216–232.

———. *Responsibility to Protect: The Global Effort to End Mass Atrocities*. Cambridge: Polity Press, 2009.

———. "Responsibility to Protect or Trojan Horse? The Crisis in Darfur and Humanitarian Intervention after Iraq." *Ethics and International Affairs* 19, no. 2 (2005): 31–54.

Blumer, Herbert. *Symbolic Interactionism: Perspective and Method*. Berkeley: University of California Press, 1986.

Böhme, Hartmut. "Gewalt im 20 Jahrhundert: Demozide in der Sicht von Erinnerungsliteratur, Statistik und qualitativer Sozialanalyse." *Figurationen* (1999): 139–157. doi:10.7788/figurationen.1999.0.0.139.

Brock, Lothar. "Frieden durch Recht. Zur Verteidigung einer Idee gegen die harten Tatsachen der internationalen Politik." *HSFK Standpunkte. Beiträge zum demokratischen Frieden* 3 (2004): 1–12.

Chomsky, Noam. "The Skeleton in the Closet: The Responsibility to Protect in History." In *Critical Perspectives on Responsibility to Protect: Interrogating Theory and Practice*, edited by Philip Cunliffe, 11–18. Abingdon, UK: Routledge, 2011.

Collier, Ruth Berins, and David Collier. *Shaping the Political Arena: Critical Junctures, the Labor Movement, and Regime Dynamics in Latin America*. Princeton, NJ: Princeton University Press, 1991.

Cooper, Richard H., and Juliette V. Kohler. "Responsibility to Protect: The Opportunity to Regulate Atrocity Crimes in the Past." In *Responsibility to Protect: The Global Moral Compact for the 21st Century*, edited by Richard H. Cooper and Juliette V. Kohler, 1–14. Basingstoke, UK: Palgrave Macmillan, 2009.

Cunliffe, Philip. "Introduction." In *Critical Perspectives on Responsibility to Protect. Interrogating Theory and Practice*, edited by Philip Cunliffe, 125–139. Abingdon, UK: Routledge, 2011.

Danish Institute of International Affairs. *Humanitarian Intervention: Legal and Political Aspects*. Copenhagen, DK: 1999. http://www.diis.dk/files/media/publications/import/extra/humanitarian_intervention_1999.pdf.

Elias, Norbert. *The Civilizing Process*. Vol. 1, *The History of Manners*. Oxford: Blackwell, 1969.

Evans, Gareth. "Responsibility to Protect: From Idea to an International Norm." In *Responsibility to Protect: The Global Moral Compact for the 21st Century*, edited by Richard H. Cooper and Juliette V. Kohler, 15–30. Basingstoke, UK: Palgrave Macmillan, 2009.

Finnemore, Martha. "Constructing Norms of Humanitarian Intervention." In *The Culture of National Security. Norms and Identity in World Politics*, edited by Peter J. Katzenstein, 153–187. New York: Columbia University Press, 1996.

Freedman, Lawrence. *The Transformation of Strategic Affairs*. London: Routledge, 2006.

Gow, James, and Milena Michalski. *War, Image and Legitimacy: Viewing Contemporary Conflict*. London: Routledge, 2007.

Habermas, Jürgen. "Bestialität und Humanität: Ein Krieg an der Grenze Zwischen Recht und Moral." *Zeit Online*, April 29, 1999. http://www.zeit.de/1999/18/199918.krieg_.xml: 3.

Hahn, Ulrich. "Responsibility to Protect (R2P): Ein Neuer Rechtfertigungsversuch für Militärische Interventionen." *Forum Pazifismus: Zeitschrift für Theorie und Praxis der Gewaltfreiheit* 22, no. 2 (2009): 33–35.

Haid, Michael. "Persilschein für Interventionen in Bürgerkriegen? Die Resolution 1973 (2011) des UN-Sicherheitsrates." *AUSDRUCK. Magazin der Informationsstelle-Militarisierung EV* 2 (2011): 9–13.

Hehir, Aidan. *The Responsibility to Protect: Rhetoric, Reality and the Future of Humanitarian Intervention*. Basingstoke, UK: Palgrave Macmillan, 2012.

———. "The Responsibility to Protect in International Political Discourse: Encouraging Statement of Intent or Illusory Platitudes?" *International Journal of Human Rights* 15, no. 8 (2011): 1331–1348.

Heinze, Eric A. *Waging Humanitarian War: The Ethics, Law, and Politics of Humanitarian Intervention*. Albany: State University of New York Press, 2009.

Hobbes, Thomas. *Leviathan*, edited by C. B. Macpherson. Middlesex, UK: Penguin Books, 1968.

ICISS. *The Responsibility to Protect: Report of the International Commission on Intervention and State Sovereignty*. Ottawa: International Development Research Centre, 2001.

Imbusch, Peter. *Moderne und Gewalt. Zivilisationstheoretische Perspektiven auf das 20 Jahrhundert*. Wiesbaden, DE: VS Verlag, 2005.

Independent International Commission on Kosovo (IICK). *Kosovo Report: Conflict, International Response, Lessons Learned*. Oxford: Oxford University Press, 2000.

Kahl, Martin, and Ulrich Teusch. "Sind die Neuen Kriege Wirklich Neu?" *Leviathon* 32, no. 3 (2004): 382–401.

Kaldor, Mary. *A Decade of Humanitarian Intervention: Global Civil Society*. Oxford: Oxford University Press, 2001.

———. *New and Old Wars: Organised Violence in a Global Era*. Cambridge: Polity, 1999.

Kant, Immanuel, and Thomas Kingsmill Abbott. *Fundamental Principles of the Metaphysics of Morals*. Raleigh, NC: Alex Catalogue, 1785.

Kantner, Cathleen, and Sammi Sandawi. "Der Nationalstaat und das Militär." In *Militärsoziologie-Eine Einführung,* edited by Nina Leonhard and Ines-Jacqueline Werkner, 24–49. Wiesbaden, DE: VS Verlag, 2005.

Kubler, George. *The Shape of Time: Remarks on the History of Things*. New Haven, CT: Yale University Press, 1970.

Kümmel, Gerhard. "Auftrag und Aufgaben des Militärs im Wandel." In: *Militärsoziologie-Eine Einführung,* edited by Nina Leonhard and Ines-Jacqueline Werkner, 50–67. Wiesbaden, DE: VS Verlag, 2005.

———. "Militärische Aufträge und die Legitimation der Streitkräfte." In *Handbuch Militär und Sozialwissenschaften,* edited by Sven Bernhard Gareis and Paul Klein, 111–118. Wiesbaden, DE: VS Verlag, 2004.

Mamdani, Mahmood. "Responsibility to Protect or Right to Punish?" In *Critical Perspectives on Responsibility to Protect: Interrogating Theory and Practice*, edited by Philip Cunliffe, 125–139. Abingdon, UK: Routledge, 2011.

Mann, Michael. *The Sources of Social Power: A History of Power from the Beginning to A.D. 1760*. Cambridge: Cambridge University Press, 1986.

Münkler, Herfried. *Die Neuen Kriege*. Reinbeck, DE: Rororo, 2002.

Münkler, Herfried, and Karsten Malowitz. "Humanitäre Interventionen: Bedeutungen, Entwicklungen und Perspektiven eines Umstrittenen Konzepts-Ein Überblick." In *Humanitäre Intervention: Ein Instrument Außenpolitischer Konfliktbearbeitung*, edited by Herfried Münkler and Karsten Malowitz, 7–27. Wiesbaden, DE: VS Verlag, 2008.

Murray, Robert. "Humanitarianism, Responsibility or Realty? Evaluating Intervention as State Strategy." In *Libya: The Responsibility to Protect and the Future of Humanitarian Intervention*, edited by Aidan Hehir and Robert Murray, 15–33. Basingstoke, UK: Palgrave Macmillan, 2013.

Nonhoff, Martin. "Konstruktivistisch-Pragmatische Methodik: Ein Plädoyer für die Diskursanalyse." *Zeitschrift für Internationale Beziehungen* 18, no. 2 (2011): 91–107.

Pieterse, Jan Nederveen. "Sociology of Humanitarian Intervention: Bosnia, Rwanda and Somalia Compared." *International Political Science Review* 18, no. 1 (1997): 71–93.

Rausch, Anne. *Responsibility to Protect*. Frankfurt, DE: AM, Peter Lang, 2011.

Reeb, Hans-Joachim. "Öffentlichkeit als Teil des Schlachtfeldes. Grundlagen der Kriegskommunikation aus Militärischer Perspektive." In *Krieg als Medienereignis II: Krisenkommunikation im 21 Jahrhundert*, edited by Martin Löffelholz, 97–214. Wiesbaden, DE: VS Verlag, 2004.

Schetter, Conrad. "Von der Entwicklungszusammenarbeit zur Humanitären Interventionen. Die Kontinuität einer Kultur der Treuhandschaft." In *Interventionskultur: Zur Soziologie von Interventionsgesellschaften*, edited by Thorsten Bonacker, Michael Daxner, Jan H. Free, and Christoph Zürcher, 31–48. Wiesbaden, DE: VS Verlag, 2010.

Shaw, Martin. *The New Western Way of War: Risk-Transfer War and Its Crisis in Iraq*. Cambridge: Polity Press, 2009.

———. *Post-Military Society: Militarism, Demilitarization and War at the End of the Twentieth Century*. Philadelphia, PA: Temple University Press, 1991.

Sofsky, Wolfgang. *Traktat über die Gewalt*. Frankfurt, DE: AM, Fischer Taschenbuch Verlag, 2005.

Steinhoff, Uwe. *On the Ethics of War and Terrorism*. Oxford: Oxford University Press, 2007.

Thakur, Ramesh. *The United Nations, Peace and Security*. Cambridge: Polity Press 2006.

UN. "2005 World Summit Outcome." Resolution adopted by the General Assembly 60/1. 2005, Sixtieth session Agenda items 46 and 120, October 24, 2005.

Weber, Mathias. *Der UNO-Einsatz in Somalia. Die Problematik einer "Humanitären Intervention."* Denzlingen, DE: MW Verlag, 1997.

Weller, Christoph. "Zivile Konfliktbearbeitung: Begriffe und Konzeptentwicklungen." In *Zivile Konfliktbearbeitung. Aktuelle Forschungsergebnisse (INEF-Report 85/2007)*, edited by Christoph Weller, 9–16. Duisburg, DE: Institut für Entwicklung und Frieden, Universität Duisburg-Essen, 2007.

Wheeler, Nicholas J. *Saving Strangers: Humanitarian Intervention in International Society*. Oxford: Oxford University Press, 2000.

Wilson, Stephanie. *Effectiveness, Legitimacy, and the Use of Force in Modern Wars: The Relentless Battle for Hearts and Minds in NATO's Wars over Kosovo*. Wiesbaden, DE: VS Verlag, 2009.

2 Responsibility to Protect

The Paradox of International Intervention in Africa

Dauda Abubakar

WITH THE END of the Cold War and transitions to democratic rule in Africa in the early 1990s, many countries face challenges of violent internal conflicts arising from diverse sources including ethnoreligious tensions, predatory struggles over state power and resources by elites, and greed and bad governance.[1] African conflicts are rooted not only in the legacies of colonial rule, oppression by ruling elites, and uneven development, but also in contested issues of participation in the democratic process, identity politics, citizenship rights, land, and self-determination.[2] With the increase in magnitude of civilian casualties in African conflicts, debates have emerged about the notion of state sovereignty and international humanitarian intervention. Advocates of the Westphalian principle of sovereignty and noninterference contend that the state has exclusive authority over its territorial border as well as the welfare of its citizens. However, cosmopolitan supporters of the doctrine of responsibility to protect (R2P) contend that with the rising tide of war crimes and genocide in Africa's collapsed states, sovereignty may no longer be sacrosanct in international society.[3] Sovereignty, they argue, entails moral responsibility, and where the state fails or is unwilling to protect its citizenry, the international community has the normative obligation to intervene and rescue victims of armed conflict.

However, when the principle of human protection is applied inconsistently in African conflicts through the narrow lens of major power geostrategic and economic interests, it undermines R2P as a supposedly altruistic endeavor designed to save humanity from extermination by authoritarian regimes. As I demonstrate later in the two cases of international humanitarian intervention in Darfur and Libya, major power geostrategic interests significantly influenced the calculations of actors in the decision to either support or dither over intervention, based on their perceived narrow strategic and economic interests. Such an approach to morality in international society, as Roland Paris contends, raises certain fundamental tensions within the logic of R2P, such as (1) the mixed-motives problem, (2) the conspicuous harm problem, and (3) the inconsistency problem.[4] We could add a fourth paradox, which I describe as the collateral damage or proportionality problem, whereby interveners may use excessive force in humanitarian rescue that undermines the initial goal of human protection. While I concede that some African conflicts involve human rights violations and crimes against humanity that violate international law, the root causes of these conflicts are more complex than the narratives in which they are framed by the powerful states in international society, NGOs, and other human rights activists that advocate for intervention.[5] This chapter explicates the paradoxes, contradictions, and tensions in international humanitarian intervention through the analytical lens of the doctrine of R2P. In both the Darfur and Libya crises that I examine in this chapter, there were internal civil wars in which rebel groups were challenging authoritarian regimes; there were also allegations of human rights violations, atrocities against civilians, and the threat to regional security and stability. Also in both cases, there were efforts by the African Union (AU), the United Nations (UN), and the European Union (EU) to resolve humanitarian catastrophes using the doctrine of R2P. What factors influenced the decision and policies of the international community (including African countries and the AU) toward these conflicts? To what extent did narrow self-interests (or mixed motives) of permanent members (P5) of the UN Security Council affect the response of the international community toward the crises? In what ways could the doctrine of R2P be reconstituted so that it is applied consistently to ensure the protection of innocent civilians in armed conflict? I elaborate in the chapter that Darfur-Sudan reveals an instance of humanitarian catastrophe unleashed on the citizenry by the state in which there was little or no political will for robust international humanitarian intervention because of the mixed-motives problem of P5 members. In the case of Libya, I argue that although the North Atlantic Treaty Organization (NATO)–led humanitarian intervention, Operation Unified Protector, may have begun as an altruistic initiative for civilian protection from mass slaughter by an authoritarian regime, the disproportionate use of force, nonetheless, went beyond the tenets of UN Security Council resolution 1973, culminating in regime change and the death of Muammar Gaddafi at the hands of the rebels. The unintended consequences of Operation Unified Protector, such as the death of innocent civilians in Sirte, the collapse of the Gaddafi regime, and the proliferation of heavy weapons in the Sahel region and the destabilization of Mali, as well as the continuing instability in Libya as a result of destructive factional violence between various militia groups, indicate the limits and structural tensions within the R2P doctrine. As I demonstrate later in the chapter, NATO intervention in Libya reveals not only the mixed-motives and inconsistency problems of R2P but also the collateral damage or proportionality problem whereby Libya's

military and economic infrastructures were destroyed through NATO's disproportionate use of force.

There has been an extensive scholarly debate around the efficacy and limitations of the doctrine of R2P. Cosmopolitan advocates of R2P doctrine and liberal
intervention contend that sovereignty is not sacrosanct and should not be a stum-
bling block for saving strangers from "barbarism," ethnic cleansing, and human
rights violations. According to these scholars, states are not only political entities
but also moral agents in international society and have the obligation for protecting "shared humanity" and its universal values as enshrined in international law.
However, some critics of unilateral intervention argue that for the last four centuries, the 1648 Westphalian doctrine of sovereignty, equality of state actors, and
noninterference in the internal affairs of states has been the foundational architecture for stability in international society. Any attempt to jettison sovereignty
and the principle of noninterference in favor of the doctrine of R2P and the use of
force in international humanitarian intervention, the critics contend, would not
only "blast open a gaping hole in the foundation of democratic theory" but also
inscribe democratic deficit by diluting the relationship of representation between
people (citizens) and the state. In the words of Philip Cunliffe, "Sovereignty pre-
serves the freedom of a people to be self-determining, not the impunity of the
state apparatus" and that to jettison absolute sovereignty is "to erode the idea of
representative government and the self-determination of nations. As sovereignty
inheres in the relationship between people and the state . . . then the idea of sovereignty already answers the question of who should alleviate human suffering
or stamp out gross abuses of human rights: it is the people themselves who must
impose their will on the state."[6]

The French and American revolutions of the eighteenth century that over-
threw oppressive regimes are clear historical antecedents of how popular struggles for universal human rights and self-determination primarily rests with the
people themselves. Representative democratic institutions emerged out of these
struggles that eventually consolidated the institutions of the rule of law, justice,
and accountability to the people, as we know it today in Western democracies.
However, the doctrine of R2P and coercive humanitarian intervention flips this
historical evidence upside down by asserting that the emancipation and protection of the victims of human rights violations should be the responsibility of the
international community. As Adam Branch perceptively asserts, "Instead of af-
firming popular sovereignty and the political agency of the people," sovereignty
as responsibility "argues that the right to judge, reform, or reconstitute the state
passes not *inwards* to the people, but *outwards* to foreign states and organizations, whose right and responsibility it becomes to intervene."[7] As I show later, in
spite of the foregoing criticisms, the doctrine of R2P, if properly reconstituted to
take on board the notion of popular sovereignty and democratic accountability,

could provide the framework for ameliorating human suffering and the protection of civilians in armed conflicts. As I will show in the comparative analyses of Darfur and Libya, the inconsistency problem in the application of the doctrine of R2P reveals some of its internal tensions and paradox. However, it is pertinent to note that recent research and nuanced analyses of the notion of new humanitarianism indicate that external intervention in Sierra Leone's devastating civil war led to the restoration of peace, security, and democratic order.[8] But there are also other conflicts in Africa, such as Darfur and Libya, where humanitarian intervention under the rubric of R2P has left the civilian population trapped in perpetual violence. Before examining the two cases, it is important to briefly outline the core tenets of R2P as well as its antecedents.

The Doctrine of R2P and Its Tenets

In a 1996 book titled *Sovereignty as Responsibility: Conflict Management in Africa*, Francis Deng and his colleagues from the Brookings Institution introduced the notion of sovereignty as responsibility. The central thrust of their argument is that following the end of the Cold War and the subsequent withdrawal of superpowers from the continent, most African states faced exponential economic, political, and legitimacy crises that degenerated into violent conflicts. They contend that these violent internal conflicts arising from state failure, elite predatory rule, and collapse are the primary sources of not only human suffering and gross violations of human rights, but also the destruction of civilian lives, internal displacement, refugee crises, and the erosion of developmental capacity of Africa's postcolonial states. For Deng, the principle of sovereignty as responsibility requires that since African regimes have failed to ensure the protection of their citizens, the international community has the moral obligation to intervene and protect the lives of innocent victims of genocide and crimes against humanity.[9] Drawing from Deng's sovereignty as responsibility construct, the then secretary-general of the United Nations, Boutros Boutros-Ghali, in his *Agenda for Peace*, declared that for those African people who have been "orphaned by state collapse, the only alternative source of protection, relief assistance, and rehabilitation toward a self-reliant development has to be the international community." He went further to assert that "the time of absolute and exclusive sovereignty . . . has passed" and called for humanitarian interventions that will not only ensure global peace and security but defend human rights even where it entails the violation of the Westphalian doctrine of state sovereignty and noninterference.[10] For Michael Ignatieff, complex humanitarian crises provide the paradigmatic terrain of humanity, where the failure of state order and rule of law has unleashed victims of violent ethnic cleansing.[11] Similarly, the former secretary-general of the UN Kofi Annan, in an address to the General Assembly in 2000, challenged world leaders: "If humanitarian intervention is, indeed, an unacceptable assault on sovereignty, how should we respond to Rwanda, to a Srebrenica—to gross and systematic violations of human rights?"[12] The devastating 1993 crises in Somalia and ethnic cleansing in Bosnia and Kosovo that prompted NATO's unilateral intervention in 1999, the brutal 1990s civil wars in Sierra Leone and Liberia, and the catastrophic Rwanda genocide of 1994, which shocked the conscience of the international community by its failure to "save" the Tutsis from slaughter, are some of the key historical precedents that prompted the government of Canada to announce at the 2000 UN General Assembly the establishment of the International Commission on Intervention and State Sovereignty (ICISS). Cochaired by Gareth Evans and Mohamed Sahnoun, ICISS submitted its report to the UN secretary-general titled *The Responsibility to Protect*, which reformulated the philosophical foundations of the doctrine of sovereignty as autonomy and non-interference in international society. Drawing its inspiration from Deng's conceptualization of sovereignty as responsibility, ICISS contends that

> while the state whose people are directly affected has the default responsibility to protect, a residual responsibility also lies with the broader community of states. This fallback responsibility is activated when a particular state is clearly either unwilling or unable to fulfill its responsibility to protect or is itself the actual perpetrator of crimes or atrocities; or where people living outside a particular state are directly threatened by actions taking place there. This responsibility also requires that in some circumstances action must be taken by the broader community of states to support populations that are in jeopardy or under serious threat.[13]

In reformulating the 1648 Westphalian doctrine of sovereignty, which holds that states are autonomous and have the legitimate authority over the internal affairs of their territory and population (internal or de facto sovereignty) and that they are the legal agents of that constituted territorial entity in international society (external or de jure sovereignty), ICISS introduced a fundamental principle by asserting that the international community has the moral obligation to intervene in the internal affairs of a state where the citizenry are at risk of genocide, war crimes, and grotesque human rights violations. But ICISS also provides a nuanced caveat, particularly with regard to the use of coercive humanitarian intervention by stating that "coercive measures may include political, economic or judicial measures, and even in extreme cases—but only extreme cases—they may also include military action. As a matter of first principles, in the case of reaction just as with prevention, less intrusive and coercive measures should always be considered before more coercive and intrusive ones are applied." Furthermore, ICISS notes that "tough threshold conditions should be satisfied before military intervention is contemplated," and it identifies six core principles that should guide any form of humanitarian intervention. These are first, the right authority (who can authorize military intervention); second, the just cause principle (what kind of harm is sufficient to trigger military intervention overriding the nonintervention principle); third, the right intention (intervention must be to halt human suffering, while "overthrow of regimes is not, as such, a legitimate objective"); fourth, the principle of last resort (premised on the assumption that diplomatic, economic, and other nonmilitary tools for peaceful resolution must first be explored); fifth, the principle of proportionality (interveners should endeavor to use coercive measures only to secure the humanitarian objective at stake while limiting collateral damage to civilians); and sixth, the reasonable prospects principle (the use of force can be justified only if it stands a reasonable chance of halting or averting the atrocities that triggered the intervention in the first place).[14] As the ICISS report clearly indicates, "military intervention is not justified if actual protection cannot be achieved, or if the consequences of embarking upon the intervention are likely to be worse than if there is no action at all."[15] As I elaborate later in the chapter, the cases of Darfur and, particularly, Libya provide empirical context for a nuanced interrogation of the dilemmas embedded in the doctrine of R2P, particularly in the realm of its application as a guiding framework for humanitarian intervention in African conflicts.

It is also important to note that apart from stating the foregoing six principles, the doctrine of R2P as articulated in the 2001 ICISS report is primarily anchored on three foundational tenets or pillars. These include first, the "responsibility to prevent," which is premised on the assumption that sovereign states have the responsibility to ensure that domestic crises do not escalate into violent conflicts that threaten innocent civilian population and human rights violations. The second pillar, "responsibility to react" is based on the principle that in the event of a sovereign state failing or being unwilling to protect its citizenry, the international community has the obligation to intervene and avert human suffering. However, ICISS clearly provides specific principles that should guide the use of force for humanitarian purposes in discharging this obligation. The use of force can be applied only as a last resort when other options of negotiated settlement have been exhausted. The key question for us here is: to what extent do humanitarian interveners in African conflicts comply with these enunciated principles? The third foundational pillar of R2P is the "responsibility to rebuild."[16] This pillar is a crucial component of the doctrine of R2P, which requires that after conducting coercive intervention, the international community has a responsibility for supporting the state in reconstructing its physical infrastructures, reconciliation, and strengthening institutions of democratic accountability and rule of law that would ensure good governance, peace, and development. Although the AU intervened in Darfur, while NATO used coercive intervention in Libya to effect regime change, the two cases of humanitarian intervention reveal not only the inconsistency problem of the doctrine of R2P but also the mixed-motives and conspicuous harm problems of R2P. In the case of Darfur, for example, the African Union Mission in Sudan (AMIS), which was dispatched to protect civilians in internally displaced persons (IDPs) camps, not only was poorly equipped and small in number, but its rules of engagement were circumscribed that they should not directly confront the Janjaweed militia nor the rebel groups that were all involved in perpetrating violence against the people of Darfur. The absence of a robust AU diplomatic or military strategy to avert civilian suffering increased the harm for the people of Darfur instead of alleviating it. Issues of economic exclusion, infrastructural development, and inclusion in the Sudanese political decision making were never on the agenda of AMIS, which is contrary to the principles of pillar three—the responsibility to rebuild. In the case of NATO's intervention in Libya, the driving force behind the coalition's use of disproportionate military force against Gaddafi was primarily to obliterate Libya's defense system and economic infrastructures, strengthen the rebels, and ultimately ensure regime change, rather than protecting innocent civilians caught in the fighting. In the end, more harm than good has been done to Libya and its citizenry, who continue to be terrorized by armed militia in a state that is crippled and on the verge of collapse. Thus, an important lesson from NATO's intervention in Libya is that R2P is instrumentalized in the discourse of humanitarianism, whereby Western culpability and complicity in exacerbating disorder in Africa is projected as saving humanity from itself.[17] Like Darfur with respect to pillar three, the responsibility to rebuild, Libya and the welfare of its citizenry may not have been taken seriously in the agenda of the international community. UN Security Council resolution 1973, which authorized NATO's intervention in Libya, primarily emphasized pillar one—the responsibility to react—without significantly exploring the option of a negotiated settlement as advocated by the AU. The disproportionate use of military power against Gaddafi's forces created more political instability and harm than good for the civilian population in Libya, who, in the first place, are the initial focus of NATO's Operation Unified Protector.[18] As General Charles Bouchard, the commander of NATO's 2011 operation later observed, "the international role in Libya after the regimes fall was insufficient to accomplish the stability . . . objective we set for ourselves."[19]

The response of African states as well as the AU toward NATO's use of force to effect regime change in Libya was largely framed within the principles of R2P, particularly the notion that diplomatic, political, and economic options should first be explored, rather than unilateral use of force. While African states strongly hold on to the principle that sovereignty and noninterference in internal affairs of other states are sacrosanct, they also have the AU Constitutive Act of 2002, which endorses the doctrine of R2P. For example, article 4(h) of the AU Constitutive Act provides for the right of the AU to intervene in a member state under "grave circumstances" such as war crimes, genocide, and crimes against humanity upon the recommendation of the AU Peace and Security Council (PSC). The Constitutive Act of the AU as well as the Ezulwini Consensus of 2005 are the two key documents that clearly articulate the position of African states on issues of international humanitarian intervention under the doctrine of R2P. For example, in the section on collective security and the use of force, the Ezulwini Consensus acknowledges that although the UN General Assembly and the UN Security Council have an important role to play in the implementation of R2P, the fact that they are often far from the scenes of African conflicts makes it imperative that the AU be empowered to take actions with the approval of the UN Security Council, although in certain situations, such approval could be granted after the conflict has been resolved. For example, during the Sierra Leone and Liberia civil wars, the Economic Community of West African States Monitoring Group (ECOMOG) intervened to stabilize the situation, and the UN Security Council granted its consent after the operation had been completed. This innovative component of the Ezulwini Consensus, as part of the broader African Peace and Security Architecture (APSA), not only indicates the significant role of regional organizations such as the AU, Economic Community of West African States (ECOWAS), Inter-Governmental Authority on Development (IGAD), and the Southern African Development Community (SADC) in determining how R2P is implemented in African conflicts, but it also specifies the obligation of the UN and international community toward such undertaking. The AU through the Ezulwini Consensus clearly accepts the three interrelated pillars of R2P described earlier. However, the Ezulwini Consensus also makes it emphatically clear that R2P "should not be used as a pretext to undermine the sovereignty, independence and territorial integrity of states."[20]

During the Darfur crisis the AU established AMIS to ensure the protection of civilians trapped in the conflict between the government of Sudan and the two rebel movements—the Sudan Liberation Movement/Army (SLM/A) and the Justice and Equality Movement (JEM). It is important to note also that while AU's humanitarian intervention in Darfur involved the deployment of troops, their rules of engagement were limited to civilian protection, rather than the use of force against the rebels or the Janjaweed militia. Furthermore, AU member states also engaged in diplomatic initiatives such as the Abuja Peace Conference along with the Darfur Peace Agreement (DPA) to ensure a peaceful resolution of the conflict. The AU was also able to convince President Omar al-Bashir of Sudan to allow humanitarian agencies to provide much-needed relief materials to IDPs in their camps. Although the AU peace initiatives did not yield many results due to the recalcitrance of some of the rebel leaders, who insisted that the UN, United States, and EU should be involved in the negotiations and material support, it nevertheless indicates that regional organizations could play some significant role in the implementation of R2P doctrine as a framework for international humanitarian intervention.[21] The EU, United States, and Canada provided token financial and technical support to AMIS and the Darfur peace negotiation process but did not commit significant ground troops for a robust humanitarian mission in Darfur, citing AU's administrative incompetence and the credibility of AMIS.[22] While AU's strategy of negotiated settlement in the Darfur crisis is commendable, the drawback is that it also shielded President al-Bashir from indictment by the International Criminal Court (ICC), thereby failing to address part of the causes of the crisis in Darfur, in line with the tenets of R2P. In the case of Libya, however, NATO not only committed significant resources in terms of air power against the Gaddafi regime but also provided the rebel movements with arms and armaments as well as intelligence information in the war against Gaddafi. Furthermore, although the AU insisted, in line with R2P principles, on seeking diplomatic, political, and economic options first before the use of force in Libya, NATO was more concerned with the pursuit of unilateral military action rather than a negotiated settlement in the Libyan conflict.

It is pertinent to note that in spite of the humanitarian interventions by the international community through the AU, NATO, and UN in the Darfur and Libyan crises, which aimed at protecting civilians from harm, both Libya and Darfur remain engulfed in violence and insecurity. The anticipated outcome of R2P doctrine in the form of civilian protection as well as rebuilding infrastructures, reconciliation, and good governance have not materialized in either Darfur or Libya. How does the application of R2P affect the outcomes of humanitarian intervention in African conflicts? To what extent do the problems of mixed motives of interveners, disproportionality in the use of force, and collateral damage impact the trajectories of humanitarian intervention under the rubric of R2P? As I will show later, in both Darfur and Libya, the problem of harm to civilians and the risks of state failure persist. In the sections that follow, I examine these two cases in depth with the aim of peering through the complexities of international humanitarian interventions in Africa and the ramifications of the application of R2P as a framework for civilian human protection in armed conflicts.

Darfur: Insurgency and Political Violence in Sudan

Since independence from British colonial rule in 1956, Sudan has been at war, especially with the southern provinces that have been marginalized in the postcolonial period. In 2005, the Sudan People's Liberation Movement (SPLM/A) signed the Comprehensive Peace Agreement (CPA) with the government of al-Bashir, thus paving the way for the resolution of the southern conflict. However, by 2003, decades of marginalization of the western province of Darfur triggered another major conflict that led to a protracted civil war and the extermination of innocent civilians. While there have been debates on whether the actions of the government of Sudan along with its Janjaweed allies in Darfur amounted to genocide or not, I contend that although the issue of legal definition is pertinent, it may distract from addressing the primary problem in the conflict, namely, the protection of innocent civilian population from extermination by their own government.

The UN International Commission on Darfur, chaired by Antonio Cassese, provides some insight into the magnitude of the mass atrocities that were committed in Darfur by the government of Sudan through its Janjaweed militia as well as the two rebel movements, namely, SLM/A and JEM. The commission estimates that approximately 2.27 million people (out of the total population of 6.3 million) were affected by the Darfur conflict, including casualties ranging from 218,000 to 306,000; 1.65 million internally displaced persons; and 203,000 refugees in Chad.[23] The commission revealed several things: first, both the government of Sudan and the Janjaweed militia "are responsible for serious violations of international human rights and humanitarian law amounting to crimes under international law." Second, the Janjaweed militia and government forces conducted "indiscriminate attacks, including killing of civilians, torture, enforced disappearances, destruction of villages, rape and sexual violence, pillaging and forced displacement throughout Darfur." Third, the vast majority of the victims have been from African ethnic groups in Darfur such as the Fur, Zaghawa, Massalit, Jebel, and Aranga, to mention a few. Finally, the conduct of such a widespread destruction and systematic displacement of innocent civilians "may amount to crimes against humanity." The commission went further to conclude that international offenses such as the crimes against humanity and war crimes that have been committed in Darfur may be no less serious and heinous than genocide and that actions must be taken urgently to end these violations.[24] Thus, from the findings of the Cassese Commission, it seems that although the legal concept of genocide may not apply to the Darfur conflict as such, it is nevertheless obvious that there were mass atrocities against innocent civilians ranging from war crimes and ethnic cleansing to crimes against humanity. In what ways did regional actors such as AU and the international community respond to the Darfur conflict where war crimes and crimes against humanity were committed by both government forces and the rebels? Were the responses by the AU and international community consistent with the core tenets of R2P? To what extent did the mixed-motives, inconsistency, and conspicuous harm problems affect the response of UN Security Council members, especially in terms of the R2P doctrine?

The causes of the Darfur conflict are intricately connected to the history of colonial and postcolonial Sudan, particularly the Turko-Egyptian legacies of slavery and slave raiding in the predominantly African South and Darfur regions by Arabs and the British indirect rule policy under the Anglo-Egyptian Condominium. British indirect rule not only reinforced a native administrative system based on native chieftaincy and ownership of land (or *dar*), but also utilized the "Closed Districts Ordinance" of 1922 that cordoned the South from the North and also parcelized and retribalized Darfur. The exclusion of a majority of the people in Sudan under both colonial and postcolonial regimes from access to power and social and economic resources in Khartoum entrenched regional grievances within the society against the central government. Mahmood Mamdani eloquently provides an incisive analysis of the processes of the British colonial policy of indirect rule, which primarily relies on the use of traditional institutions to ensure local governance, taxation, land administration, and the enforcement of law and order. As he puts it, the system of native administration enforced under colonial rule in Sudan and other British territories resulted in an unintended consequence, namely, the allocation of native authorities along "tribal" lines. Thus, ethnic groups with native authority are regarded as "indigenes," while migrant groups became "settlers." The implication of this policy for the Darfur conflict is that it exacerbated disputes over land ownership and citizenship rights, particularly between Arab pastoralists and African sedentary farmers.[25] Furthermore, the onset of drought and desertification in the Sahel region further deepened conflicts over pasture and water among the various communities.[26]

British colonial education policy privileged the children of traditional rulers, thereby exacerbating social and economic hierarchies in postcolonial Sudan. In 1938, the British governor of Darfur asserted that "We . . . have been able to limit education to the sons of Chiefs and native administration personnel and can confidently look forward to keeping the ruling classes at the top of the elementary tree for many years to come."[27] Thus, at independence in 1956, the dominant riverine Arab elite who took over from the British defined Sudan's national identity in terms of being Arab and Islamic.[28] According to scholars such as Alex DeWaal, Arabism in postcolonial Sudan increasingly assumes a hierarchy of peoples, which in turn reflects the constitutive histories of unequal privilege and power relations.[29] In terms of resource distribution and infrastructural development, the postcolonial regimes concentrated power and national wealth at the central capital in Khartoum, while peripheral regions such as Darfur, southern provinces, Kordofan, and Nuba were virtually excluded. The marginalization of the periphery is at the center of the grievances not only of South Sudan but also the Darfur insurgency by SLM/A and JEM that exploded in 2003. With the increasing availability of oil wealth, the postcolonial elite in Sudan turned the state and its resources into a channel for private enrichment, to the detriment of the citizenry in the periphery.[30] The ascendance of Sudan into the rentier club of oil-producing states further exacerbated tensions between the central government and peripheral provinces in the country over resource allocation.[31] China remains a key player in Sudan's oil industry through its control of about 40 percent of the consortium in Great Nile Oil Corporation (the national oil company of Sudan). In 1995, Sudan exported 96 percent of its petroleum products to China, amounting to $3.4 billion in revenue. In 2007, even as thousands of civilians in Darfur were being exterminated by the Janjaweed militia, China's special envoy to Darfur, Liu Giu Jin, toured the ravaged region and declared that "the situation in Darfur is now basically normal."[32] According to Allison Ayers, the availability of revenue earnings from oil provided the al-Bashir government with much-needed funds for the procurement of arms and ammunitions to sustain its devastating counterinsurgency war of ethnic cleansing against the people of Darfur.[33]

Although humanitarian relief agencies continued to provide aid to refugees, a robust international humanitarian intervention to halt the war crimes and restore order could not materialize in Darfur. In mid-2004, the AU deployed a token ill-equipped mission composed of 60 monitors and 300 troops, which was later expanded to 7,000 troops under AMIS. However, AMIS was constrained not only by its lack of capabilities, but also by the mixed-motives problem. The mandate of the mission was primarily as an "observer," and it did not "have a mandate to go out and proactively protect civilians. In fact it can only protect civilians when they are being attacked in its presence, and only if it feels it has enough troops to intervene—and too often it does not."[34] Even when the African Union/UN hybrid operation in Darfur (UNAMID) took over from AMIS in 2007 and deployed around 17,000 troops, the problems of poor capacity to properly protect civilians persisted. Another dimension of the mixed-motives problem and inconsistency in the Darfur crisis relates to the role of Russia, as P5 member of the UN Security Council. According to Cristina Badescu and Linnea Berghlom, Russia has been an important supplier of arms and armaments to President al-Bashir's government and was reluctant to support any form of robust humanitarian intervention by the international community that might lead to regime change, with possible loss of a lucrative market and payment for earlier contracts. Furthermore, as Paul Williams and Alex Bellamy argue, Russia's opposition to intervention in Darfur stems from the substantial commercial interest in Sudan, where it sold around $150 million worth of military hardware and signed an oil deal with the al-Bashir government worth $200 million.[35] The mixed-motives problem was also evident in the position taken by United States government in the Darfur crisis.

In his testimony before the United States Senate Foreign Affairs Committee in 2004, Secretary of State Colin Powell affirmed that "genocide has been committed in Darfur, and that the government of Sudan and the Janjaweed bear responsibility—and genocide may still be occurring."[36] In 2007, the United States Congress passed the Sudan Accountability and Divestment Act, which required all companies applying for United States government contracts to "prove that they were not conducting business in Sudan." Also, President George W. Bush announced a series of sanctions targeting high-ranking Sudanese government officials as well as companies operating in Sudan. The United States also cooperated with the UN Security Council in referring the Darfur situation to the ICC, which issued an arrest warrant for President al-Bashir and two top government officials. It was also obvious to the UN Security Council, from the findings of the 2005 International Commission of Inquiry into Darfur (ICID), EU, and AU, that while the Darfur conflict may not be labeled as "genocide," there were, indeed, war crimes and crimes against humanity committed by the Janjaweed militia against the innocent civilian population. In line with the premise and tenets of R2P, the government of Sudan was neither willing to protect nor committed to protecting the civilian population in Darfur. However, the international community dithered over Darfur, and by the time the AU sent its token monitors (i.e., AMIS) into the region, thousands of innocent civilians had been killed, while over 1.2 million have been forced into IDP camps in neighboring Chad. An important question therefore arises: why was there no robust international humanitarian intervention in Darfur, in line with the R2P doctrine and AU's Constitutive Act, even when it was obvious that the government of Sudan was unwilling to protect civilians?

I contend that there are three fundamental reasons for this inconsistency and paradox that explain the actions of some P5 members of the UN Security Council. First, China, as a permanent member of the UN Security Council with veto power, was not willing to allow any robust intervention in Sudan because of its interests and investment in the oil industry. Second, the United States was already preoccupied with its so-called Global War on Terror campaign in Afghanistan and Iraq. Furthermore, as Badescu and Bergholm indicate, the United States was not willing to put pressure on the regime in Khartoum because Sudan was providing intelligence information on the possible whereabouts of Osama bin Laden, who had earlier lived in Sudan from 1992 to 1998. For example, in 2005, the then head of Sudan's intelligence service, Salah Gosh, was invited to the United States for consultations with the CIA on antiterrorism matters.[37] Furthermore, United States policy makers may have refrained from taking robust humanitarian action in Darfur or insisting on firmer action against al-Bashir by the ICC because the United States had declined to ratify the Rome Statute that established the ICC. A related explanation is that the United States and Western governments, along with IGAD, have invested considerable diplomatic and financial capital in the mediation of the north-south conflict in Sudan (Machakos-Naivasha peace process) and would not want it to be destroyed by Sudan's other conflicts, such as Darfur. A third factor that militated against effective humanitarian response to the Darfur crisis is the recalcitrance of the al-Bashir regime to allow any form of robust UN peacekeeping force on the grounds that it would violate the sovereignty of Sudan. Thus, despite the obvious reality of human suffering in Darfur-Sudan, the international community (including AU) could not effectively ameliorate the situation because of the mixed-motives problem of some P5 members of the UN Security Council. Darfur, like the situation in Syria where over 300,000 civilians have been killed and over 1 million people are refugees, shows the embedded inconsistencies and paradox of R2P. In the final analysis, the people of Darfur were left with an ill-equipped AU mission, whose limited mandate could not effectively protect civilians in the embattled region. In terms of R2P doctrine, the Darfur crisis raises the dilemma of the mixed-motives problem, whereby the major powers are more concerned with protecting self-interests rather than saving humanity. As Nick Grono perceptively argues, the tragic reality of Darfur, is that the region "does not matter enough, and Sudan matters much, for the international community to do more to stop the atrocities."[38] For DeWaal, Darfur represents the complexities of African conflicts as well as the limits and paradox of the doctrine of R2P as a framework for curtailing war crimes, ethnic cleansing, and crimes against humanity. If Darfur, as discussed above, reveals the challenges of the mixed-motives problem and inconsistencies embedded in the strategic logic of R2P doctrine, the case of Libya raises the paradox of collateral damage or proportionality problem in humanitarian intervention.

Libya, NATO, and the Collateral Damage Problem

The application of the doctrine of R2P in the Libya crisis arose from UN Security Council resolution 1973, which mandated NATO to implement a "no-fly zone" for the purpose of protecting civilians from Gaddafi's forces. However, as I discuss below, NATO's disproportionate use of force in the Libyan conflict exceeded the initial mandate granted by the UN Security Council. There are three key questions I seek to examine: First, does UN Security Council authorization for humanitarian engagement provide a legitimate basis for supporting rebel movements, disproportionate use of force, or regime change in a sovereign state? Second, in what way do the problems of collateral damage and mixed motives during civilian protection in armed conflicts impact the future legitimacy of R2P in international society? Third, to what extent was pillar three of the R2P doctrine—responsibility to rebuild—observed in the actions of NATO after the 2011 Libya Operation Unified Protector? It is important to note from the outset that the outbreak of the crisis in Libya is part of the larger Arab Spring revolt by opposition groups in Middle East and North African countries against dictatorships and their demand for democratization of the political space.

Specifically in North Africa, the Arab Spring began in Tunisia with the self-immolation of one Mohammed Bouzazi. It gradually spread to Egypt, Libya,

Bahrain, Syria, and other Middle Eastern countries. However, unlike Egypt and Tunisia, where there was no external military intervention, the uprising in Libya degenerated into civil war that prompted foreign intervention by NATO under the doctrine of R2P that culminated into violent regime change.[39] The rebellion against Gaddafi that started in Benghazi is intricately woven with the history of state formation in Libya. Prior to Italian colonial occupation in 1911, the geographical space that became Libya was composed of three Ottoman provinces of Cyrenaica, Fezzan, and Tripolitania. While Cyrenaica was under the monarchy of King Muhammad Idris Sanusi, the western province of Tripolitania formed the autonomous Tripolitania Republic in 1918. The Sanusiyya monarchy based in Cyrenaica and the Tripolitania Republic constituted the bastion of nationalist opposition to Italian colonial occupation. In its brutal campaign against the Libyan people, Italy exterminated about half a million people, while another 60,000 perished in concentration camps.[40] The three provinces were eventually amalgamated to form the present state of Libya. Between 1943 and 1951, Libya was administered by Britain and France. After independence in 1951, political power was handed back to the Sanusiyya monarchy, which was overthrown by Gaddafi in the 1969 military coup.

With the ascendance of Gaddafi and the availability of oil wealth in the 1970s, Libya experienced impressive socioeconomic transformation, urbanization, expansion of higher education, health services, and the emergence of a middle class. Between 1950 and 2010, Libya's population increased from 1 million to 6.5 million. In Tripoli, the population increased from 130,000 in 1951 to 1.8 million in 2010, while in the eastern city of Benghazi, the population increased from 70,000 to 650,000.[41] With abundant wealth from the export of oil and natural gas resources to Europe, the Libyan state subsidized social services such as health, transportation, and education, thereby improving the livelihood of the citizenry. For example, in 2011 Libya's Human Development Index of 0.760 was ranked at number 54 out of 187 countries, which was better than most African and Middle Eastern countries. Between 1980 and 2011 life expectancy increased in Libya from 60.1 years to 74.8 years, while the adult literacy rate reached an impressive 88.9 percent. In 2010, gross national income per capita was $15,767, which was far greater than that of all sub-Saharan African countries.[42]

In spite of these impressive accomplishments under Gaddafi, the centralization of power and restriction of the political space increasingly created dissatisfaction with the ideology of personal rule. For the people of Cyrenaica, the Gaddafi regime that sacked the Sanusiyya monarchy, which hitherto had its headquarters in Benghazi, was fundamentally illegitimate. By the 1990s, there emerged a formidable opposition group called the Libyan Islamic Fighting Group (LIFG) led by Abd al-Hakim Bilhaj, a veteran of the Afghan war. LIFG drew most of its support from eastern cities such as Baida, Darnah, and Ajdabiyya in Cyrenaica.

As the base of the Sanusiyya Movement that fiercely fought Italian colonization through heroes such as Omar Mukhtar, Benghazi and the province of Cyrenaica in general became the rallying heartland for opposition against Gaddafi's autocracy. The Gaddafi regime responded to LIFG with a harsh crackdown. Several of its leaders were incarcerated and tortured in the Abu Salim prison in Tripoli. As a result of LIFG uprisings in 1998, the Gaddafi regime conducted aerial bombardments in Cyrenaica and declared a state of emergency in the eastern city of Darnah.[43] In 1996 a protest in the Abu Salim prison led to the massacre of about 1,200 incarcerated political prisoners. According to Ali Ahmida, it was a commemorative protest organized on February 15, 2011, by the families of the Abu Salim prison massacre victims in Benghazi and the arrest of their lawyer Fathi Terbal that triggered a confrontation with Gaddafi's security forces and the subsequent rebellion that metamorphosed into a revolution calling for the overthrow of the regime.[44] According to James Pattison, as the confrontation escalated approximately 10,000 people were killed.[45] The increase in civilian casualties and Gaddafi's threat to wipe out the opposition made the Libyan conflict a challenge for regional organizations as well as the UN. The League of Arab States (LAS) and the AU responded differently to the unfolding civil war and threat of humanitarian catastrophe in Libya.

At the outset of the Libyan crisis, the AU clearly stated its position that since the conflict was an internal political matter in a sovereign state, it should be resolved through negotiated political settlement. In an effort to find a diplomatic solution to the crisis, AU established a High Level Committee composed of South Africa, Mauritania, Mali, Uganda, and Republic of Congo. The mandate of the committee was to: (1) facilitate the cessation of hostilities, (2) ensure that Libyan authorities cooperated in allowing timely delivery of humanitarian assistance, (3) encourage Libyan authorities to protect foreign nationals including African migrants, and (4) ensure that the Gaddafi regime implemented political reforms that would facilitate a resolution of the crisis. However, AU's proposal for a peaceful negotiated settlement of the conflict was rejected by the Interim National Transition Council (NTC). In a meeting with members of the AU High Level delegation in Benghazi, Mustafa Abdel Jalil, chair of the TNC, insisted that the AU road map to negotiated settlement was not acceptable because it did not include the immediate departure of Gaddafi. According to Jalil, "Qaddafi must leave immediately if he wants to survive."[46] In its efforts to defuse the mounting violence, the AU at its Extraordinary Summit on May 25 proposed an "inter-positioning force" in the Misrata area that would monitor a ceasefire between Gaddafi forces and rebel forces, to be monitored by the AU, UN, and LAS. According to DeWaal, this option could not materialize because no African country was ready to volunteer troops and the much-needed funding from EU was delayed. As the rebel forces entered into Tripoli, the internal dynamics of the

Libyan conflict decisively swung in the TNC's favor. Some African countries such as Ethiopia and Nigeria not only recognized the TNC, but also urged the AU to do the same. In the end, AU's strategy of negotiated settlement did not yield significant success because neither Gaddafi nor the TNC was willing to enter into a ceasefire. Nonetheless, from the perspective of the doctrine of R2P as elaborated in the ICISS report, AU's position on the Libya conflict is consistent with the principle that diplomatic and political options must first be explored; if negotiated settlement fails, then force could be applied as a last resort. While the AU strategy emphasized dialogue and mediation as an appropriate channel for the resolution of the Libyan conflict, the LAS opted for a more coercive approach by calling for the imposition of a no-fly zone over Libya's air space.

From the onset of the Libyan conflict, members of the LAS were eager to ensure some form of regime transformation in that country because of Gaddafi's tacit support for Western intervention in Iraq, which led to the overthrow of a Sunni-Arab regime under Saddam Hussein. The first major response of LAS in February 2011 was the suspension of Libya's membership from the organization. Furthermore, during its Extraordinary Ministerial Meeting held in Cairo on March 12, 2011, LAS not only urged Libyan authorities to respect international law by ending "crimes against the Libyan people," but also emphatically called on the UN Security Council "to bear its responsibilities towards the deteriorating situation in Libya, and to take the necessary measures to impose immediately a no-fly zone on Libyan military aviation, and to establish safe areas in places exposed to shelling as precautionary measure that allows the protection of the Libyan people and foreign nationals residing in Libya, while respecting the sovereignty and territorial integrity of neighboring States."[47] Also, LAS urged for a coordinated effort by UN, AU, Organization of Islamic Conference (OIC), and EU in finding a solution to the Libyan conflict.

Five days after the LAS ministerial session that called for the imposition of a no-fly zone over Libya's airspace, the UN Security Council adopted resolution 1973, which explicitly authorized a "ban on all flights in the airspace of the Libyan Arab Jamahiriya to help protect civilians . . . and civilian populated areas under attack . . . including Benghazi, while excluding a foreign occupation force of any form on any part of Libyan territory."[48] Two days after the passage of the UN Security Council resolution, NATO military forces began air bombardment against Libya's air defenses. However, this military operation authorized by the UN Security Council meant that the UN had initiated a war against a sovereign state and the incumbent regime premised primarily on the R2P principle of protecting civilians. It is also a war that has been initiated in the name of civilian protection against the wishes of an incumbent government of a sovereign state. According to Alan Kuperman, NATO's intervention and support for Libya's rebels not only led to the overthrow of Gaddafi but also extended the duration of the conflict, thereby increasing the number of civilian casualties. For example, UN Human Rights Council's investigation found that twenty NATO airstrikes killed sixty civilians and injured another fifty-five. Also, on August 8, 2011, another NATO bomb killed thirty-four civilians and injured thirty-eight. By assisting the rebels through airstrikes, rather than seeking a negotiated settlement as proposed by AU, NATO elongated the duration of the Libya conflict, thereby increasing the magnitude of collateral damage to human lives and property. As Kuperman indicates, "Repeatedly, NATO would bomb Libyan forces, enabling the rebels to advance on populated areas [such as coastal towns of Misrata, Bani Walid, Sirte, and Ras Lanuf], until the government counterattacked—with each round of combat inflicting casualties on both fighters and noncombatants." Consequently, estimated casualties in the Libya conflict reached between 8,000 and 11,500.[49] Rebels also expelled 30,000 (mostly black) African guest workers on the grounds that they were "mercenaries" supporting the Gaddafi regime. Furthermore, in April 2012, Human Rights Watch reported that violence against innocent civilians around Misrata persisted and "appear[ed] to be so widespread and systematic that [it] may amount to crimes against humanity." NATO's humanitarian intervention in Libya indicates the dilemmas of the R2P doctrine whereby interveners may go beyond the initial intent of UN Security Council resolution to pursue a self-serving agenda of regime change. NATO's disproportionate use of force, even when Gaddafi's forces were in retreat, exacerbated collateral damage against both combatants and noncombatants, thereby defeating the initial objective of civilian protection as enunciated in UN resolution 1973 that authorized the intervention in the first place.

The NATO intervention raises some basic questions: What are some of the interests of the major actors in Libya's conflict? And what are the implications of the actions for the future legitimacy of R2P doctrine in international society? First, NATO countries, especially United States, Great Britain, and France, had grudges against Gaddafi because of his role in sponsoring the Pan-Am Airline bombing over Lockerbie, Scotland, in which several citizens of the United States perished. Second, Britain and France were interested in regime change not only to open up access for their corporations to Libya's vast oil and gas reserves but also to ensure that a new regime in Tripoli would curb the rising tide of illegal migration into Europe. EU countries had tried to get Gaddafi to crack down on illegal migration from sub-Saharan Africa through Libya, but he had not taken any serious action in that direction. Third, since the 1980s, Western countries had accused Gaddafi's Libya of being a "state sponsor of terrorism." Hence, UN Security Council resolution 1973 provided a convenient opportunity for regime change in Tripoli. As for LAS, particularly Sunni Gulf States such as Saudi Arabia, Qatar, and Kuwait, intervention in the Libya conflict provided the window to unseat Gaddafi, who supported the overthrow of Saddam Hussein's Sunni regime in Iraq. Second, leaders of the Gulf States were opposed to Gaddafi because of his persistent critical attitude that Arab leaders have aligned themselves with Western countries, thereby failing to take a decisive stance to resolve the Palestinian national question. Third, the leaders of Qatar and Saudi Arabia, in particular, were eager to support the demise of Gaddafi because of his alleged involvement in a plot to assassinate King Abdullah (while he was the crown prince); and fourth, Gaddafi arrogantly embarrassed the emir of Qatar, Sheikh Hammad bin Khalifa al-Thani, at the 2009 Arab summit in Doha, Qatar. In the case of the AU, their position for a negotiated settlement was premised on the principle that the conflict between Gaddafi and the rebels was an internal sovereign matter that should be settled through diplomacy rather than the use of force. Furthermore, because of the legacy of colonial domination, African states are generally suspicious of any form of external intervention, knowing that the logic of imperialism has historically been rationalized as a project of "human" civilization and emancipation from "barbarism." As President Jacob Zuma of South Africa stated, "We strongly believe that the resolution [1973] is being abused for regime change, political assassinations and foreign military occupation" and that the use of force for humanitarian cause in Libya might hamper the future prospect for legitimate use of the R2P doctrine to save civilians from harm.[50]

In both Darfur and Libya, the doctrine of R2P seems to be applied inconsistently, thereby raising the problem of its efficacy as an international norm that will ensure neutrality and the protection of innocent civilians from war crimes and crimes against humanity. While in the case of Darfur, most of the P5 countries had a mixed-motives problem that constrained the prospects for a robust and effective humanitarian intervention that could have saved the lives of thousands of civilians, in Libya, NATO's disproportionate use of air power in support of rebellion exacerbated collateral damage and harm to civilians, thereby eclipsing the initial intent of UN Security Council resolution 1973. Although the AU deployed a nimble peacekeeping force in Darfur (even when there was no peace to keep), AMIS was limited due to lack of financial resources to accomplish its goals of saving innocent civilians from harm. Even UNAMID had similar problems. Both Darfur and Libya reveal the tensions within the logic of R2P doctrine that make its utilization as a tool for saving humanity highly problematic. First is the mixed-motives problem, whereby state actors may either support or derail humanitarian action based on self-interested motivation. Second is the inconsistency problem, in which interveners may be enthusiastic in utilizing disproportionate force for regime change, as in Libya, while dithering in Darfur where there was obvious outbreak of ethnic cleansing, war crimes, and crimes against humanity. Third is the collateral damage and conspicuous harm problem, by which I refer to the situation where the outcome of supposed humanitarian action leaves behind a trail of continuing violence, political uncertainty, instability, and anarchy. In Darfur, for example, most of the refugees that were displaced during the peak of the violence still remain in IDP camps, and instability persists in the region. The case of Libya is even worse, because the NTC government that replaced the Gaddafi regime has not been able to establish a stable government. Most of the armed militia groups retain their heavy weapons and have been fighting each other for control of cities, territory, and oil terminals. Since the 2011 NATO operations in Libya, the country has not had a central government. There have been two parliaments in the country—one located in Tripoli and the other in Al Bayda. Also, Benghazi remains the site of a fierce battle between the forces of General Khalifa Haftar and Ansar al-Sharia militants. With the political vacuum created as a result of NATO's regime change in Libya, other external jihadi groups such as Islamic State in Syria and the Levant (ISIL) have joined the fight, thereby exacerbating the anarchy and disintegration of the country. A closely related unintended consequence of NATO's actions in Libya is that several weapons from Gaddafi's stockpiles have spread into Sahelian countries, thereby fueling violence in Mali and northeastern Nigeria. It is estimated that about 15,000 man-portable surface-to-air missiles (MANPADs), capable of shooting down civilian and military aircraft, are unaccounted for after the fall of the Gaddafi regime. In both Darfur and Libya, interveners seem to have neglected pillar three of the R2P doctrine that enjoins them to support the state in rebuilding its infrastructures, political inclusion, and the reconstruction of institutions of democratic accountability, good governance, and the rule of law. The failure of interveners in Darfur and Libya to follow through with the principle of rebuilding state institutions to facilitate economic development exacerbated the chasm between the citizenry and the government, thereby deepening the democratic deficit. By refracting sovereignty outward to the international community rather than inward to the people within the country, the principle of sovereignty as responsibility in R2P seems to undermine an essential ingredient of popular democratic sovereignty, which historically rests with the people.

Conclusions

The cases of humanitarian intervention in Darfur-Sudan and Libya examined in this chapter suggest that the R2P doctrine has internal tensions and inconsistency that limit its efficacy as a norm in international society. Although the crisis in Darfur was characterized by instances of ethnic cleansing, war crimes, and crimes against humanity, Western powers did not provide significant support for the AU mission to stop the carnage. Rather, the actions of the P5 members of the UN Security Council over the Darfur crisis were hampered by the mixed-motives problem, such as access to Sudan's oil and lucrative commercial market for weapons as well as securing intelligence for prosecuting the War on Terror.

The irony is that it is those weapons (supplied by Russia and China) the al-Bashir government channeled to the Janjaweed militia that perpetrated war crimes in Darfur. For Western powers, Darfur is a case of "African solutions for African problems"; hence there was dithering over robust humanitarian intervention. However, in Libya, there was a swift response by NATO, LAS, and the United States in the imposition of the no-fly zone and bombardment of Gaddafi's forces and military installations. Although the AU advocated for a negotiated political settlement, Western powers were eager to use force, which culminated in regime change. NATO's bombardment and supply of armaments to the rebels not only escalated and elongated the duration of the conflict, but also dissuaded the NTC from seeking a negotiated settlement. Thus, humanitarian intervention in Libya through the doctrine of R2P became a smokescreen for regime change. This, obviously, sets a dangerous precedent because it undermines the legitimacy of R2P, exacerbates the inconsistency problem, and subverts the efficacy of an international norm for resolution of humanitarian crises. Although the AU Constitutive Act acknowledges and supports the principles of R2P, African states were, nonetheless, weary of NATO's disproportionate use of force against an incumbent leader of a sovereign state. African Peace and Security Architecture, as articulated in AU Constitutive Act, recognizes the imperatives of civilian protection from war crimes, genocide, and crimes against humanity. It also acknowledges that African states have an obligation to intervene in member countries where there is an obvious case of genocide and violations of international humanitarian law. Thus, one of the primary reasons why most African leaders opposed NATO's military intervention and the use of force against Gaddafi is that they preferred the utilization of a diplomatic approach through AU's stipulated mechanisms of internal conflict resolution as enshrined in the Constitutive Act. Simply put, the position taken by the AU on Libya's crisis seems to be more consistent with the doctrine of R2P than NATO's disproportionate use of force, which obliterated not only Gaddafi but even more tragically the fabric of Libya's national cohesion, statehood, and unity. NATO's bombardment of Libya and the subsequent triumph of the rebels set that country on the path of incipient turmoil, insurgent militia violence, insecurity, and the breakdown of the rule of law, with catastrophic implications for the civilian population in the country.

In terms of civilian protection, the case of Libya reveals a certain fundamental paradox because not only did it culminate in the overthrow and assassination of Gaddafi, but NATO's actions fueled internal political violence among competing militia factions that continues to rage unabated. While the intent of UN Security Council resolution 1973 was primarily to facilitate the protection of civilians using the no-fly zone in the Libyan conflict, NATO's bombardment of military forces and command centers resulted in unintended civilian casualties. In November 2011, NATO's secretary-general Anders Fogh Rasmussen claimed that the operation in Libya was conducted "very carefully, without confirmed civilian casualties."[51] However, when confronted with field evidence collected by Human Rights Watch, NATO spokeswoman Oana Lungescu conceded, "From what you have gathered on the ground, it appears that innocent civilians may have been killed or injured, despite all the care and precision."[52] President Obama lamented that the failure of US and its NATO allies to plan for post-Gaddafi Libya has plunged the country into a "mess" and that the decision to use coercive intervention was the "worst mistake" of his presidency.[53] As Yahia Zoubir and Erzsebet Rozsa persuasively put it: "Far from resolving the conflict, the no-fly zone and the incessant bombings by NATO forces created a situation of no return, for they thwarted any political solution and gradually demonstrated that the intent was no longer . . . to protect civilians . . . but to bring about regime change, for which neither NATO nor any other country was mandated under the said resolution."[54] By using UN Security Council resolution 1973 to unleash disproportionate violence in the Libya crisis, NATO countries undermined a core ethical foundation of R2P, namely, the protection of civilian population vulnerable to the threat of mass atrocities. Instead of being a neutral broker for peaceful resolution of the conflict, NATO tipped the balance of forces in favor of the insurrection, thereby setting a dangerous precedent in African conflict resolution.

In Darfur, the mixed-motives problem, as discussed earlier, constrained P5 countries from providing robust support for AU's initiative through AMIS and UNAMID in the region. Since the United States was more concerned with its War on Terror, it was willing to align itself with the al-Bashir government (which is responsible for the violent counterinsurgency war in Darfur) as a source of vital intelligence on terror cells. Russia and China were motivated mainly by their commercial interests in Sudan's arms market and oil resources. The lesson of Darfur and Libya is that although Western countries and the P5 members of the UN Security Council may express disgust at human suffering perpetrated by governments and rebel groups against innocent civilians, the response to such human rights violations by the international community, more often than not, is constrained by narrow self-interest. In the final analysis, R2P doctrine becomes instrumentalized, while the use of disproportionate force, as in Libya, deepens collateral damage and political instability rather than the restoration of peace, order, and stability.

Notes

1. Souare, *Civil Wars and Coup d'Etat in West Africa*, 41–72.
2. See especially Autesserre, *The Trouble with the Congo*; Autesserre, *Peaceland*; Fearon and Laitin. "Ethnicity, Insurgency and Civil War," 76; Marshall-Fratani, "The War of Who Is Who," 12; Ekeh, "Colonialism and the Two Publics," 95; Nzongola-Ntalaja, "Citizenship, Politi-

cal Violence, and Democratization in Africa," 405; Young. "Deciphering Disorder in Africa?" 536; Ake, *Democracy and Development in Africa*, 10.

3. The 2005 World Summit Outcome would eventually adapt *The Responsibility to Protect: Report of the International Commission on Intervention and State Sovereignty* (ICISS 2001), which articulated the doctrine of responsibility to protect. For further details on cosmopolitan logic and R2P see Kaldor, *New and Old Wars*; Power, *A Problem from Hell*, 54; Deng et al., *Sovereignty as Responsibility*, 1. For a coherent and incisive critique of cosmopolitan logic and R2P, see Hehir, "The Permanence of Inconsistency," 139; Hehir, *Humanitarian Intervention*, 83–126.

4. Paris, "The Responsibility to Protect and the Structural Problems of Preventive Humanitarian Intervention," 576.

5. For debates on humanitarian intervention, see Mamdani, "The Responsibility to Protect or the Right to Punish?," 53–67; Mamdani, *Savior and Survivors*; Hehir, *Humanitarian Intervention*, 282–304; Kuperman, "A Model of Humanitarian Intervention?," 108; Ayoob, "Humanitarian Intervention and State Sovereignty," 85; Cuncliffe, "Dangerous Duties," 83; Branch, "The Irresponsibility of R2P in Africa," 275; Wheeler, *Saving Strangers*, 125.

6. Cuncliffe, "Dangerous Duties," 55–79.

7. Branch, "The Irresponsibility of R2," 269–303. For further critical perspectives on humanitarian intervention in Africa, see Bush, Martineillo, and Mercer, "Humanitarian Imperialism," 358; Wai, "The Empire's New Clothes," 487.

8. Bah, "The Contours of New Humanitarianism," 2–6. Libya, however, reveals the dilemmas of the use of force, especially when it degenerates into regime change, thereby violating international law. NATO used military force in Libya without AU's consent, but with a tacit approval of the League of Arab States (LAS).

9. Deng's argument, on the conditionality of sovereignty, as the case of Libya demonstrates, can easily be abused in pursuit of an illegitimate agenda of regime change.

10. Boutros-Ghali, *"An Agenda for Peace."*

11. For further comparative analyses of effects of identity-driven violent conflicts in the Balkans, see Ignatieff, *The Warrior's Honor*, 34–62; on the superficial and ahistorical narrative of violence in Africa, see Kaplan, "The Coming Anarchy."

12. For further details, see Annan, *Millennium Report of the Secretary General of the UN.*

13. ICISS, *The Responsibility to Protect*, 17.

14. The ICISS report is clear on the conditions that would trigger humanitarian intervention.

15. This perspective on humanitarian intervention enunciated in the ICISS report clearly makes the use of force conditional, rather than a general rule to be defined by interveners who may have a self-serving agenda at stake in a conflict. The notion of last resort is crucial.

16. The third pillar of R2P, responsibility to rebuild, emphasizes the obligation of interveners in the restoration of social, economic, and political normalcy after the conflict. See ICISS, *The Responsibility to Protect*, especially 39–43.

17. See Wai, *The Empire's New Clothes*; and the engaging book, Zubairu Wai, *Epistemologies of African Conflicts*, 120–121.

18. Aiden Hehir provides a cogent analysis of the paradox of NATO's operation in Libya, which culminated in doing more harm than good, which the UN resolution 1973 anticipated. Hehir, *Humanitarian Intervention*.

19. Coming from the commander of NATO Forces in Libya, this statement is telling, indeed, about the failure of the strategy.

20. The AU, which is the successor regional organization to the Organization of African Unity (OAU), has been conscious of Africa's hard-won political independence from colonial rule. AU's position on Libya has been anchored on the Ezulwini consensus, which clearly re-

flects the doctrine of R2P. African Union Executive Council 7th Extraordinary Session, Ezulwini Consensus, Ext/EX.CL/2, Addis Ababa, 2005.

21. DeWaal, "Darfur and the Failure of Responsibility to Protect," 1040; DeWaal, "My Fears, Alas, Were Not Unfounded."

22. Badescu and Bergholm, "The Responsibility to Protect and the Conflict in Darfur," 289.

23. UN, "Report of International Commission of Inquiry on Darfur to the UN Secretary-General."

24. Ibid., 3.

25. Mamdani, *Savior and Survivors.*

26. Nelson Kasfir deploys a neo-Malthusian explanation of the Darfur conflict. See particularly Kasfir, "Sudan's Darfur," 197.

27. Collins, *A History of Modern Sudan,* 277.

28. Jok, *Sudan,* 25.

29. Sharkey, "Arab Identity and Ideology in the Sudan," 28. For a nuanced analysis of racial identity formation and the Darfur conflict, see DeWaal, "Who Are the Darfurians." Some works that have examined the Darfur conflict from the perspective of R2P include Sarkin, "The Responsibility to Protect and Humanitarian Intervention in Africa," 376. For a more incisive historical and structural analysis of Sudan's complex civil war and insurgency, see Ayers, "Sudan's Uncivil War," 156.

30. The "greed and grievance" discourse in the analyses of African conflicts can be found in the works of Bayart, Ellis, and Hibou, *The Criminalization of the State in Africa,* 35; Berdal and Malone, *Greed and Grievance,* 28; and Millikin, *State Failure, Collapse and Reconstruction,* 10.

31. On the application of the rentier thesis to African postcolonial states, see Ross, "A Closer Look at Oil, Diamonds and Civil War," 269; Ross, "How Do Natural Resources Influence Civil War?" 46; Ross, "Does Oil Hinder Democracy," 338.

32. Gerard Prunier provides a detailed account of Darfur as an instance of genocide. See Prunier, *Darfur,* 178–179.

33. Ayers, "Sudan's Uncivil War," 156.

34. Nick Grono's incisive critique of R2P is developed in Grono, "The International Community's Failure to Protect," 262.

35. Williams and Bellamy, "The Responsibility to Protect and the Crisis in Darfur," 34. For further critical analyses on the limits of R2P and humanitarian intervention in Africa, see Bellamy, "Responsibility to Protect or Trojan Horse?," 35; and "Whither the Responsibility to Protect?," 157.

36. Robert Collins provides a refreshing account of the genocide debate on the Darfur crises in his book *Modern Sudan,* 292.

37. For further details see Belloni, "The Tragedy of Darfur and the Limits of the Responsibility to Protect," 339; and Lanz, "Save Darfur," 232.

38. Grono, *Failure to Protect,* 623.

39. For a detailed account of overthrow of Gaddafi's regime, see Zoubir and Rosza, "The End of the Libyan Dictatorship," 1267.

40. Ali Ahmida, "Libya, Social Origins of Dictatorship, and the Challenge of Democracy," 72.

41. Ibid., 74.

42. United Nations Development Project, *Human Development Report,* 2.

43. Detailed analyses of the historical processes and struggles of state formation in Libya can be found in the works of Alia Brahimi, "Libya's Revolution," 616–617; Fredric Wehrey, *The Struggle for Security in Eastern Libya* 4–8.

44. Ahmida, "Libya, Social Origins of Dictatorship," 74.

45. Pattison, "Outsourcing the Responsibility to Protect," 1–31.
46. DeWaal, "The African Union and the Libya Conflict of 2011," 2.
47. See League of Arab States, *Resolution Number 7360*, March 2011, 5.
48. UN, "Security Council Resolution," S/RES/1973, 2011, 5.
49. Kuperman, "NATO Intervention in Libya," 25.
50. Ibid., 30.
51. Chivers and Schmitt, "In Strikes on Libya by NATO, an Unspoken Civilian Toll."
52. Human Rights Watch, "Unacknowledged Deaths," 23.
53. Malloy and Treyz. "Obama Admits Worst Mistake of his Presidency."
54. Zoubir, "The End of the Libyan Dictatorship."

References

Ahmida, Ali. "Libya, Social Origins of Dictatorship, and the Challenge of Democracy," *Journal of the Middle East and Africa* 3 (2012): 70–81.
Ake, Claude. *Democracy and Development in Africa*. Washington, DC: Brookings Institution, 1996.
Annan, Kofi. *Millennium Report of the Secretary General of the UN. We the People: The Role of the UN in the 21st Century*. United Nations Document A/54/20. 2000. http://www.un.org/en/events/pastevents/pdfs/We_The_Peoples.pdf.
Autesserre, Severine. *Peaceland: Conflict Resolution and the Everyday Politics of International Intervention*. New York: Cambridge University Press, 2014.
———. *The Trouble with the Congo: Local Violence and the Failure of International Peacebuilding*. New York: Cambridge University Press, 2010.
Ayers, J. Allison. "Sudan's Uncivil War: The Global-Historical Constitution of Political Violence." *Review of African Political Economy* 37, no. 124 (2010): 153–171.
Ayoob, Mohammed. "Humanitarian Intervention and State Sovereignty." *International Journal of Human Rights* 6, no. 1 (Spring 2002): 81–102.
Bah, Abu Bakarr. "The Contours of New Humanitarianism: War and Peacebuilding in Sierra Leone." *Africa Today* 60, no. 3 (2013): 2–26.
Bayart, Jean-Francois., S. Ellis, and B. Hibou, *The Criminalization of the State in Africa*. Bloomington: Indiana University Press, 1998.
Badescu, G. Cristina, and Linnea Bergholm. "The Responsibility to Protect and the Conflict in Darfur: The Big Let-Down." *Security Dialogue* 40, no. 3 (June 2009): 287–309.
Bellamy, J. Alex. "Responsibility to Protect or Trojan Horse? The Crisis in Darfur and Humanitarian Intervention after Iraq." *Ethics and International Affairs* 19, no. 2 (2005): 31–53.
———. "Whither the Responsibility to Protect? Humanitarian Intervention and the 2005 World Summit." *Ethics and International Affairs* 20, no. 2 (2006): 143–169.
Bellamy, J. Alex, and Paul D. Williams. "The New Politics of Protection: Cote d'Ivoire, Libya and Responsibility to Protect." *International Affairs* 87, no. 4 (2011): 825–850.
Belloni, Roberto. "The Tragedy of Darfur and the Limits of the Responsibility to Protect." *Ethnopolitics* 5, no. 4 (2006): 327–346
Berdal, Matts, and David M. Malone, eds. *Greed and Grievance: Economic Agendas in Civil Wars*. Boulder, CO: Lynne Rienner, 2000.
Boutros-Ghali, Boutros. *"An Agenda for Peace," Report of the Secretary-General*. United Nations Document A/47/277-S/24111. http://www.un.org/doc/SG/agpeace.html.
Brahimi, Alia. "Libya's Revolution." *Journal of North African Studies* 16, no. 4 (2011): 605–624.

Branch, Adam. 2011. "The Irresponsibility of R2P in Africa." *Journal of Intervention and State Building*, Special Issue (2011): 269–303

Bush, Ray, Giuliano Martineillo, and Claire Mercer. "Humanitarian Imperialism." *Review of African Political Economy* 38, no. 129 (2011): 357–365.

Chivers, C. J., and Eric Schmitt. "In Strikes on Libya by NATO, an Unspoken Civilian Toll." *New York Times*, December 17, 2011. http://www.nytimes.com/2011/12/18/world/africa/scores-of-unintended-casualties-in-nato-war-in-libya.html?_r=0.

Collins, Robert O. *A History of Modern Sudan*. New York: Cambridge University, 2008.

Cuncliffe, Philip. "Dangerous Duties: Power, Paternalism and the Responsibility to Protect." *Review of International Studies* 36 (2010): 79–96.

Deng, Francis, et. al. *Sovereignty as Responsibility: Conflict Management in Africa*. Washington, DC: Brookings Institution Press, 1996.

DeWaal, Alex. "The African Union and the Libya Conflict of 2011." World Peace Foundation, *Reinventing Peace*, December 19, 2012. https://sites.tufts.edu/reinventingpeace/2012/12/19/the-african-union-and-the-libya-conflict-of-2011/.

———. "Darfur and the Failure of Responsibility to Protect." *International Affairs* 83, no. 6 (2007): 1039–1054

———. "My Fears, Alas, Were Not Unfounded: Africa's Responses to the Libya Conflict." In *Libya, the Responsibility to Protect and the Future of Humanitarian Intervention*, edited by A. Hehir and R. W. Murray, 58–82. New York: Palgrave Macmillan, 2013.

———. "Who Are the Darfurians: Arab and African Identities, Violence and External Engagement." *African Affairs* 104, no. 415 (2005): 181–205.

Ekeh, Peter. "Colonialism and the Two Publics in Africa: A Theoretical Statement," *Comparative Studies in Society and History* 17, no. 1 (1975): 91–112.

Fearon, James, and David Laitin. "Ethnicity, Insurgency and Civil War." *American Political Science Review* 97, no. 1 (2003): 75–90.

Grono, Nick. "The International Community's Failure to Protect." *African Affairs* 105, no. 421 (2006): 621–630.

Hehir, Aidan. *Humanitarian Intervention: An Introduction*. New York: Palgrave Macmillan, 2013.

———. "The Permanence of Inconsistency: Libya, the Security Council and the Responsibility to Protect." *International Security* 18, no. 1 (Summer 2013): 137–159.

Human Rights Council. *Report of the International Commission of Inquiry on Libya*. A/HRC/19/68. March 2, 2012.

Human Rights Watch. "Unacknowledged Deaths: Civilian Casualties in NATO's Air Campaign in Libya." May 2012. http://www.hrw.org/sites/default/files/reports/Libya.

Ignatieff, Michael. *The Warrior's Honor: Ethnic war and the Modern Conscience*. New York: Henry Hold, 1997.

International Commission on Intervention and State Sovereignty. *The Responsibility to Protect: Report of the International Commission on Intervention and State Sovereignty*. Ottawa: International Development Research Centre, 2001.

Jok, Maduk Jok. *Sudan: Race, Religion and Violence*. Oxford: One World Book, 2007.

Kaplan, Robert. "The Coming Anarchy: How Scarcity, Crime, Overpopulation and Disease Are Rapidly Destroying the Social Fabric of Our Planet." *Atlantic Monthly* 273, no. 2 (1994): 44–76.

Kaldor, Mary. *New and Old Wars: Organised Violence in a Global Era*. Cambridge: Polity, 1999.

Kasfir, Nelson. "Sudan's Darfur: Is It Genocide." *Current History*, May 2005, 195–202.

Kuperman, J. Alan. "A Model Humanitarian Intervention? Reassessing NATO's Libya Campaign." *International Security* 38, no. 1 (Summer 2013): 105–136.

———. "NATO Intervention in Libya: A Humanitarian Success?" In *Libya, the Responsibility to Protect and the Future of Humanitarian Intervention,* edited by Aidan Hehir and R. W. Murray, 25. New York: Palgrave Macmillan, 2013.

Lanz. David. "Save Darfur: A Movement and Its Discontents." *African Affairs* 108, no. 443 (2009): 669–677.

League of Arab States. *Resolution Number 7360.* March 2011.

Malloy, Allie, and Catherine Treyz. "Obama Admits Worst Mistake of his Presidency." *CNN* April 11, 2016, http://www.cnn.com/2016/04/10/politics/obama-libya-biggest-mistake.

Mamdani, Mahmood. "The Responsibility to Protect of the Right to Punish?" *Journal of Intervention and Statebuilding* 4, no. 1 (2010): 53–67.

———. *Savior and Survivors: Darfur, Politics and the War on Terror.* New York: Pantheon books, 2009.

Marshall-Fratani, R. "The War of Who Is Who: Autochthony, Nationalism, and Citizenship in the Ivorian Crisis." *African Studies Review* 49, no. 2 (2006): 9–43.

Millikin, Jennifer, ed. *State Failure, Collapse and Reconstruction.* Malden, MA: Blackwell, 2003.

Nzongola-Ntalaja, Georges. "Citizenship, Political Violence, and Democratization in Africa." *Global Governance* 10 (2004): 403–409.

———. "The Politics of Citizenship in the Democratic Republic of Congo." In *Making Nations, Creating Strangers: States and Citizenship in Africa,* edited by Sara Dorman et al., 69– 80. Leiden: Brill, 2007.

Paris, Roland. "The Responsibility to Protect and the Structural Problems of Preventive Humanitarian Intervention." *International Peacekeeping* 21, no. 5: (2014): 569–603.

Pattison, James. "Outsourcing the Responsibility to Protect: Humanitarian Intervention and Private Military and Security Companies." *International Theory* 2, no. 1 (2011): 1–31.

Prunier, Gerard. *Darfur: A 21st Century Genocide.* 3rd ed. New York: Cornell University Press, 2008.

Power, Samantha. *A Problem from Hell: America and the Age of Genocide.* New York: Basic Books.

Ross, Michael. "A Closer Look at Oil, Diamonds, and Civil War." *Annual Review of Political Science* 9 (2006): 265–300.

———. "Does Oil Hinder Democracy." *World Politics* 53 (2001): 325–361.

———. "How Do Natural Resources Influence Civil War? Evidence from Thirteen Cases." *International Organization* 58 (2004): 35–67.

Sarkin, Jeremy. "The Responsibility to Protect and Humanitarian Intervention in Africa." *Global Responsibility to Protect* 2 (2010): 371–387.

Sharkey, J. Heather. "Arab Identity and Ideology in the Sudan: The Politics of Language, Ethnicity and Race." *African Affairs* 107, no. 426 (2008): 21–43.

Souare, K. Issaka. *Civil Wars and Coup d'Etat in West Africa: An Attempt to Understand the Roots and Prescribe Possible Solutions.* Lanham, MD: University Press of America, 2006.

United Nations. "Report of International Commission of Inquiry on Darfur to the UN Secretary-General." January 25, 2005. http://www.un.org/News/dh/sudan/com.

———. "Security Council Resolution." S/RES/1973, 2011. UN.org/doc/UNDOC/GEN/GEN/No5/564/35/pdf.

United Nations Development Project, *Human Development Report.* New York: United Nations, 2011.

Wai, Zubairu. "The Empire's New Clothes: Africa, Liberal Interventionism and Contemporary World Order." *Review of African Political Economy* 41, no. 142 (2014): 483–499.

———. *Epistemologies of African Conflicts: Violence, Evolutionism, and the War in Sierra Leone.* New York: Palgrave, 2012.

Wehrey, Fredric. "The Struggle for Security in Eastern Libya." Washington, DC: Carnegie Endowment for International Peace, September 2012.

Wheeler, Nicholas. 2000. *Saving Strangers: Humanitarian Intervention in International Society.* Oxford: Oxford University Press, 2000.

Williams, Paul, and Alex Bellamy. 2005. "The Responsibility to Protect and the Crisis in Darfur." *Security Dialogue* 36, no. 1 (2005): 27–47.

Young, Crawford. 2002. "Deciphering Disorder in Africa: Is Identity the Key?" *World Politics* 54 (2002): 532–557.

Zoubir, Yahia H,. and Erzsebet N. Rozsa. "The End of the Libyan Dictatorship: The Uncertain Transition." *Third World Quarterly* 33, no. 7 (2012):1267–1283.

3 Dancing Boys and the Moral Dilemmas of Military Missions

The Practice of Bacha Bazi *in Afghanistan*

Michelle Schut and Eva van Baarle

> There he [lieutenant of the Afghan National Army] was, in bed with a "chai boy" in the spoons position. I thought: "Bloody hell, with a child? Is that normal?" But in their eyes it is normal. It is their culture, so you just close the door, because what else can you do? You can't really pull that guy out of bed, but those are the moments when you really want to do something.
>
> Major in the Marine Corps, serving as a member of an
> Operational Mentoring and Liaison Team

In 2010, THE PBS *Frontline* news program in the United States brought the harrowing situation of the dancing boys in Afghanistan to worldwide attention by broadcasting a documentary titled *The Dancing Boys of Afghanistan*.[1] In the documentary, Afghan journalist Najibullah Quraishi sketches the lives of these often impoverished young "entertainers," who live in the service of affluent and influential Afghans. The boys are dressed as women and wear makeup in order to perform dances for their masters. This is, however, not as innocent as it seems, as the boys are then taken to the home of the highest bidder. This practice, in which an adult man (*bacha baz*) has a sexual relationship with a preadolescent boy (*bacha bereesh*, boys without beards) is called *bacha bazi* (Persian for "boy play"). The boy is taken into the family or social circle of the man and is sometimes given some form of special payment and/or financial support for his family. The boy is a status symbol and sexual partner to the influential men in question.

The Dancing Boys of Afghanistan documentary gave rise to significant responses. The documentary was, however, not the first time that Western media channels had highlighted this practice.[2] In 2009, Travis Schouten, a former corporal of the Canadian Armed Forces, reported on the rape of an Afghan boy by members of the Afghan National Security Forces (ANSF) on a Canadian compound just outside Kandahar. The events, reported in the *Ottawa Citizen* of September 19, 2009, had taken place in 2006.[3] While the Canadian Armed Forces tried to keep a lid on the incident and the North Atlantic Treaty Organization (NATO) ignored the affair, Schouten endeavored to bring the issue to the public's attention. Moreover, he wanted clear guidelines to be drawn up on what action military personnel should take and whom they should report to in the event of witnessing sexual abuse.[4] He was not the only one to express concern. NATO personnel in Afghanistan have similar stories to tell. They talk of catamites or "chai boys" (tea boys), that is, boys wearing makeup who are the servants of, among others, police and army commanders and who do more "chores" than just making the tea. These stories inspired us to study the practice of bacha bazi.

There are some studies and more documentaries highlighting the practice of bacha bazi.[5] However, little attention is given to how international military personnel operating in this region approach the issue, which in their eyes is a morally and culturally critical situation. In her work on the International Criminal Court (ICC) and war crimes in the Democratic Republic of Congo, Milli Lake specifically addressed the issue of sexual and gender-based violence, including that against boys.[6] However, her work dealt with sexual and gender-based violence typically committed by combatants and the prosecution of those crimes under international law. Her work does not address the roles of international forces or their responsibility and efforts to prevent the crimes. Our work examines the responsibility and efforts of international forces in Afghanistan to deal with sexual violence against boys.

Since there is a remarkable lack of gender-specific data on sexual violence toward men in the international military operations literature, our aim is to contribute to the discourse on the responsibility to protect (R2P) doctrine, concentrating on gender-based violence toward boys in the armed conflict in Afghanistan.[7] In Afghanistan, large sections of vulnerable civilians are exposed to moral dangers, including sexual violence, which can be explained by the complete collapse of the state and society after decades of war. The focus in this chapter is on how Dutch military personnel act when faced with sexual violence regarding young boys, having the responsibility to protect and at the same time also having to maintain good relations with their local partners. First, we describe a number of theoretical notions. Secondly, we examine the background of bacha bazi in Afghanistan and the Dutch and international guidelines regarding bacha bazi. Finally, we discuss what Dutch military personnel did when faced with bacha bazi and give a number of recommendations for future international missions.

Moral Dilemmas: Morally and Culturally Critical Situations

The practice of bacha bazi contradicts the legal standards and moral values of most individual members of the Dutch military on how to behave toward children. Moral and cultural values are considered to be relative, in terms of both time and place. Values define what is important and right and serve as the basis of norms within societies.[8] While moral values can be personal or group based, cultural values belong to a specific group of people. Cultural values deal not only with morals, but also with "knowledge, art, belief and any other capabilities and habits acquired by man as a member of society."[9] In the eyes of our respondents, sexual contact with children, both girls and boys, is unacceptable. Dutch military personnel experienced bacha bazi as a morally and culturally critical situation.[10] These are defined as situations in which the conduct of the local population in a deployment area (i.e., a different culture) is experienced as conflicting with one's own personal moral and cultural values. The issue of bacha bazi is one of the morally and culturally critical situations most mentioned by our respondents, members of the Royal Netherlands Army with deployment experience in Afghanistan.

Some members of the Dutch military experience these situations as a moral dilemma, owing to the fact that some of their local counterparts may be involved. We define a moral dilemma as a situation in which there is a conflict between two or more moral values that cannot be respected simultaneously.[11] Dealing with moral questions requires moral competence.[12] Moral competence involves people knowing what is expected of them and being prepared to act accordingly. Several elements are important for moral competence. First is becoming aware of your own values and the values that may be at stake in a given situation. One can gauge the moral dimension of a situation only if one is capable of recognizing the values that are being violated. The next step is to make a judgment about the situation and communicate it. The final step is the preparedness to act on the judgment and be accountable for the choice made in the given situation.[13]

Although a number of military personnel feel that values clash in the case of bacha bazi, they are not clear on what action they should take. Some respondents indicated that the chai boys are part of Afghan culture and used this argument as a reason for taking no action. A particular view of Afghan culture and the difference with Western culture is constructed, in which the phenomenon of chai boys are viewed as normal in the context of Afghanistan.[14] This can be framed as orientalism, which according to Edward Said has "less to do with the regions and people they essentialize, exoticize and objectify than with the conditions under which the discourses were produced."[15] This is also a clear culturally and morally relativist point of view. Moral and cultural relativism is based on the observation that different cultures have different moral standards, which is merely descriptive. Normative moral relativism holds that because nobody is right or wrong, we ought to tolerate the behavior of others even when we disagree with their morality.[16] There are several important drawbacks to moral relativism. For example, you can never criticize cultures (including your own, even if slavery or genocide takes place), making moral change very problematic.[17] As Russell Blackford notes, it is important that we do not tolerate everything, nor should we adopt a quietism about moral traditions that cause hardship and suffering. Equally, we should not passively accept the moral norms of our own societies when they are ineffective, counterproductive, or simply unnecessary.[18]

Method

Twenty-nine semi-structured interviews were conducted with Dutch military personnel on morally and culturally critical situations they encountered during their deployments. Of the twenty-nine respondents, twenty-two had been deployed to Afghanistan (to Kabul, Kandahar, Uruzgan, Deh Rawod, and Mazar-e Sharif, among other places) for at least one term (three to six months). During the interviews only open questions were asked, such as, "Can you give us examples of cultural differences which conflict with your values?" The Dutch respondents mentioned young boys who were sexually assaulted in Afghanistan. Although we did not ask about sexual violence explicitly, it was mentioned as a morally and culturally critical situation with great regularity. Based on the data, we decided to focus on this particular morally and culturally critical situation. As described, we followed the grounded theory approach.[19]

Similarly, during lessons organized by the military in dealing with dilemmas and moral judgments, Dutch military personnel are asked to identify a moral dilemma that they have encountered in their military practice.[20] Course participants often refer to bacha bazi as a moral dilemma. As in the interviews we conducted, course participants are not asked explicitly about bacha bazi, yet they often mention it. On the basis of this information, five additional in-depth interviews were conducted with Dutch military personnel who had been deployed to Afghanistan and who had specifically referred to the practice of bacha bazi during the military lessons. Furthermore, sixteen interviews about morally and culturally critical situations were held with Dutch police trainers in Kunduz. Of the total of fifty interviews, forty-five of the interviewees were men and five were women, varying in rank from private to colonel and being from all four services of the Royal Netherlands Army. The interviews were recorded and the transcriptions sent to the interviewees for a member check. Names and other means of identification were changed in order to guarantee anonymity of those interviewed.

Furthermore, a study was carried out using the literature available on bacha bazi in general and on specific Afghan, Dutch, and international guidelines regarding bacha bazi. It is striking that scholarly literature on the subject is restricted to research from the eighteenth and nineteenth centuries. Currently, the issue is receiving attention mainly from international and nongovernmental organizations. In addition to accessing the available literature, a short field study was conducted in the Kunduz area in October 2012. Observations were made at the Afghan Uniform Police (AUP) training areas and two group discussions were held with patrolmen of the AUP in Kunduz, representing various ranks, age groups, and ethnicities. Nine in-depth interviews were held with various parties. Six interviews were conducted with officers of the ANSF working at the Ministry of Interior Affairs in Afghanistan or for various police services, such as the Afghan National Civil Police in the Kabul region. Permission was not given to record a number of these interviews on account of Afghan Ministry of Defense restrictions and the protection of privacy. Two interpreters from the Kunduz area, working at that time for NATO, were also interviewed. Finally, an Afghan humanitarian aid worker, who had been active in both the United Kingdom and Afghanistan, was also interviewed. We also spoke to a NATO interpreter. Detailed notes were made during all of these interviews. All of these interviews were about respondents' views on bacha bazi and the reactions of international military personnel confronted with bacha bazi situations.[21]

The field study was hampered by the unstable security situation. As a result, conducting interviews with the local civilian population was too dangerous, and the first author could travel outside the base only with the help of the Dutch military. The quality and kind of data collected are also influenced by the complex relationships resulting from the different aspects of our identity in different contexts.[22] We are aware that our "multiple positionalities" (i.e., gender, nationality, and civilian status) influenced our research process.[23] As female civilian researchers in a masculine military context, we are also aware of our own position, in Afghanistan as well as in the Netherlands defense establishment. For example, Dutch military respondents sometimes assumed that we as civilian women (one of us being a mother) would find it shocking to hear that the practice of bacha bazi gradually becomes more or less normal to them.

It is a fact that that our work was to a certain extent facilitated by the International Security Assistance Force (ISAF). The translators we used were working for NATO and physical access and safety were provided by the Dutch military. All of these unavoidable factors may have influenced our data.[24] On the ground, we were automatically associated with, and even perceived to be, Western peacekeepers. Moreover, Afghan respondents were giving their answers on the question of bacha bazi to a female Dutch researcher from their positions as security officials. It is possible that they simply gave politically correct answers. A further complicating factor is that the practice of bacha bazi is an open secret in Afghanistan and it is not talked about in public.[25] This was vividly demonstrated during a group interview with AUP officers in Kunduz. After one young policeman in the group, who had seen the bacha bazi phenomenon during a party in a rural area, responded that "it is OK," the rest of the group immediately reacted by saying "no, it is not OK" and then quickly started talking about something else, avoiding the subject.

Bacha Bazi

In Afghanistan, young boys are sometimes kidnapped, taken as orphans, or sold by their parents to be used for entertainment and sex. Over half of our Afghan respondents indicate that these boys are abused. The boys, who are sometimes no more than eleven years old, are selected for their height and beauty. The young boys are valued for "their beauty and, implicit in this . . . , the promise of erotic fulfilment and pleasure."[26] The more attractive the boy, the more prestige the adult man (bacha baz) "owner" receives. To the bacha baz, the boy is a status symbol. Boys who are good performers are respected and often have the chance to give dancing lessons, earn a reasonable wage, and, in some cases, become a bacha baz themselves. It is a vicious circle.[27] For most of the other boys, however, future prospects are less rosy. They are left without education or money. Moreover, they are stigmatized, which makes it even harder to earn a living.

The issue of bacha bazi should be understood in its context, most notably the state of the Afghan security sector, civil-military relations in Afghanistan, Afghan history, and the social conditions in Afghanistan. Violence against civilians, including sexual violence, tends to be more common in armed forces or armed groups and in societies with dysfunctional accountability and command structures.[28] It is also important to note that attention for men and boys as victims of sexual and gender-based violence is relatively new. Recent reports indicate that the problem might be dramatically underestimated.[29]

In the existing literature on the subject of bacha bazi, various explanations are mentioned. Afghanistan's turbulent history is quoted as one of the main reasons for large numbers of boys being vulnerable to sexual abuse. In general terms, the protection of boys by the family is reduced, and large numbers of boys are out in the open looking for work or they become migrants.[30] The distinction between the private and public domains in Afghan culture, particularly regarding showing affection, is another explanation given for the existence of bacha bazi.[31] As noted by John Frederick, "While affectionate behaviour between males and females in public is not tolerated, between males it is openly demonstrated."[32]

Another notable explanation in literature for bacha bazi is that it could be viewed as an Afghan custom owing to the fact that it is said to have been practiced as early as the Middle Ages.[33] There are various expressions of the beauty of boys in old poems, songs, and texts, proving that the practice has existed for centuries.[34] For example, there is a written text dating back to 1041 CE describing the adoration of young boys: "You know how deep was the love in your eyes kindled within my soul, or how great was my suffering! Bless my beloved! He wished to visit me but could not come near me because of his tear-drowned eyes . . . wine made him obedient to all my wishes."[35] Presently, statements concerning the beauty of young boys are also made in public, as can be seen in a documentary called *Taliban Country*, where Jan Mohammed, at that time governor and chief of police, says the following about the photographs of young boys found at a suspect's house: "Where did you find these boys? O Allah, what good looks! Aren't they heavenly creatures? What beautiful boys they are. I wish I was young again. They are more beautiful than ten women. . . . We will take him [the suspect] along with us and for a few nights he will keep us entertained."[36] Although the literature and examples show that the practice exists, we would be hesitant to refer to it as Afghan culture. First of all, it is likely that the practice is not an accepted social norm, nor is it the main culture in Afghanistan. It can simply be a subculture of wealthy and influential men. Moreover, this can be a practice that they can continue due to the security gap and disintegration of the state and society after decades of war. Above that, this practice also seems to contradict Islamic norms in Afghanistan. For example, the boys may often be considered to have breached their family's honor, or commit suicide, which suggests that the practice is far from being well accepted in Afghan culture.

Bacha bazi is not called homosexuality in Afghanistan. Homosexuality is sex between men, but young boys are not yet men. These boys have a feminized role in terms of appearance and conduct.[37] The male perpetrator is masculinized as the practice gives him (more) power.[38] As stated by Charli Carpenter, "The violence is gender-based owing to configurations of gender ideas that justify or naturalize it."[39] Since pederasty and pedophilia are not applicable to boy play in Afghanistan, we will continue to use the term "bacha bazi" or "boy play."[40]

Perception of Bacha Bazi in Afghanistan

Currently, there is no legislation in force that explicitly refers to bacha bazi, but there are regulations concerning anal sex, pederasty, sexual abuse, and the exploitation of children, including the Rome Statute of the ICC.[41] Although Afghan legislation does not specifically mention the term "bacha bazi," it does state that child abuse and pederasty are punishable offenses. Furthermore, Afghanistan has signed international treaties and has a policy to protect children, including the National Plan of Action against Child Trafficking 2004, the National Strategy for Children at Risk 2008, the United Nations Convention on the Rights of Children, and the South Asian Association for Regional Cooperation's Convention on Preventing and Combating Trafficking in Women and Children for Prostitution. Though it is clear that bacha bazi is against Afghan law, in practice the law is often not enforced.

According to the Afghan respondents, the big problems are that the numbers of police personnel are too low and the authorities are unable to mete out the applicable punishments. This is characteristic for a fragile state such as postwar

Afghanistan, where security sector reform has failed to facilitate good governance and police reform.[42] The security gap and weakness of government make
the arrest and punishment of the bacha baz by ANSF personnel and the Afghan
authorities difficult. Currently, the practice of bacha bazi is said to be on the rise
again, owing to the fact that the bacha baz is not prosecuted by the Afghan government, since most government organizations are still mainly located in urban
areas and provincial administrative centers.[43] A further factor is that the safe
shelters for these boys are located only in the major city. Respondents pointed
out that shelters do help the boys make a better future. Since the boys typically
cannot return to their families because their own honor and their families' honor
has been tarnished, it seems that shelter would be the best solution for dealing
with the current problem.

A critical question that came out in our study is whether the practice is accepted by a broad segment of the population or whether it is accepted only by
male local leaders. According to Shivananda Khan, in some parts of Afghanistan
bacha bazi is normal: "Sexual exploitation and/or abuse of adolescent males by
older men . . . can, in some parts of the country, be considered a social norm
within certain segments of Afghanistan society, particularly among certain populations."[44] However, Catherine Norman's report on the Afghan police in Helmand shows that families actively complain about the behavior of the Afghan
police, who are known to rape boys.[45] Furthermore, some modern Afghan songs
explicitly demonstrate that many Afghans find the practice disgusting. A clear
example can be found in the lyrics of a song by Suhell and Umaira Sadiqzadah
simply titled "Bacha Bazi": "Enough with this boy play / Our country's name has
gone bad / You have taken the boys' respect and honor away / With this nasty
act you are not getting anywhere."[46] Just as the aforementioned lyrics to modern
popular songs, the servants of the law also speak out against bacha bazi. Moreover, 80 percent of the Afghan respondents in our study stated that bacha bazi is
an immoral practice. They indicate that it contravenes the Islamic religion and
that the practice goes against Islamic law and Afghan law. One of the respondents
was particularly firm and fierce in his reaction to this practice among people he
described as "bad people, who act like beasts."

Boy play is not restricted to Afghanistan. Some versions of the practice have
been noted in other Asian countries such as Pakistan, India, and Bangladesh.[47]
The practice was, for centuries, also institutionalized in ancient Greece, particularly in Athens and Thebes.[48] Although our study is not about boy play as it was
practiced in ancient Greece, it is interesting to note that there are quite a number of similarities between boy play in ancient Greece and the practice of bacha
bazi in Afghanistan. Boy play remained quite common for thousands of years
in ancient Greece, even though the practice was criticized. It seems that it was
only after the rise of Christianity and St. Paul's strong criticism of homosexual-

ity and pederasty that a major social shift against boy play took place.[49] How boy play is really perceived is dependent on the zeitgeist. As Foucault has pointed out both in the *History of Sexuality* (1976) and in *Discipline and Punish* (1975), we should be aware that, roughly since the nineteenth century, we have been not only influenced but also disciplined by the proliferation of the modern categories of anomaly—delinquents, the pervert—which "the technologies of discipline and technology are supposed to eliminate but never do."[50]

Bacha Bazi and International Military Personnel Guidelines

While there is no official policy regarding bacha bazi for international military personnel, several guidelines have been issued on how to behave during missions in Afghanistan. In this section, we look briefly at the primary tasks of ISAF military personnel in Afghanistan, the legal framework of the mission in Afghanistan, and the current guidelines regarding bacha bazi. These tasks, mission goals, and legal framework are closely related to the considerations and the actual behavior of military personnel in the field including when they are faced with morally and culturally critical situations.

Since the fall of the Taliban regime in 2001 and the appointment of Hamid Karzai as president of Afghanistan, the Netherlands has been part of ISAF. ISAF operates with the consent of the Afghan government of Karzai. The mission was authorized by the UN Security Council based on Chapter VII of the UN Charter. As part of ISAF, the Royal Netherlands Army has carried out a number of different missions in various provinces in Afghanistan. Its primary tasks are to assist the Afghan government in extending its authority throughout the country, carry out security operations in concert with the Afghan National Army in order to promote stability in the country, and support the Afghan National Police by disarming illegal combatants.[51]

UN resolutions give ISAF a role in protecting human rights and civilians. UN Security Council resolution 2011, for example, states, "Reaffirming that all parties to armed conflict must take all feasible steps to ensure the protection of affected civilians, especially women, children and displaced persons, calling for all parties to comply with their obligations under international humanitarian and human rights law and for all appropriate measures to be taken to ensure the protection of civilians."[52] However, ISAF troops are also guests in a sovereign state that has a police force at its disposal for law enforcement. The Afghan police have authority in the area of criminal investigation, which Dutch military personnel do not have. The reality is that there is a security gap in Afghanistan, which is one of the reasons why Western military personnel were recently training Afghan police officers.[53] A case of bacha bazi will, in the first instance, be judged by Afghan law. This was also the message the commander and the legal adviser gave to one of the teams of the Netherlands Police Training Group in Kunduz. He stated that "as Dutch nationals, and more specifically, as military personnel with a police observing, mentoring and liaison task, we do not have the right to take action if activities take place that are against Afghan law. It is our task to observe how the Afghan police deal with the situation and then to discuss their approach with them and provide them with further training." Although this was a clear description of the task in hand, the commander also had some clear advice for his personnel: "If you catch them red-handed, I will back your intervention."

In the Netherlands, all persons being deployed to another country are given information about the deployment area during mission-specific training, which is provided by the Cultural and Historical Background and Information Section of the Royal Netherlands Army. In these kinds of trainings, participants are told that bacha bazi occurs in Afghan society and are also shown footage from, among other things, *The Dancing Boys of Afghanistan* documentary. Despite this mission-oriented information and other initiatives taken by individual commanders, the Royal Netherlands Army has not drawn up specific guidelines for Dutch military personnel on what action to take when they encounter bacha bazi. The senior leadership within the defense establishment now also recognizes the moral dilemma posed by bacha bazi, particularly when a member of personnel witnesses sexual abuse. Bacha bazi is now seen as an important issue, which is one of the reasons why attention was given to it during the recent police training mission in Kunduz. The issue was discussed during the workup period of Dutch military personnel and in the training program for Afghan police personnel. In the police training program, Afghan police personnel were given lessons on investigative procedures and Afghan legislation regarding sexual abuse of women and children.[54]

The failure of the Royal Netherlands Army to provide guidelines for military personnel has shifted the responsibility for how to act in bacha bazi situations to the men and women in the field. As we gathered from both the literature and our contacts with various colleagues in the United States and Canada working in the field of ethics at the various defense academies, all coalition partners have failed to provide adequate policies for dealing with bacha bazi. In the United States, the subject seems to be avoided. American soldiers and marines have been instructed not to intervene, in some cases, even when their Afghan allies have abused boys on military bases.[55] Canada has a similar policy of "don't look, don't tell."[56] In 2011, a study was published on the crisis in trust and cultural incompatibility.[57] According to this study, reports have been received from United States and Canadian military personnel regarding Afghan security personnel raping young boys.[58] In Canada, there was a great deal of media exposure for the case reported by Schouten in *Ottawa Citizen*. In 2008, the Canadian minister of defense, Peter

Mackay, announced that "troops will not turn a blind eye to the abuse of children. Let us be clear: in no way, shape or form have Canadian soldiers and certainly the Canadian government ever condoned or excused allegations of sexual abuse against children in this country or anywhere else."[59] Given the fact that bacha bazi is illegal in Afghanistan and the international forces are there to support the local forces in the development of law, one could argue that there appears to be no moral dilemma. However, there is a clash of values between supporting the development of law and addressing the violation of the physical integrity of the boys on the one hand and on the other hand, the military mission's need to maintain good relations with local leaders, who may be involved in bacha bazi.

Bacha bazi still poses a critical question for the military intervention in Afghanistan. In particular, how should military personnel be prepared for dealing with bacha bazi? Should they be expected to intervene? Up until now, we have been unable to find concrete guidelines on these relevant questions. Guidelines could, for instance, include the recommendation to report cases of sexual and gender-based violence to local or international humanitarian organizations. The UN High Commissioner for Refugees (UNHCR) has developed several guidelines for its own personnel on how to access survivors, facilitate reporting, provide protection, and deliver essential medical, legal, and social services.[60] As noted previously, by this failure to provide guidelines, moral responsibility seems to be shifted to the individual members of the military who encounter this practice and are consequently faced with a moral dilemma.[61] That demands much of the moral competence of military personnel. However, it is clear that Afghan laws, including those relating to sexual contact with boys, must be enforced and adhered to by all persons in Afghanistan.

Understanding Bacha Bazi: The Perspective of Dutch Military Personnel

The main question in this chapter is how Dutch military personnel act when they encountered bacha bazi during their deployment in Afghanistan. We address this question by examining the views of Dutch military personnel, as a case study, on what international forces experienced and their responses to the bacha bazi problem. In particular, we seek to know whether Dutch military personnel see bacha bazi as a moral dilemma and the actions they typically take when faced with bacha bazi.

Bacha bazi is one of the critical situations frequently mentioned by Dutch respondents in discussions of culture and morality during their service in Afghanistan. Dutch soldiers call the boys involved in bacha bazi chai boys, catamites, or flower boys. The local term, bacha bazi, was not used by any of the Dutch respondents. A colonel who had been deployed to Uruzgan recounted, "We had a clear case of it in the Afghan Security Guard, a boy wearing nail varnish and the rest, with a voice to match." According to all Dutch respondents, these well-kept boys of approximately nine to ten years of age, not only make tea for senior police officers and dress up and dance for elderly men, but also are sexually abused. One Dutch female major tried to sum up the "positive" side of the bacha bazi phenomenon. She noted that "it is an honor for a boy to be selected, as it increases their status. They are given beautiful clothes and are paid. So there are some advantages for the boys. Unfortunately, they have to do something in return. I imagine that it is not very nice for chai boys working at police stations, because they have to be available to the whole group." Most respondents from the Royal Netherlands Army see the practice in a more negative light. A lieutenant colonel who had served in Kandahar and Uruzgan said, "After a party, the big shots take the boy away with them and have him sit on their laps, followed by the rest of it." Often, the sexual abuse of these boys is only a supposition, as the lieutenant colonel further indicates: "I saw boys wearing makeup and dancing during a party, but anything else was no more than suspicion on my part." However, there are accounts of Dutch soldiers who certainly have observed abuse taking place, such as a major who heard boys screaming during the night.

Dutch soldiers emphasized that the boys are a status symbol to the men they work for. Several Dutch respondents went on to say that the Afghans they had spoken to had told them that the practice is a result of the difference between men and women. As also noted by one of the respondents, "women are for reproduction, men are for love and pleasure." The strict separation of men and women was also referred to: "The stricter the division between men and women as prescribed by religion, the more often you will see this kind of thing happening." A number of the military personnel we interviewed thought that bacha bazi is a legal practice in Afghanistan, but the majority knew that it is illegal. According to them, the problem is that many Afghans are illiterate and are consequently ignorant of the legislation in place. These examples can be interpreted as orientalist archetypes. Afghans are portrayed by our Dutch interviewees as "starkly different from and utterly inferior to Westerners."[62]

A number of military personnel experience the bacha bazi phenomenon as a shock or as a moral dilemma. This results not only from the practice clashing with their personal values, but also from the fact that they were unprepared by the Dutch military to deal with this phenomenon. From the start, little attention was given to the subject during pre-deployment training for Afghanistan. As a Dutch respondent stated, "During mission-specific training, we didn't discuss this subject at all. But we did learn that we must respect local culture." Consequently, for a number of personnel, an encounter with bacha bazi becomes a moral dilemma because they are unsure how best to deal with it. During one lesson on ethics given by one of the commanders at the Police Training Group in Kunduz, a captain raised the issue. He had personally experienced the dilemma while deployed in another part of Afghanistan and had wished to see the Royal Netherlands Army put a number of guidelines in place on how to deal with bacha bazi.

Handling the Bacha Bazi Moral Dilemma

Dealing with bacha bazi can prove to be a dilemma in terms of what action to take. Dutch soldiers often had to deliberate the values that are important to them. One commander gave an account of how he had gone with a provincial recon-struction team (PRT) to attend a meeting on power supply. On that occasion, a roughly ten-year-old boy, who was under the influence of drugs, started to dance for them. As the Dutch commander stated,

> He had a lot of scarfs with him and during his dance he started to throw them towards us. The interpreter explained that the one who gets the most scarfs is allowed to go with the boy. . . . Suddenly, I noticed that all of the scarfs had been thrown towards me. I found this an embarrassing situation and said, via the interpreter, that I respected their culture, but this is not the way we treat children. Fortunately, this worked out OK. Later, I was told that I had done nothing wrong and that we could carry on with our business there. Personally, I felt quite powerless as any action you take might have serious consequences.

In terms of moral competence, this soldier is aware of the clash of values such as the humane treatment of children and good relations with local commanders. Therefore, he experiences this situation as difficult and even as a moral dilemma. He communicates his judgment, that he rejects this way of treating children, but at the same time is uncertain about the consequences on the relations with the local commanders.

Cultural difference has been a frequently mentioned reason by Dutch military personnel for not intervening in bacha bazi situations. As one respondent stated, "It is a custom there, a fact of life. It is their culture. I won't be able to change it on my own." Another lieutenant from the Marine Corps noted, "You have to put your Western views aside." During the course of time, soldiers started to see the custom, initially perceived as "strange," as a normal event. As a re-spondent stated, "The peculiar thing is that it becomes more and more normal, which is a phenomenon known as mission creep. . . . After six months, you start to adjust and start to assimilate local customs" and "we practically never talked about it, you get used to it."

In addition to the value of respecting local culture, other values are given as a reason for not intervening. Such reasons include consideration of the safety of Dutch troops, maintaining good relations with important and powerful men in the mission area, and the need to focus on the overall mission. As indicated by a respondent, "You have to break through a certain barrier. You have to think: 'OK, this is too disgusting for words, but he is the police commander with jurisdiction in this area and I need information . . . so don't think about the little boy, don't do it!'" Dutch soldiers developed strategies for when to respond or not respond. As one respondent summed it:

> When they [the Afghans] all seem to get together, such as on Thursday eve-nings . . . don't get involved in that, particularly if there's only three or four of you. If there are about a hundred of you, you would probably say something about it. . . . It might be a different story if we saw it happening in our camp, because then they would be on our territory, but now, we are on their ground. You have to work with them, carry out tasks with them and there was also some kind of threat in the air, so you don't want to disrupt relations with them.

Soldiers learn to define the limits of their action. In the case of the above re-spondent, it is the location where the practice takes place and the mandate given to him. Others also have a clear idea of when they would intervene, namely if, as stated by a respondent, "he starts to play dirty games in my presence, I will certainly speak out" and "if you see someone being abused or see someone bleed-ing owing to others getting too romantic with them, then you have a right to say 'Look at this blood! Why don't you stop this? The boy is going to the medical post and he won't be coming back. Go and make your own tea.'" Other members of the military were unaware of their own moral limits, until they were asked about them in the interviews. In some cases, Dutch or coalition soldiers did intervene. As a captain from the Marine Corps who was acting as force protection for the Americans stated: "We received a message saying that there was a chai boy at a police post. We went over there and I really thought that the American officer was going to execute someone. . . . We had caught him red-handed, he really had a boy there. I thought it was all over for the police commander. . . . I was pleased to see the boy being taken away and returned to his family." In some cases, stories like these had unhappy endings, as some boys were murdered on account of hav-ing tarnished their families' honor, while other boys committed suicide.

Another interesting matter is how the Afghan security troops think that for-eign forces who witness bacha bazi should respond. According to the Afghan respondents, the law and the religion of Islam forbid this practice and action should be taken, but both the aid worker and the Afghan security officers re-marked that it is not the responsibility of military personnel to intervene in the local system of social values. The Afghan respondents stated that even if military personnel witness a case of bacha bazi, they are not permitted to intervene di-rectly, but must call the 119 emergency phone line or inform the local police and subsequently support the action that the local police take. A lieutenant colonel of the Afghan National Civil Order Police quoted an example of complaints re-ceived at the Afghan Ministry of the Interior about a certain colonel, who was dismissed from his post—even though the case was not proven. Although the criminal investigation and judicial chains are still being built up in Afghanistan, international military personnel may not take over criminal investigation and judicial tasks. At most, they may only support the local police when encountering a case of bacha bazi, as they do not have enough capacity. The Afghan respondents have a clear vision of how international forces should respond when confronted with bacha bazi, which is reflected neither in guidelines of the Royal Netherlands Army nor in NATO policy.

As already mentioned, NATO and the Royal Netherlands Army have not put any guidelines in place regarding what actions should be taken in bacha bazi situations. According to one interviewee, who had been the commander of Multinational Base Tarin Kowt (MNBTK), there was only one way to proceed:

> Act on the basis of common sense. Because there was no specific instruction in place on how to deal with it [the bacha bazi phenomenon], I began to discuss the subject with my colleagues during the workup period. . . . One thing we wanted to avoid at all costs was a press report on the subject. We amended the Standard Operating Procedures and Standard Operating Instructions for MNBTK (regarding access to the base etc.) to include a line stating that minors are not welcome at MNBTK. We subsequently also requested the OMLT to ensure that no children entered the ANA and ANP camps.

During the decompression phase at the end of the mission, the Royal Netherlands Army does little about its personnel's experiences with bacha bazi. According to a number of military personnel, the workup and decompression periods are not geared toward other cultures. As noted by a respondent: "All of your standards and values are called into question there. . . . You have to be prepared for that kind of thing. . . . It is extremely tough, dealing with your own standards and values in a totally different culture such as Afghanistan. You have to be continually aware of local culture. I thought it poor that this type of thing is not discussed after the mission: there is no debriefing."

Conclusions

The practice of bacha bazi is common in Afghanistan. Although this practice is forbidden by Afghan law, owing to the weakness of the security sector and government enforcement, perpetrators are not punished. Guidelines from NATO or the Royal Netherlands Army on how to act when confronted with bacha bazi during military deployments do not exist. During the pre-deployment training, there is only a short explanation of bacha bazi. This could be one of the reasons why Dutch military personnel, and more broadly international military personnel, feel uncertain, some even shocked, when faced with this situation during deployment.

The Dutch soldiers who took part in this study specifically named bacha bazi as a morally and culturally critical situation when asked about behavior of local people in Afghanistan that conflicted with their personal moral values. A number of military personnel experienced it as a moral dilemma, but are unable to explain which particular values clash with their values. Values such as safety and respect for culture, which lean toward nonintervention, are often mentioned. Values that lean toward intervention, such as human dignity and the physical integrity of young boys, are only named by one or two of the interviewees. As a result they are not able to make a morally responsible and conscious consideration for which they could take full responsibility and be accountable for to both themselves and to others. They therefore lack a number of crucial skills regarding the moral competence required to deal appropriately with moral dilemmas.

Both the Royal Netherlands Army and individual members of the Dutch military refer to bacha bazi as a deep-rooted practice in Afghan culture that is seen as normal. This assumption is not entirely correct as, despite its long history and widespread exposure, the practice is prohibited from both the religious and legal points of view. Furthermore, some Afghans themselves publicly speak out against bacha bazi and are also making efforts to combat the practice. The reason mostly cited by many members of the military for not intervening in bacha bazi situations is cultural and moral relativism (i.e., "it is the culture"). Dutch military personnel also assert that they would not be able to change anything just by themselves and therefore chose to do nothing to address bacha bazi. However, cultures are not static and can change, as evident from the boy play practice in ancient Greece.

The nonrecognition of bacha bazi as a moral issue or the normalization of bacha bazi through the blurring of moral standards or keeping a moral distance could be seen as a way of coping with the bacha bazi.[63] However, for people with that attitude, the danger of moral blindness lurks. This means that the moral dimensions (and the related values) of situations are not recognized, which makes it difficult for them to make a conscious choice. In other words, the soldier is not capable of acting with moral competence. This might also be said of NATO and the Royal Netherlands Army, which have not issued guidelines to their military personnel. Both of these state entities, seeking to build a safe and democratic Afghanistan, have shifted an important human rights responsibility of state actors to their individual soldiers. NATO and the Royal Netherlands Army failed to adequately recognize or respond to bacha bazi. Both institutions do, however, have a duty to train their military personnel and deliver on the core principles of human rights embedded in their international mandate to intervene in Afghanistan.

As many respondents suggested during our study, we draw attention to the need for more concrete policies to be developed to address these kinds of situations during deployment. This should include training on understanding sexual and gender-based violence, without "ignoring the fact that, in conflict situations, adult men and adolescent boys also face major risks of abuse and violence based upon culturally constructed notions of gender roles."[64] This may also consist of additional training on military ethics as well as guidelines and support before, during, and after missions with regard to various morally and culturally critical situations and moral dilemmas that arise owing to differences between local practices on the one hand and on the other hand the moral values of intervening forces and the human rights principles underpinning their mandate to intervene in other countries.

Notes

1. "The Dancing Boys of Afghanistan"; Aroussi, "Women, Peace and Security," 589.
2. *The Kite Runner* (2003), a book by Khaled Hosseini, also delves into the practice of bacha bazi. The main character, Amir, sets out to search for Sohrab, the son of his best friend, who was taken by the Taliban. Amir finds Sohrab in a soldier's house, where he is forced to dance while wearing women's clothes. After Amir has rescued Sohrab from the Taliban, he says: "I'm so dirty and full of sin. The bad man and the other two did things to me" (278).
3. Pugliese, "Former Soldier Still Fights to Protect Afghan Boys from Abuse"; Pugliese, "Sex Abuse and Silence Exposed."
4. "'T Shouten."
5. Jalalzai, *Child Sex, Bacha Bazi and Prostitution in Afghanistan*; Leatherman, *Sexual Violence and Armed Conflict*.
6. Lake, "Ending Impunity for Sexual and Gender-Based Crimes," 1–32.
7. Carpenter, "Recognizing Gender-Based Violence against Civilian Men and Boys in Conflict Situations," 97.
8. Frey, *Eye Juggling*; Verweij, "Morele Professionaliteit In de Militaire Praktijk," 126–138.
9. Frey, *Eye Juggling*; Verweij, "Morele Professionaliteit in de Militaire Praktijk."
10. Maas, "Confrontaties Met Moreel Kritische Situaties."
11. Statman, *Moral Dilemmas*, 32; Baarda and Verweij, "Military Ethics, 2.
12. Karssing, *Morele Competentie in Organisaties*, 39; Widdershoven,"Reflectie als Interventie"; Wortel and Bosch, "Strengthening Moral Competence," 17–35; Van Luijk and Dubbink, "Moral Competence," 11–17.
13. Verweij, "Het Belang Van Militaire Ethiek Voor de Krijgsmacht," 28–30; Wortel, "Strengthening Moral Competence."
14. Stanski, "'So These Folks are Aggressive,'" 73–94.
15. Said, *Orientalism*, 95. Also see Stepputat, "Knowledge Production in the Security-Development Nexus," 440.
16. Levi, *Moral Relativism*; Lukes, *Moral Relativism*; Whetham, "The Challenge of Ethical Relativism in Coalition Operations," 302–316.
17. Levi, *Moral Relativism*; Lukes, *Moral Relativism*; Rachels and Rachels, *The Elements of Moral Philosophy, Europe*.
18. Blackford, "Book Review: Sam Harris' The Moral Landscape," 53–62.

19. Strauss and Corbin, "Grounded Theory Methodology," 191–210; Strauss and Corbin, *Basics of Qualitative Research*.

20. Given during the "Train the Trainer" Course in Military Ethics for Non-Commissioned Officers and during lessons on ethics that are part of Intermediate Defence Studies.

21. Apart from four of the five additional in-depth interviews, all interviews with Dutch military personnel and with Afghan respondents were conducted by the first author, Michelle Schut, in the context of her PhD research on morally and culturally critical situations in the interaction with the local population during military deployment. Schut, "Soldiers as Strangers: Morally and Culturally Critical Situations during Military Missions."

22. Loftsdóttir, "Never Forgetting?" 303–317.

23. Schön, *The Reflective Turn*, 164; Henry, Higate, and Sanghera, "Positionality and Power," 467–482.

24. Henry, "Positionality and Power."

25. At the beginning of the interviews, respondents were reluctant and careful in their answers.

26. De Lind van Wijngaarden and Bushra, "Male Adolescent Concubinage in Peshawar, Northwestern Pakistan," 1068.

27. Schuyler, *Turkistan*, 133.

28. Baaz and Stern, "The Complexity of Violence"; Horwood, *The Shame of War*.

29. Carpenter, "Recognizing Gender-Based Violence," 83–103; United Nations High Commissioner for Refugees, *UNHCR Issues Guidelines on Protection of Male Rape Victims*; United Nations High Commissioner for Refugees, *Working with Men and Boy Survivors of Sexual and Gender-Based Violence in Forced Displacement*; Stor, "The Rape of Men."

30. Slugget, *Mapping of Psychosocial Support for Girls and Boys Affected by Child Sexual Abuse*; Khan, *Everybody Knows, but Nobody Knows*, 19; Frederick, *Sexual Abuse and Exploitation of Boys in South Asia*, 32; Lee-Koo, "Not Suitable for Children," 478.

31. Khan, *Everybody Knows, but Nobody Knows*; De Lind van Wijngaarden, "Male Adolescent Concubinage."

32. Frederick, *Sexual Abuse and Exploitation of Boys in South Asia*.

33. Jenkins, *Male Sexuality, Diversity and Culture*; Leatherman, *Sexual Violence*; Khan, *Rapid Assessment of Male Vulnerabilities*.

34. De Lind van Wijngaarden, "Male Adolescent Concubinage."

35. Khan, *Rapid Assessment of Male Vulnerabilities*.

36. "Taliban Country."

37. Khan, *Rapid Assessment of Male Vulnerabilities*; De Lind van Wijngaarden, "Male Adolescent Concubinage."

38. Skjelsbaek. "Sexual Violence in Times of War," 69–84.

39. Carpenter, "Recognizing Gender-Based Violence."

40. Jenkins, *Male Sexuality, Diversity and Culture*; Khan, *Rapid Assessment of Male Vulnerabilities*.

41. Penal Code 1975, Section 427; Civil Code, Section 249; Labour Code, Constitution of Afghanistan, Section 49.

42. Sedra, "Security Sector Reform in Afghanistan," 94–110; Murray, "Police-Building in Afghanistan," 108–126; Friesendorf, "Paramilitarization and Security Sector Reform," 79–95.

43. Barfield, *Afghan Customary Law and Its Relationship to Formal Judicial Institutions*, 26.

44. Khan, *Everybody Knows, but Nobody Knows*.

45. Norman, *What Do Afghans Want from the Police?*

46. "Bacha Bazi By Suhell & Umaira Sadiqzadeh."

47. Frederick, *Sexual Abuse and Exploitation of Boys in South Asia*; De Lind van Wijngaarden, "Male Adolescent Concubinage."

48. Percy, *Pederasty and Pedagogy in Archaic Greece.*
49. Ibid.
50. Rabinow, *The Foucault Reader.*
51. Ducheine and Pouw, *Research Paper Operaties in Afghanistan*, 332.
52. UN, "Approving Extension of International Security Assistance Force in Afghanistan."
53. A security gap exists if, in a postconflict situation, there are no or insufficient numbers of security troops in place to restore and maintain public order. Dziedzic, "Introduction," 3–18.
54. *Trainer's Guide*, chapter 4.3, "Sexual Abuse of Women and Children." This is a guide constructed by the Netherlands for Dutch police trainers in Afghanistan, in possession of the author.
55. Goldstein, "U.S. Soldiers Told to Ignore Sexual Abuse of Boys by Afghan Allies."
56. Westhead, "Don't Look, Don't Tell, Troops Told."
57. Bordin, "A Crisis of Trust and Cultural Incompatibility."
58. Ibid.
59. Freeze, "Report Cites 'Crisis in Trust' between Afghans and NATO."
60. UN High Commissioner for Refugees, *UNHCR Issues Guidelines*; UN High Commissioner for Refugees, *Working with Men and Boy Survivors.*
61. Although Dutch military forces will start leaving Afghanistan this year, they are likely to continue to encounter (similar) morally and culturally critical situations during future deployments to foreign countries.
62. Stanski, "So These Folks Are Aggressive."
63. Bandura, "Selective Activation and Disengagement of Moral Control," 27–46; McAlister, Bandura, and Owen, "Mechanisms of Moral Disengagement in Support of Military Force," 141–165.
64. Carpenter, "Recognizing Gender-Based Violence," 95.

References

Aroussi, Sahla. "Women, Peace and Security; Addressing Accountability for Wartime Sexual Violence." *International Feminist Journal of Politics* 13, no. 4 (2011): 576–593.
Baarda, Theodoor A., and Desiree E. M. Verweij. "Military Ethics: Its Nature and Pedagogy." In *Military Ethics: The Dutch Approach, a Practical Guide*, edited by Theadoor A. Baarda and Desiree E. M. Verweij, 1–23. Leiden, NL: Martinus Nijhoff, 2006.
"Bacha Bazi by Suhell and Umaira Sadiqzadeh." YouTube video, 3:50. Posted by 552004aa, September 16, 2010. http://www.youtube.com/watch?v=0daKxBzjq40.
Bandura, Albert. "Selective Activation and Disengagement of Moral Control." *Journal of Social Issues* 46, no. 1 (1990): 27–46.
Barfield, Thomas. *Afghan Customary Law and Its Relationship to Formal Judicial Institutions.* Washington, DC: United States Institute for Peace, 2003.
Blackford, Russell. "Book Review: Sam Harris' The Moral Landscape." *Journal of Evolution and Technology* 21, no. 2 (2010): 53–62.
Bordin, Jeffrey. "A Crisis Of Trust And Cultural Incompatibility: A Red Team Study of Mutual Perceptions of Afghan National Security Force Personnel and U.S. Soldiers in Understanding and Mitigating the Phenomena of ANSF Committed Fratricide-Murders." May 12, 2011. http://www2.gwu.edu/~nsarchiv/NSAEBB/NSAEBB370/docs/Document%2011.pdf.
Carpenter, Charli. "Recognizing Gender-Based Violence against Civilian Men and Boys in Conflict Situations." *Security Dialogue* 37, no. 1 (2006): 83–103.

The Dancing Boys of Afghanistan. PBS *Frontline.* www.pbs.org/wgbh/pages/frontline/dancingboys/.

De Lind van Wijngaarden, Jan Willem, and Bushra Rani. "Male Adolescent Concubinage in Pesha-war, Northwestern Pakistan." *Culture, Health and Sexuality: An International Journal for Research, Intervention and Care* 13, no. 9 (2011): 1061–1072.

Ducheine, Paul A. L., and Eric H. Pouw. *Research Paper Operaties in Afghanistan: Rechtsbases en Rechtsregimes.* Breda, NL: Netherlands Defence Academy, 2009.

Dziedzic, Michael J. "Introduction." In *Policing the New World Order: Peace Operations and Public Security,* edited by Robert B. Oakley, Michael J. Dziedzic and Elliot M. Goldberg, 3–18. Washington, DC: National Defense University Press, 1998.

Eriksson Baaz, Maria, and Maria Stern. "The Complexity of Violence: A Critical Analysis of Sexual Violence in the Democratic Republic of Congo (DRC)." Nordiska Afrikainstitutet/Nordic Africa Institute, *SIDA,* May 2010. http://www.diva-portal.org/smash/get/-diva2:319527/FULLTEXT02.pdf.

Frederick, John. "Sexual Abuse and Exploitation of Boys in South Asia: A Review of Research Findings, Legislation, Policy and Programme Responses." UNICEF Innocenti Research Centre, 2010. https://www.unicef-irc.org/publications/pdf/iwp_2010_02.pdf.

Freeze, Colin. "Report Cites 'Crisis in Trust' between Afghans and NATO." *Globe and Mail,* June 22, 2012.

Frey, Rodney. *Eye Juggling: Seeing the World through a Looking Glass and a Glass Pane: A Workbook for Clarifying and Interpreting Values.* Lanham, MD: University Press of America, 1994.

Friesendorf, Cornelus. "Paramilitarization and Security Sector Reform: The Afghan National Police." *Journal of International Peacekeeping* 18, no. 1 (2011): 79–95.

Goldstein, Joseph. "U.S. Soldiers Told to Ignore Sexual Abuse of Boys by Afghan Allies." *New York Times,* September 20, 2015.

Henry, Marsha, Paul Higate, and Gurchaten Sanghera. "Positionality and Power: The Politics of Peacekeeping Research" *International Peacekeeping* 16, no. 4 (2009): 467–482.

Horwood, Christopher. *The Shame of War: Sexual Violence against Woman and Girls in Conflict.* Malta: Integrated Regional Information Networks / United Nations Office of the Coordination of Humanitarian Affairs, 2007.

Hosseini, Khaled. *The Kite Runner.* London: Bloomsbury, 2003.

Jalalzai, Musa Khan. *Child Sex, Bacha Bazi and Prostitution in Afghanistan: Male Prostitution, Forced Marriages, Play Boy, Women, Arms and Drug Trafficking.* Saarbrücken, Germany: Lambert Academic, 2011.

Jenkins, Carol. *Male Sexuality, Diversity and Culture: Implications for HIV Prevention and Care.* Geneva, Switzerland: UNAIDS, 2014.

Karssing, Edgar. *Morele Competentie in Organisaties.* Assen: Van Gorcum, 2000.

Khan, Shivananda. *Everybody Knows, but Nobody Knows: Desk Review of Current Literature on HIV and Male-Male Sexualities, Behaviours and Sexual Exploitation in Afghanistan.* NAZ Foundation International, 2008.

———. *Rapid Assessment of Male Vulnerabilities to HIV and Sexual Exploitation in Afghanistan.* NAZ Foundation International, 2009. http://www.aidsdatahub.org/everybody-knows-but-nobody-knows-desk-review-of-current-literature-on-hiv-and-male-male-sexualities-behaviours-and-sexual-exploitation-in-afghanistan-naz-foundation-international.

Lake, Milli. "Ending Impunity for Sexual and Gender-Based Crimes: The International Criminal Court and Complementarity in the Democratic Republic of Congo." *African Conflict and Peacebuilding Review* 4, no. 1 (2014): 1–32.

Leatherman, Janie L. *Sexual Violence and Armed Conflict*. Cambridge: Polity Press, 2011.

Lee-Koo, Katrina. "Not Suitable for Children: The Politicisation of Conflict-Affected Children in Post-2011 Afghanistan." *Australian Journal of International Affairs* 67, no. 4 (2013): 475–490.

Levi, Neil. *Moral Relativism: A Short Introduction*. Oxford: Oneworld, 2002.

Loftsdóttir, Kristín. "Never Forgetting? Gender and Racial-Ethnic Identity during Fieldwork." *Social Anthropology* 10, no. 3 (2002): 303–317.

Lukes, Steven. *Moral Relativism*. New York: Picador, 2008.

Maas, Sofie. "Confrontaties Met Moreel Kritische Situaties: Overwegingen, Emoties en Handelingen Van Docenten." PhD diss., Radboud University Nijmegen, 2010.

McAlister, Alfred, Albert Bandura, and Steven Owen. "Mechanisms of Moral Disengagement in Support of Military Force: The Impact of 9/11." *Journal of Social and Clinical Psychology* 25, no. 2 (2006): 141–165.

Murray, Tonita. "Police-Building in Afghanistan: A Case Study of Civil Security Sector Reform." *Journal of International Peacekeeping* 13, no. 1 (2007): 108–126.

Norman, Catherine. *What Do Afghans Want from the Police? Views from Helmand Province*. Center for Naval Analysis and Solutions, 2012. https://www.cna.org/CNA_files/PDF/D0026181.A2.pdf.

Percy, William A. *Pederasty and Pedagogy in Archaic Greece*. Chicago: University of Illinois Press, 1996.

Pugliese, David. "Former Soldier Still Fights to Protect Afghan Boys from Abuse." *Ottawa Citizen*, September 19, 2009.

———. "Sex Abuse and Silence Exposed: DND Brass Told of Rape of Boys by Afghan Allies." *Ottawa Citizen*, September 21, 2009.

Rabinow, Paul. *The Foucault Reader*. New York: Pantheon Books, 1984.

Rachels, James, and Stuart Rachels. *The Elements of Moral Philosophy, Europe*. London: McGraw-Hill Education, 2011.

Said, Edward W. *Orientalism: Western Representations of the Orient*. Harmondsworth, UK: Penguin, 1985.

Schön, Donald A. *The Reflective Turn: Case Studies in and on Educational Practice*. New York: Teachers College Press, 1991.

Schut, Michelle. "Soldiers as Strangers: Morally and Culturally Critical Situations during Military Missions." PhD diss., Radboud University Nijmegen, 2015.

Schuyler, Eugene. *Turkistan: Notes of a Journey in Russian Turkistan, Khokand, Bukhara, and Kuldja*. London: Sampson Low, Marston, Searle & Rivington, 1876.

Sedra, Mark. "Security Sector Reform in Afghanistan: The Slide towards Expediency." *International Peacekeeping* 13, no. 1 (2006): 94–110.

Skjelsbaek, Inger. "Sexual Violence in Times of War: A New Challenge for Peace Operations?" *International Peacekeeping* 8, no. 2 (2001): 69–84.

Slugget, Cath. *Mapping of Psychosocial Support for Girls and Boys Affected by Child Sexual Abuse in Four Countries in South and Central Asia: Afghanistan, Bangladesh, Nepal and Pakistan*. Save the Children, 2003. http://resourcecentre.savethechildren.se/sites/default/files/documents/2973.pdf.

Stanski, Keith. "'So These Folks Are Aggressive': An Orientalist Reading of 'Afghan Warlord.'" *Security Dialogue* 40, no. 1 (2009): 73–94.

Statman, Daniel. *Moral Dilemmas*. Value Inquiry Book Series 32. Amsterdam, NL: Editions Rodopi BV, 1995.

Stepputat, Finn. "Knowledge Production in the Security-Development Nexus: An Ethnographic Reflection." *Security Dialogue* 43, no. 4 (2012): 439–455.

Stor, Will. "The Rape of Men: The Darkest Secret of War." *Guardian*, July 17, 2011.

Strauss, Anselm, and Juliet Corbin. *Basics of Qualitative Research: Techniques and Procedures for Developing Grounded Theory.* Thousand Oaks, CA: Sage, 1998.

———. "Grounded Theory Methodology." In *Handbook of Qualitative Research*, edited by Norman K. Denzin, and Yvonna S. Lincoln, 191–210. Thousand Oaks, CA: Sage, 1994.

"T Shouten." YouTube video, 3:00. Posted by Eva van Baarle, November 25, 2012. http://www .youtube.com/watch?v=9nm13pEkdEA&feature=youtu.be.

"Taliban Country." YouTube video, 10:08. Posted by Journeyman Pictures, January 18, 2008. http:// www.youtube.com/watch?v=9c18CKwlAGQ.

United Nations. "Approving Extension of International Security Assistance Force in Afghanistan, Security Council Welcomes Agreement to Transfer Security Lead to Afghan Forces." Press release. https://www.un.org/News/Press/docs/2011/sc10408.doc.htm.

United Nations High Commissioner for Refugees. *UNHCR Issues Guidelines on Protection of Male Rape Victims.* October 8, 2012. http://www.unhcr.org/5072bfa69.html.

———. *Working with Men and Boy Survivors of Sexual and Gender-Based Violence in Forced Displacement.* July 2012. http://www.refworld.org/cgi-bin/texis/vtx/rwmain?docid=5006aa262.

Van Luijk, Hans, and Dubbink, Wim. "Moral Competence." *European Business Ethics Cases in Context* 28 (2011): 11–17.

Verweij, Desirée E. M. "Het Belang Van Militaire Ethiek Voor de Krijgsmacht." *Carré* 7/8 (2005): 28–30.

———. "Morele Professionaliteit In de Militaire Praktijk." In *Werkzame Idealen; Ethische Reflecties op Professionaliteit*, edited by Jos Kole en Doret de Ruyter, 126–138. Assen, NL: Van Gorcum, 2007.

Westhead, Rick. "Don't Look, Don't Tell, Troops Told." *Star*, June 16, 2008.

Whetham, David. "The Challenge of Ethical Relativism in Coalition Operations." *Journal of Military Ethics* 7, no. 4 (2008): 302–316.

Widdershoven, Guy. "Reflectie als Interventie." *Oration*, Vrije Universiteit Amsterdam, September 9, 2010. http://dare.ubvu.vu.nl/bitstream/handle/1871/19122/Oratie_Widdershoven .pdf?sequence=1.

Wortel, Eva M., and Jolanda Bosch. "Strengthening Moral Competence: A 'Train the Trainer' Course on Military Ethics" *Journal of Military Ethics* 10, no. 1 (2011): 17–35.

4   Managerial Capacity in Peacekeeping Operations

The Case of EUFOR

Unsal Sigri, M. Abdulkadir Varoglu,
and Ufuk Basar

THE SCOPE OF international interventions in civil wars began to change in cor-respondence with the end of the Cold War. Following the end of the Cold War, civil wars became one of the prominent threats to global peace and security. In this milieu internal conflicts within states cause disruption and instability in the international system, which sometimes necessitate international intervention.[1] Conflicts among ethnic groups within falling states or among hostile states cause regional chaos and bloodshed. Millions of people have been displaced, have per-ished, or became refugees as a result of post–Cold War civil wars, which are often referred to as new wars.[2]

Civil wars with devastating consequences have taken place in the Balkans, Africa, and the Middle East. The United Nations (UN) and other international organizations and coalitions have been conducting peacekeeping operations since 1948 in response to civil wars.[3] Since their inception, however, the way peacekeeping operations' management has been conducted has been the subject of debate among scholars, policy makers, and security experts. Two issues that are frequently discussed are (1) the management of the use of force by peacekeep-ers, which is critical for the effectiveness of the overall operation on the ground, and (2) proper use of limited resources.[4] The success or failure of a peacekeeping operation usually depends on how well it is managed. In a typical peacekeep-ing operation, peacekeepers at all levels often face political, bureaucratic, and resource constraints. As such, successful management of a peacekeeping opera-tion requires the security staff, both on the ground and at the headquarters, to be skilled enough to overcome the constraints and solve unexpected obstacles. Ar-guably, successful peacekeeping operations can be accomplished only by this kind of managerial skills, regardless of the complexity and multidimensionality of the peacekeeping operation.[5] Proper management of peacekeeping operations and successes in peacekeeping operations have broad implications for international security beyond the specific case of any one peacekeeping mission. Successful peacekeeping missions add to the popular support for international interventions, especially in humanitarian crises where major powers may not have direct interests that compel them to intervene. Similarly, mismanaged peacekeeping operations are likely to undermine popular support for international intervention, even in cases where there are compelling humanitarian needs. Understanding the factors that contribute to successful peacekeeping is an important way to develop best practices and increase the likelihood of more popular support for international peacebuilding through the application of the responsibility to protect (R2P) doctrine.[6] One notable case of managerial challenges and some successes in peacekeeping is the case of Bosnia-Herzegovina.

The Bosnia-Herzegovina war (1992 to 1995) is one of the most brutal ethnic conflicts after the end of the Cold War. The war ended with intervention of the North Atlantic Treaty Organization (NATO), which took over from the UN. Many of the problems associated with the Bosnian war are the result of poor managerial capacities of successive peacekeeping operations, most notably Implementation Force (IFOR), Stabilization Force (SFOR), and European Force (EUFOR).[7] While the lack of proper managerial capacity was devastating, an interesting phenomenon is the way peacekeepers on the ground adjusted and improvised to overcome systemic challenges. This raises an important question about not only the managerial skills security officers bring with them to civil war situations but also the managerial skill they accrue from their experiences while serving in peacekeeping operations and how those new skills can contribute to the overall success of the peacekeeping operation.

This chapter assesses the development of peacekeepers' managerial skills during peacekeeping operations and its broader implications for peacekeeping and international interventions in new war situations. The chapter is based on a study of EUFOR Operation Althea. The research was conducted among EUFOR peacekeepers using David Kolb's experiential learning model. The first part of the chapter discusses the meaning and evolution of peacekeeping operations and provides background information on EUFOR Operation Althea. Next, the chapter examines the managerial characteristics of peacekeeping operations and the capacity-building role of peacekeeping operations. Finally, the chapter presents and analyzes the data. The findings of the study point to the implications of accrued managerial skills for peacekeeping and security personnel, which is an area that needs further research.

Peacekeeping Operations and Their Challenges

Peacekeeping operations are a form of peace support operations. At the core of such operations is the aim of enhancing the effectiveness of the diplomatic efforts of peacemaking and peace enforcement. The spectrum of peace support operations ranges from observation missions to robust peacekeeping missions under Chapter VII of the UN Charter.[8] Peacekeeping operations evolved in three generations. The first, traditional peacekeeping, dates back to the beginning of the Cold War. The core missions of traditional peacekeeping are to separate warring parties through the deployment of lightly armed and impartial international troops and observation or monitoring of peace agreements or ceasefires. Consent of the warring parties, impartiality, and limited use of force (i.e., only in case of a threat to self-security) are prominent conditions of traditional peacekeeping.[9] The United Nations Emergency Force (UNEF) in Sinai, the United Nations Peacekeeping Force in Cyprus (UNFICYP), and the United Nations Disengagement Observer Force in Golan Heights (UNDOF) are examples of traditional peacekeeping. In sum, the first generation of peacekeeping operations was limited to creating a buffer between conflicting parties through the deployment of lightly armed and neutral peacekeepers, who observe and monitor the terms of existing peace agreements. Post–Cold War civil wars are significantly different from previous wars in which traditional peacekeeping missions have operated.[10] Traditional peacekeeping missions have been unable to effectively maintain ceasefire and significantly reduce violence, which in some cases results in catastrophes such as the massacre in Srebrenica. The second generation of peacekeeping operations evolved under these new circumstances.[11] The United Nations Assistance Group (UNTAG) for Namibia, the United Nations Operations in Mozambique (UNOMOZ), and the United Nations Transitional Authority in Cambodia (UNTAC) are some examples of second-generation peacekeeping operations. As distinct from the traditional peacekeeping, peacekeepers serving in second-generation peacekeeping operations strive to resolve conflicts between warring parties, in addition to their observation and monitoring missions.[12] The force formations of peacekeepers are larger in size, and troops are equipped and armed with heavy weaponry in order to deter the belligerents and end the conflict. Peacekeepers are typically deployed in conditions where conflict has not ceased.[13] International organizations and states intervene in the conflicts typically on the basis of UN Security Council authorization, and in most cases without the approval of belligerents. In contrast to traditional peacekeeping, second-generation peacekeeping operations are multidimensional. In addition to their monitoring mandate, new dimensions of finding solutions to conflicts and minimizing the need for peacekeeping are often added to the tasks of second-generation peacekeeping operations.

Second-generation peacekeeping missions were significantly challenged in meeting their expanded tasks. This difficulty has given birth to a third generation of peacekeeping operations. The aims of the third-generation peacekeeping operations are generally to stabilize and rebuild war-torn countries. The composition of the troops and contingents has significantly changed in comparison to the previous generation of peacekeeping operations. Police units, members of nongovernmental organizations, and humanitarian workers now take part in missions along with military peacekeepers.[14] By using a combination of military and civilian capabilities synchronously, peacekeepers strive to enforce ceasefires, end conflicts, sustain peace agreements, and rebuild war-torn states. As distinct from the previous-generation peacekeeping operations, other international and regional organizations also conducted peace operations under the UN mandate. Some notable cases of third-generation peacekeeping operations include the United Nations Mission in Sierra Leone (UNAMSIL), United Nations Mission in the Central African Republic and Chad (MINURCAT), United Nations Operations in Burundi (ONUB), and United Nations Operations in Somalia (UNOSOM). Throughout this evolution process, the mission of international peace operations has been transformed from peacekeeping to peace enforcement and peacebuilding.[15] This evolution of international peace operations also requires a critical examination of the managerial capacities of peacekeepers in order to understand the nature and impacts of peacekeeping operations and develop adequate policies for future missions.

Third-generation peacekeeping operations face numerous problems, most notably communication and adaptation, that are directly connected to the challenges of multidimensionality, flexibility, and cultural diversity.[16] There are indications that peacekeepers with specific soft skills can overcome some of these problems. This study directly addresses this issue by examining the extent to which peacekeepers possess some of the soft skills needed to overcome communication and adaptation problems and thereby accomplish successful peacekeeping operations. In particular, the study focuses on soft skills such as adaptation, building of good relations with locals and with other peacekeepers, stress management, and cultural awareness. The study was conducted among peacekeepers serving under Operation EUFOR Althea in Bosnia-Herzegovina, which is one notable example of third-generation peacekeeping operations.

Emergence and Progress of Operation EUFOR Althea

Following Bosnia-Herzegovina's declaration of independence from the Federation of Yugoslavia in March 1992, an ethnic war began between Croats, Serbs, and Bosniaks in Bosnia-Herzegovina and continued brutally until 1995. The war ended with the NATO military intervention, which was followed by the 1995 Dayton Peace Accord. A new constitution for Bosnia-Herzegovina was created in Dayton, Ohio, United States, under which the Serb Republic and Bosniak-Croat Federation were merged into one state. The Serb Republic and Bosniak-Croat

Federation were tied into a weak central government of Bosnia-Herzegovina. Before the ethnic violence began in 1992, Yugoslavia was a federation comprising five states (i.e., Bosnia-Herzegovina, Croatia, Macedonia, Slovenia, and Serbia, comprising Kosovo and Montenegro as autonomous regions) and several ethnic groups (e.g., Albanians, Bosniaks, Croats, Macedonians, Magyars, Montenegrins, Serbs, Slovenes, and Turks). Albanians were living mainly in Kosovo and Macedonia; Bosniaks were living mainly in Bosnia-Herzegovina and slightly in other states of the federation; Croats were living mainly in Croatia and Bosnia-Herzegovina; Macedonians were living mainly in Macedonia; Magyars were living mainly in the Vojvodina region of Serbia; Montenegrins were living mainly in Montenegro and slightly in Serbia; Serbs were living mainly in Serbia, Bosnia-Herzegovina, and slightly in other states of the federation; Slovenes were living mainly in Slovenia; and Turks were living mainly in Kosovo and slightly in Macedonia. Slovenia and Croatia, which declared independence in June 1991, were the first federated states to secede from the federation. However Serbs who lived in Croatia frowned on the declaration of secession. This dispute marked the beginning of the war, with fighting between Croat and Serb militias in August 1991. That fighting between Croats and Serbs ended with the intervention of UN peacekeepers in the winter of 1992.[17] At the time of this initial fighting between Croats and Serbs, the government of Bosnia-Herzegovina was composed of Bosniaks, Croats, and Serbs. Upon the declarations of independence from the Federation of Yugoslavia by Slovenia and Croatia, Serbs in Bosnia-Herzegovina declared that they wanted Bosnia-Herzegovina to remain within the Federation of Yugoslavia. This declaration of allegiance to the Federation of Yugoslavia by the Serbs was an effort to preempt any attempt by Bosniaks and Croats in Bosnia-Herzegovina to declare the independence of Bosnia-Herzegovina from the Federation of Yugoslavia. Relying on the 1991 decision of the European Community granting recognition to any former state of the Federation of Yugoslavia that declared independence, Bosniaks and Croats in Bosnia-Herzegovina held a referendum for the independence of Bosnia-Herzegovina in March 1992. Bosnian Serbs boycotted the referendum in opposition to the pro-independence movement. In April 1992, the Bosnian Serbs militia and the Yugoslav National Army launched coordinated and planned attacks throughout Bosnia-Herzegovina, which later on turned into ethnic cleansing. The attack began a few days before the recognition of the independence of Bosnia-Herzegovina by the European Community and the United States. More than 90,000 people were killed in the brutal civil war. UN peacekeepers, who were deployed in Bosnia-Herzegovina in 1992, were unable to prevent the Serbian attacks. The inability of UN peacekeepers to deal with the civil war opened the way for NATO intervention to end the war in Bosnia-Herzegovina. The NATO intervention changed the balance of power among the warring factions. All sides agreed to an initial peace agreement in Dayton on November 21, 1995. Subsequently, the final peace agreement was signed in Paris on December 14, 1995.[18]

According to the Dayton Peace Agreement, Bosnia-Herzegovina kept its borders as they existed before the breakup of the Federation of Yugoslavia. However, the new Bosnia-Herzegovina comprised two decentralized and semi-autonomous states: (1) the Federation of Bosnia-Herzegovina, dominated mostly by Bosniaks and Croats, and (2) Republika Srpska, dominated mostly by Serbs. The Federation of Bosnia-Herzegovina got 51 percent of the total territory of the entire Bosnia-Herzegovina, while the remaining 49 percent went to Republika Srpska.[19] The Federation of Bosnia-Herzegovina comprises ten cantons, some of which dominated by Croats and others by Bosniaks. Each of the two federating states of the new Bosnia-Herzegovina has its own parliaments and presidents, which enables it to establish relations with neighboring countries while respecting the territorial integrity of Bosnia-Herzegovina. In addition, each federating state has the right to establish agreements with other countries and international organizations with the consent of the central government of Bosnia-Herzegovina. The central government is responsible for foreign policy, customs policy, monetary policy, immigration, and refugee and asylum policy. Decisions of the central government are taken by the majority of the members of the federal parliament. However, each of the three ethnic groups (i.e., Bosniaks, Croats, and Serbs) has the right to block the decisions, if it feels threats to its vital interests.[20]

Following the ratification of the Dayton Peace Accord, the NATO Implementation Force (IFOR) was deployed in Bosnia-Herzegovina and began its mission on December 20, 1995. IFOR was composed of over 60,000 United States, European, and Russian troops. It executed the key terms of the Dayton Peace Accord, most notably de-escalation and demilitarization of each conflicting faction, repatriation of displaced people, and the establishment of a safe and secure environment. IFOR was replaced with the Stabilization Force (SFOR) on December 20, 1996. SFOR, composed of 30,000 troops, continued to provide a safe and secure environment, in which hostilities among the warring factions lessened.[21] As NATO was completing its mission, there were calls for the deployment of a European force to replace SFOR. Based on deliberations of the EU Council of Foreign Ministers in December 2002 and the June 2004 NATO summit in Istanbul, a decision was reached to replace SFOR with an EU peacekeeping force by the end of 2004. A European force was seen as more appropriate to continue the peace operation since NATO had completed its core mission of ending the civil war and preventing any intention to return to war. Based on this consensus, Operation EUFOR Althea began deploying troops on December 2, 2004. Operation EUFOR Althea took its name from the Greek goddess of healing and was authorized under UN Security Council's resolution 1575, which allows the mission to use force if necessary and act as a deterrent to any intention to return to war.[22] Although EUFOR took control of the peacekeeping operation, a small NATO element was stationed in Sarajevo to assist the central government of Bosnia-Herzegovina, provide support for the integration of country into NATO, and share intelligence with EUFOR.

EUFOR was the third-largest operation that the EU had undertaken. The main mission of EUFOR was not too different from the previous NATO operations tasked with creating and sustaining a safe and secure environment and preventing resumptions of interethnic violence. However, EUFOR was also tasked with creating and ensuring a proper atmosphere for the integration of Bosnia-Herzegovina into the Euro-Atlantic alliance. The first EUFOR military force comprised 7,000 troops, which was the same size as SFOR. As the threat of violence in Bosnia-Herzegovina decreased, the EU Council reduced the size of EUFOR in 2007 from 7,000 to approximately 2,000 troops, which could be reinforced as needed by the Over the Horizon Forces of NATO, located in Kosovo, and by the EU Operational and Strategic Reserve Forces.[23] With the troop reduction in 2007, the main elements of EUFOR (i.e., the three multinational task forces deployed in Banja Luka, Tuzla, and Mostar), were replaced with the Multinational Manoeuvre Battalion. The Multinational Manoeuvre Battalion comprised three motorized companies from Austria, Hungary, and Turkey and a reconnaissance platoon from Austria. EUFOR also included the integrated police unit and liaison observation teams (LOTs). Throughout Operation EUFOR Althea, LOTs operated as the ears and the eyes of the mission by stationing units at forty-four different points all over Bosnia-Herzegovina. In 2010, the EU Council added the mobile training teams (MTT) to EUFOR to improve the capabilities of the Armed Forces of Bosnia-Herzegovina. Arguably, EUFOR evolved from being a robust military peacekeeping force to a de facto long-term military training and assistance force.[24]

Managerial Skills in Peacekeeping

In peacekeeping operations, missions are typically executed by diverse staff from different countries. Each mission is charged with several tasks to be done in sometimes dangerous, usually challenging, and generally unstable environments. Resources for the operations are often limited. Organizational procedures and regulations of troops from different countries are frequently cumbersome. This makes it difficult to synchronize and coordinate the activities of the staff around common goals. Sometimes, these problems significantly impede the success of the overall peacekeeping mission. In such environments, adequately skilled peacekeepers play critical roles in managing situations and executing the duties of the peacekeeping mission. Effective management of peacekeeping operations has been recognized as an important condition for the success of peacekeeping missions.[25] In general, management refers to a process in which resources of an organization are used effectively to achieve the objectives of the organization. Management entails planning, organizing, executing, directing, monitoring, and evaluating functions. Each of these requires specific managerial skills.[26]

In this study, managerial skills of peacekeepers are assessed at the personal, interpersonal, and group levels. At the personal level, the study examines peacekeepers' skills of self-awareness, stress management, and effective problem solving. At the interpersonal level, we examine skills related to constructive communication, effective motivation, and effective conflict management. Management skills at the group level include effective assistance, delegation of work, teamwork, and leadership.

In terms of personal-level managerial skills, self-awareness refers to one's ability to focus attention inwardly and one's degree of attention to the perceptions of others about oneself.[27] Individuals who are more cognizant of others' perceptions about themselves and can compare themselves against salient standards, such as specific behaviors or progress toward a goal, are more prone to develop a self-awareness, whereby they can behave properly toward others and improve positive attitudes.[28] Self-awareness enables peacekeepers to act empathetically toward others such as civilians, locals, and colleagues. They build healthy relationships that can contribute to the success of peacekeeping operations.[29] Another factor with which peacekeepers have to deal is stress. Peacekeepers are usually exposed to stress factors such as hostility and dangerous warlike circumstances. Many peacekeepers witness life-threatening situations and atrocities. These traumatic experiences, continuously arduous responsibilities, and the repercussions of being away from home and family are common stress factors for peacekeepers. In this context, stress management refers to individuals' physical and psychological skills and capacity to cope with events or situations under which they feel pressured and tense. Peacekeepers' normal reactions to abnormal conditions based on the instincts of self-preservation and self-protection do help them survive. However, these kinds of reactions can consume peacekeepers' physical and mental energy.[30] Effective problem solving refers to the most important cognitive activity of individuals in daily and professional contexts. Problem solving is one of the most important learning outcomes throughout people's lives.[31] In the context of peacekeeping operations, problem-solving skills prominently affect the success of a mission. Peacekeepers generally encounter ambiguous situations in which problems occur frequently. In performing their mission tasks (e.g., distributing humanitarian supplies, disarming militia, controlling large crowds), peacekeepers interact with troops from other countries, NGOs, and locals, who may be content or discontent with the presence of the peacekeeping force. Peacekeepers frequently have to use their problem-solving skills to deal with hostilities and obstacles.[32] Problem-solving skills are key determinants of the success of peacekeeping operations.

Constructive communication, which is one of the three interpersonal-level managerial skills assessed in our research, refers to an individual's skill of building healthy relationships with others. Communication provides proper climate for effective coordination and strong relationships among people and organizations. When partners in peacekeeping operation come from varied countries or cultures, different communication patterns cause impediments in managerial processes.[33] Therefore, it is important for peacekeepers to have constructive communication skills in order to achieve mission effectiveness. Effective motivation, which is the second interpersonal managerial skill, refers to peacekeepers' self-motivation level and ability to motivate others in the ambiguous and multidimensional conditions typical of peacekeeping operations. When the peacekeepers feel that their mission has turned into an ordinary event or experience stress due to the unstable conditions and multidimensionality of peacekeeping operations, they can feel unmotivated, causing a decrease in their performance levels. In such cases, the skill of effective motivation pays dividends in directing fatigued colleagues toward mission objectives.[34] The last interpersonal managerial skill we assessed is effective conflict management, which refers to peacekeepers' skill of dealing with conflicts deriving from differences in mandates, mission objectives, and organizational cultures and the competition over resources between peacekeepers and other organizations or among peacekeepers from different countries. The more peacekeepers are skilled with conflict management, the easier it will be to accomplish the mission. In this context, peacekeepers have to be ready to handle all sorts of conflicts and compensate for other parties' lack of managerial skills. Conflict management skill plays an important role in accomplishing the objectives of peacekeeping operations.[35]

Finally, we assessed group-level managerial skills. Effective assistance refers to peacekeepers' capacity to help those who are in need and to effectively allocate tasks among team members. Helping others fosters team spirit among peacekeepers, which can have positive effects on mission success.[36] Equal and proper delegation of tasks among team members may increase effectiveness of the overall mission on the ground. However, without effective teamwork skill, neither assistance nor proper delegation of work would result in mission success. Lack of skill in teamwork is a weakness that can cause mission failure. Teamwork skill requires competencies in information exchange, coordination, assignment of roles, error checking, and motivation, which directly impact team performance and mission efficiency in a multidimensional peacekeeping environment.[37] Therefore, the teamwork skill of peacekeepers can be evaluated as one of the core competencies for the success of peacekeeping operations, which can be considered as an attribute of effective leadership skill.

Building Individual Capacity and Experiential Learning

Capacity building is the continual change that enables individuals and organizations to improve their skills, capabilities, and competencies in order to function effectively.[38] In this chapter, we assess the improvements in the managerial skills of individual peacekeepers. We directly examine the extent to which peacekeepers build individual capacity based on their experiences in a peacekeeping operation. Unlike other studies, which focus mainly on the positive military gains from peacekeeping, our work is concerned with the implications of proper management and peacekeeping success for the enhancement of international peacebuilding. As we noted, successful peacekeeping operations are more likely to provide popular support for future international humanitarian problems that may genuinely need international intervention, as was the case in Bosnia-Herzegovina. As such, our study of the relation between managerial skills and the success of peacekeeping brings a unique micro-level angle to the way we discuss international peacebuilding. To enhance international security through peacebuilding operations, we need to know the micro-level dynamics that can impede or support international peacekeeping operations.

This study draws on several works that are relevant to the question we address in this chapter. Morris Janowitz examined some of the positive effects of experience in peacekeeping operations on enhancement of peacekeepers' military skills, especially officers' leadership skills.[39] Due to the nature of peacekeeping operations, combat units and their personnel, from the platoon to company level, significantly improve their wartime skills during peacekeeping operations. Peacekeeping activities increase soldiers' experience in dealing with complex, challenging, and risky environments. Such experience instills confidence, collaboration, and teamwork, which can increase unit cohesion and overall unit readiness. Peacekeeping gives peacekeepers a chance to operate in a real, warlike environment where they may gain invaluable improvements in managerial skills.[40] In her study of United States military personnel in Macedonia, Laura Miller found that peacekeeping experience enhances soldier skills at the small-unit level and improves leadership skills among noncommissioned officers.[41]

Given the multidimensionality of third-generation peacekeeping operations, peacekeepers are trained in a variety of mission-related skills prior to deployment in order to execute a variety of tasks ranging from distributing humanitarian relief supplies to protecting refugees.[42] However, the training activities do not provide enough competency for peacekeepers as compared to the skills they develop during the actual implementation of peacekeeping operations.[43] Therefore, we measure the extent to which peacekeepers improve their above-mentioned managerial skills and build individual capacity as a consequence of their experience in peacekeeping operations.

+---+
| →   Concrete Experience   ↓ |
| |
| Active Experimentation   Reflective Observation |
| |
| ↑   Abstract Conceptualization   ← |
+---+

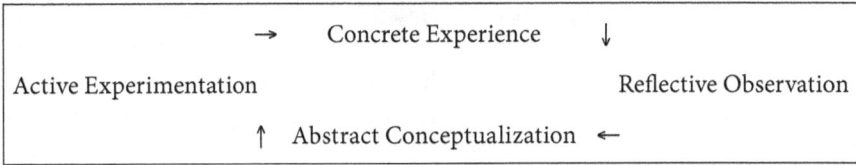

Figure 4.1. David Kolb's experiential learning model

Soft skills, which can be in the form of social, managerial, and interpersonal skills, are strongly related to emotional intelligence. Therefore soft skills can be tools of capacity building during the professional career of military personnel. They are the courteous way of presenting, interacting, negotiating, problem solving, and managing, which are essential at every level of an organization, including most prominently peacekeeping forces. Self-awareness, self-regulation, motivation, stress management, empathy, and social interaction skills are prominent soft skills.[44] In today's fast-changing world, with rapid improvement in communication technology and a shift from industrial society to information society, many military field missions and headquarters emphasize integrity, communication, and flexibility in conducting their work.[45] However, one problem that still remains is the undervaluing of the importance of soft skills. Studies continue to show that militaries need soft skills.[46]

The individual capacity-building role of peacekeeping can be examined through the notion of experiential learning. Experiential learning is the process of making meaning from direct experience for the individual.[47] Aristotle once said, "For the things we have to learn before we can do them, we learn by doing them."[48] In this manner Kolb's study on experience as the source of learning and individual development provides a very useful notion of experiential learning.[49] If we apply the example of job shadowing in peacekeeping as a method for training qualified peacekeepers based on concrete experience, we see that peacekeepers physically experience the peace operation in the here-and-now. This direct experience forms the basis for observation and reflection. Peacekeepers get the opportunity to consider what works or fails (reflective observation) and to think about ways to improve on future peacekeeping activities (abstract conceptualization). Every new peacekeeping experience is informed by a cyclical pattern of previous experience driven by the thought and reflection processes. This, in essence, is active experimentation, as Kolb points out in his work. Kolb's experiential learning model sets out four distinct learning styles, which are based on a four-stage learning cycle. In this model, immediate or concrete experiences provide a basis for observations and reflections. Moreover, observations and reflections are assimilated and distilled into abstract concepts, which produce new implications for action and new experiences (see figure 4.1).

According to Kolb, this process represents an ideal learning cycle or spiral where the learner touches all the bases. In essence, it is a cycle of experiencing, reflecting, thinking, and acting. Immediate or concrete experiences lead to observations and reflections. These reflections are then assimilated into abstract concepts with implications for action, which the person can actively test and experiment with. The net result is the creation of new experiences.[50] According to Kolb, experiential learning, as the meaning-making process of the individual's direct experience, requires certain qualities. In particular, the learner must (1) be willing to be actively involved in the experience, (2) be able to reflect on the experience, (3) possess and use analytical skills to conceptualize the experience, and (4) possess decision-making and problem-solving skills in order to use the new ideas gained from the experience. Based on Kolb's experiential learning model, Micah Jacobson and Mari Ruddy developed five practical questions to enhance the effectiveness of experiential learning: Did you notice? Why did that happen? Does that happen in life? Why does that happen? How can you use that?[51] These sorts of questions are useful for peacekeepers to ask themselves during a mission to garner the benefits of the peacekeeping operation experience for future assignments.

Method and Data

Our study is framed along Kolb's experiential learning model and the insights of Jacobson and Ruddy to assess the capacity-building skill peacekeepers accrue during peacekeeping operations.[52] In particular, the aim of our research is to determine the individual capacity-building effect of the peacekeeping experience on peacekeepers' managerial skills, most notably self-awareness, stress management, effective problem solving, constructive communication, effective motivation, effective conflict management, effective assistance, delegation of work, teamwork, and leadership. By assessing the managerial capacity building of peacekeeping operations, we hope to establish some of the critical micro-level factors that contribute to the success of peacekeeping missions. Such knowledge can be useful for planning feature operations and thereby increase the positive impacts and public perceptions of peacekeeping on international peacebuilding efforts.

This study is based on a survey conducted among fifty-three officers serving in EUFOR. The study participants were from Austria, Bosnia-Herzegovina, Czech Republic, Hungary, Macedonia, Netherlands, Romania, Spain, and Turkey. Each of the participants took part in the survey voluntarily. All of the participants are male and their age profile ranges from twenty-six to fifty-three, with an average of thirty-seven years. The total years in military service of participants

Table 4.1. Fit indexes of each scale

Scales	Δχ2/SD		GFI		CFI		RMR	
	Pre	Post	Pre	Post	Pre	Post	Pre	Post
SA	1.8	1.9	.94	.85	.95	.95	.06	.07
MS	2.6	1.1	.85	.93	.95	.98	.07	.06
EPS	1.3	1.9	.84	.88	.93	.94	.08	.07
CC	1.0	1.5	.89	.86	.98	.95	.08	.08
EM	1.8	1.5	.85	.85	.94	.95	.08	.09
ECM	2.1	2.6	.85	.83	.95	.96	.08	.07
EA	2.4	1.9	.95	.96	.96	.97	.03	.03
DoW	4.3	2.3	.92	.96	.91	.95	.07	.05
TWL	3.0	1.9	.85	.85	.94	.95	0.8	.05

range from four to thirty-five, with an average of seventeen years. All of the participants have had previous experience in peacekeeping operations. Their experience ranges from six to forty-eight months, with an average of twelve months.

The survey was conducted in Sarajevo, Bosnia-Herzegovina, between June and November 2012. Data were collected using the Assessment of Managerial Skills in Peace Operations Questionnaire developed by one of the co-authors (i.e., Unsal Sigri) who was serving as the chief of the Capacity Building Department at EUFOR headquarters. The entire questionnaire was in English due to the multinational character of peacekeeping operations and peacekeepers' high level of English proficiency. Before the survey all permissions needed were received from EUFOR authorities. The survey was conducted at two different times involving the same participants, with six months interval between the first and second survey. The pre- and post-surveys are used to assess improvements or recessions in individual capacity of each managerial skill of peacekeepers.

The questionnaire has a six point Likert-type scale (6 = strongly agree, 1 = strongly disagree) to assess the following skills: (a) self-awareness (SA), (b) managing stress (MS), (c) effective problem solving (EPS), (d) constructive communication (CC), (e) effective motivation (EM), (f) effective conflict management (ECM), (g) effective assistance (EA), (h) delegation of work (DoW), and (i) teamwork and leadership (TWL). Ascending points indicate strength of each skill. The reliability of the each scale is assessed using Cronbach's coefficient alpha at each data collection period (pre/initial and post/after six months), and coefficients vary between 0.71 and 0.88. The validity of the each scale is also assessed at each data collection period with confirmatory factor analysis, results of which verify a one-factor structure. The results of each analysis are presented in table 4.1.

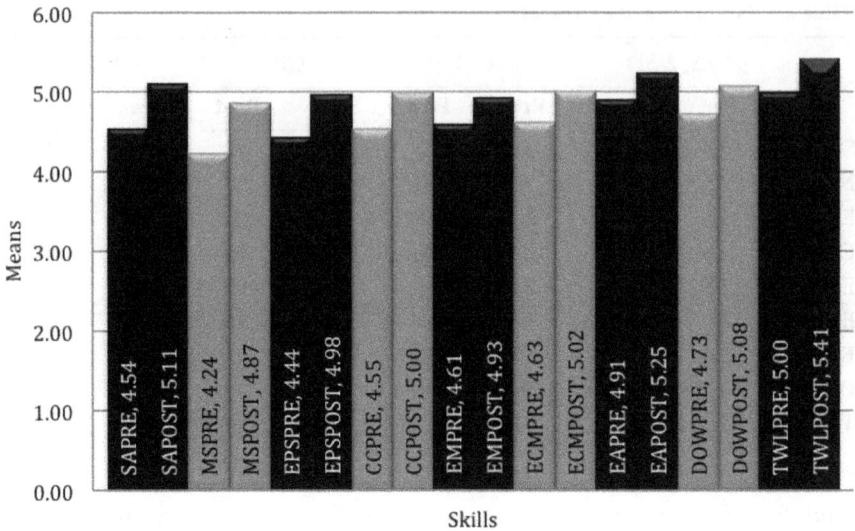

Figure 4.2. Individual capacity building

Findings and Discussion

The findings of our research indicate that peacekeeping experience leads to considerable improvement in managerial skills of peacekeepers (see figure 4.2). Each pair of bars represent one of the managerial skills we measured: self-awareness (SA), managing stress (MS), effective problem solving (EPS), constructive communication (CC), effective motivation (EM), effective conflict management (ECM), effective assistance (EA), delegation of work (DoW), and teamwork and leadership (TWL). The value on each bar indicates the pre- or post-survey strength of each managerial skill.

Our findings correspond to the finding of other studies in this area, which is an indication of the importance of the study. Janowitz finds that peacekeeping experience enhances military skills.[53] Similarly, Mark Perrin et al. report that commanders observe an overwhelming improvement in wartime skills of soldiers during deployment on peace operations.[54] Research conducted among peacekeepers serving under UNFICYP indicates that the best training in peacekeeping skills occurs in the field. As Charles Moskos suggests, our findings show that the field training that occurs during peacekeeping experience enhances the managerial skills of peacekeepers. Miller's studies of United States peacekeepers in Macedonia also reveal that peacekeeping experience improves the military and leadership skills of peacekeepers.[55] Our study adds to the findings of other studies by measuring specific skills sets that are enhanced by peacekeeping operations. More importantly, our study shifts the debate from the effects of peacekeeping on improvement in traditional military skills to discovering the set of skills that impact on the overall success of peacekeeping missions, which would be beneficial for the broader efforts to enhance international peacebuilding through effective third-generation peacekeeping missions under the doctrine of R2P.

Conclusions

In spite of the elapsed time and peacekeeping efforts since the end of the violence in Bosnia-Herzegovina, a hidden tension and hatred among the former warring factions can still be felt by peacekeepers who served in Bosnia-Herzegovina. In our opinion, normality throughout the country can be enhanced by effective implementation of the peacebuilding process. The overall peacebuilding process is carried out and coordinated mainly by peacekeepers. That's why we assert that management of Operation EUFOR Althea is one of the key elements of success in Bosnia-Herzegovina. In this context, advanced managerial capacity of peacekeepers may pay dividends and ensure the accomplishment of the mission in a shorter period of time.

As distinct from other studies, this research measures how the peacekeeping experience improves specific managerial skills, namely: self-awareness, managing stress, effective problem solving, constructive communication, effective motivation, effective conflict management, effective assistance, delegation of work, and teamwork and leadership. In addition, a new tool for measuring managerial skills was used during the actual implementation of the peacekeeping mission. The findings of this research indicate considerable improvements in managerial capacity of peacekeepers due to their experience, which may affect the training programs and training methodology of peacekeeping participating countries in the future. New pre-deployment training curriculums may be developed considering the potential improvements in managerial skills of peacekeepers, which occur during implementation of the mission. Our study supplies important fill-in for a gap in the field of management of peacekeeping operations and leaves room for further research.

Despite the crucial findings of this research, the study has some limitations. In particular, the sample is small, there were no prior studies on the same issues, and the managerial skills measured are limited. The lack of comparable studies measuring the same managerial skills means that we cannot make direct comparisons. Despite the limitations, we point to the importance of managerial skills in the accomplishment of peacekeeping operations. Our study points to the need to further study soft skills and develop improved measurement instruments in order to analyze the effects of managerial skills on mission-specific objectives. Armed forces of countries may pay attention to soft skills and improve training programs and doctrines to ensure their troops are equipped with soft skills. Such skills could only increase the success of future peacekeeping missions, which would encourage reluctant publics to support third-generation international peacekeeping missions when they are truly needed to enhance international peace and security.

With reference to the notion of experiential learning, this study notes that peacekeepers need to build managerial skills, which can be reinforced with direct and real experience in a peacekeeping operation. With the direct and real experience in a peacekeeping operation, peacekeepers may have opportunities to make discoveries and experiments with knowledge firsthand, instead of hearing or reading about other people's experiences. A job-shadowing method in peacekeeping may be an example of valuable experiential learning, which can contribute significantly to the peacekeeper's overall understanding of the real-time environment. However, such a method is not easy to implement due to time and budget limitations.

An experiential learning approach in peacekeeping training may allow participants to share knowledge and experiences and contribute dynamically to the learning process. Through this process, participants not only acquire information but also contribute to the construction of knowledge in a way that is meaningful and directly applicable to the reality of peacekeeping operations. A notable example in this direction is the Peacekeeping Training Programme of the United Nations Institute for Training and Research, which emphasizes experiential training.[56] In particular, it highlights experiential and collaborative learning focusing on the learning needs, interests, and styles of participants to ensure the relevance and retention of content. Many peacekeeping operations are forced to reinvent the wheel because of failure to capture and spread what has been learned from previous operations. This inability to exploit experiential learning has worrying implications for future peacekeeping operations. This chapter clearly points to peacekeeping operations as sources of experiential learning based on individual practices.

There is a growing attention to issues of experiential learning in peacekeeping. An International Peace Institute paper titled "Enhancing Training for Deploying the Best" indicates that more can be done to equip the right people with the right skills for UN peacekeeping operations.[57] Another study, on training needs, from the Kofi Annan International Peacekeeping Training Center points out the importance of adaptation and refinement of the management skills.[58] In Yantsislav Yanakiev's study of Bulgarian peacekeepers, 55 percent of peacekeepers mentioned the need for additional knowledge of intercultural management techniques and 37 percent of peacekeepers also said they needed communication skills.[59]

Experiential learning theory can help us understand the learning process in peacekeeping operations at a deeper and more comprehensive level. It can provide insights for improving learning and the processes in peacekeeping operations. The training programs for the peacekeepers based on experiential learning activity may aim to capture the institutional and personal learning and best practice through issue-based action research. This bottom-up and exploratory approach may result in new ways to understand and articulate the peacebuilding work that is being conducted within international peacekeeping operations.

Notes

1. Chan, "The Evolution of Peace Support Operations and Implications for the Conscript Military," 62–78.

2. Kaldor, *New and Old Wars*.

3. Chan, "The Evolution of Peace Support Operations," 63.

4. Tranca and Garon, "Fight It or Freeze It."

5. International Peace Institute, *The Management Handbook for UN Field Missions*.

6. UN, *2005 World Summit Outcome*.

7. Juhasz, "The European Union's Crisis Management Activity in Bosnia and Herzegovina."

8. Dandeker and Gow, "The Future of Peace Support Operations," 327–348.

9. Miller, "Do Soldiers Hate Peacekeeping?," 415–450.

10. Bah, "The Contours of New Humanitarianism," 2–26; Kaldor, "In Defense of New Wars," 1–16.

11. Kühne, "Peace Support Operations," 358–367.

12. Sigri and Basar, "An Analysis of Assessment of Peacekeeping Operations," 389–406.

13. Dandeker, "The Future of Peace Support Operations."

14. Bah, "Civil Non-State Actors in Peacekeeping and Peacebuilding in West Africa," 313–336.

15. Bah, "The Contours of New Humanitarianism"; Tranca, "Fight It or Freeze It."

16. Kernic, "The Soldier and the Task," 113–128.

17. Kalyvas and Sambanis, "Bosnia's Civil War," 191–229.

18. Woehrel, "Bosnia," 255–273.

19. Juncos, "The EU's Post-Conflict Intervention in Bosnia and Herzegovina," 88–108.

20. Juhasz, "The European Union's Crisis Management Activity in Bosnia and Herzegovina."

21. Knezovic, "Scanning EUFOR-Operation Althea and a Possible Croatian Role in It," 125–131.

22. Keohane, "EUFOR Althea (Bosnia and Herzegovina)," 211–220.

23. Donlon, *EUPM and EUNAVFOR*, 33–34.

24. Knauer, *EUFOR Althea*.

25. IPI, *The Management Handbook for UN Field Missions*.

26. Ülgen and Mirze, *İşletmelerde Stratejik Yönetim*.

27. Ashley and Reiter-Palmon, "Self-Awareness and the Evolution of Leaders," 2–17.

28. Caldwell, "Identity, Self-Awareness, and Self-Deception," 393–406.

29. Basset, *Growing Better Leaders for the Future.*

30. United Nations Department of Peacekeeping Operations, *UN Stress Management Booklet.*

31. Jonassen, "Toward a Design Theory of Problem Solving," 63–85.

32. Stanley, "Psychological Dimensions of Peacekeeping."

33. Griffith, "The Role of Communication Competencies in International Business Relationship Development," 256–265.

34. Jelusic, "Motivation for Peace Operations73–85.

35. Ramajaran, Bezrukova, Jehn, Euwema, and Kop, "Relationship between Peacekeepers and NGO Workers," 167–191.

36. Raver, Ehrhart, and Chadwick, "The Emergence of Team Helping Norms," 616–637.

37. Pierce, "Barriers to Adaptability in a Multinational Team."

38. Australian Volunteers International, *Information Sheet-Introduction to Capacity Building.*

39. Janowitz, *The Professional Soldier.*

40. Perrin, Eskridge, and Burghart, *Army Peacekeepers*, 1–17.

41. Miller, "Do Soldiers Hate Peacekeeping?," 438.

42. Findlay, *The New Peacekeeping and the New Peacekeepers*, 1–48.

43. Moskos, *Peace Soldiers*, 134.

44. Marques, "Understanding the Strength of Gentleness," 163–171.

45. Caforio, "The Information Society and the Changing Face of War," 129–142; Robles, "Executive Perceptions of the Top 10 Soft Skills Needed in Today's Workplace," 453–465.

46. Buhler, "The Growing Importance of Soft Skills in the Workplace," 13–15.

47. Itin, "Reasserting the Philosophy of Experiential Education as a Vehicle for Change in the 21st Century," 91–98.

48. Aristotle, *Nicomachean Ethics.*

49. Kolb, *Experiential Learning.*

50. Kolb and Kolb, *Bibliography of Research on Experiential Learning Theory and the Learning Style Inventory.*

51. Jacobson and Ruddy, *Open to Outcome.*

52. Kolb, *Experiential Learning*; Jacobson, *Open to Outcome.*

53. Janowitz, *The Professional Soldier*, 429.

54. Perrin, *Army Peacekeepers*, 8.

55. Moskos, *Peace Soldiers*, 134; Miller, "Do Soldiers Hate Peacekeeping?": 438.

56. United Nations Institute for Training and Research, "Peacekeeping Training Programme."

57. Cutillo, "Deploying the Best," 1–16.

58. Albrecht and Malan, *Training Needs Analysis.*

59. Yanakiev, "Educating Adaptable Military Leaders and Training of Teams for Coalition Operations," 203–216.

References

Albrecht, Peter, and Mark Malan. *Training Needs Analysis Workshop: (West) African Civilian Professional Staff in PSO.* Workshop Report of Kofi Annan International Peacekeeping Training Centre, Accra, Ghana, June 8–10, 2005.

Aristotle. *Nicomachean Ethics*. 350 BC. http://classics.mit.edu/Aristotle/nicomachaen.2.ii.html.

Ashley, Greg C., and Roni Reiter-Palmon. "Self Awareness and the Evolution of Leaders: The Need for a Better Measure of Self Awareness." *Journal of Behavioral and Applied Management* 14, no. 1 (2012): 2–17.

Australian Volunteers International. *Information Sheet-Introduction to Capacity Building*. 2006. http://www.australianvolunteers.com/media/511868/3-introduction-to-capacity-building -ju109.pdf.

Bah, Abu Bakarr. "Civil Non-State Actors in Peacekeeping and Peacebuilding in West Africa." *Journal of International Peacekeeping* 17 (2013): 313–336.

———. "The Contours of New Humanitarianism: War and Peacebuilding in Sierra Leone." *Africa Today* 60, no. 1 (2013): 2–26.

Basset, Richard C. *Growing Better Leaders for the Future: A Story in Optimizing Self-Awareness*. USAWC Strategy Research Project, US Army War College. 2004.

Buhler, Patricia M. "The Growing Importance of Soft Skills in the Workplace." *Supervision* 62, no. 6 (2001): 13–15.

Caldwell, Cam. "Identity, Self-Awareness, and Self-Deception: Ethical Implications for Leaders and Organizations." *Journal of Business Ethics* 90 (2009): 393–406.

Caforio, Giuseppe. "The Information Society and the Changing Face of War." In *Society, Culture and Technology at the Dawn of the 21st Century*, edited by Janusz Mucha and Katarzyna Lesczczynska, 129–142. Newcastle, UK: Cambridge Scholars, 2010.

Chan, Samuel. "The Evolution of Peace Support Operations and Implications for the Conscript Military." *Journal of the Singapore Armed Forces* 37, no. 1 (2011): 62–78.

Cutillo, Alberto. "Deploying the Best: Enhancing Training for United Nations Peacekeepers." *International Peace Institute* 5 (2013): 1–16.

Dandeker, Christopher, and James Gow. "The Future of Peace Support Operations: Strategic Peace-keeping and Success." *Armed Forces and Society* 23, no. 3 (1997): 327–348.

Donlon, Fidelma. *EUPM and EUNAVFOR. Mission in Bosnia-Herzegovina: Analytical Report*. European Commission, 2010.

Findlay, Trevor. *The New Peacekeeping and The New Peacekeepers*. Working Paper No. 1996/2. Department of International Relations, Research School of Pacific and Asian Studies: Aus-tralian National University-Canberra, 1996, 1–48.

Griffith, David A. "The Role of Communication Competencies in International Business Relation-ship Development." *Journal of World Business* 37 (2002): 256–265.

International Peace Institute. *The Management Handbook for UN Field Missions*. New York: United Nations, 2012.

Itin, Christian M. "Reasserting the Philosophy of Experiential Education as a Vehicle for Change in the 21st Century." *Journal of Experiential Education* 22, no. 2 (1999): 91–98.

Jacobson, Micah, and Mari Ruddy. *Open to Outcome*. Oklahoma City, OK: Wood 'N' Barnes, 2004.

Janowitz, Morris. *The Professional Soldier*. New York: Free Press, 1960.

Jelusic, Ljubica. "Motivation for Peace Operations." *International Review of Sociology* 17, no. 1 (2007): 73–85.

Jonassen, David H. "Toward a Design Theory of Problem Solving." *Educational Technology Re-search and Development* 48, no. 4 (2000): 63–85.

Juhasz, Krisztina. *The European Union's Crisis Management Activity in Bosnia and Herzegovina*. Paper presented at The Balkans Dialogue: Conflict Resolution and EU Accession Politics in the Balkans and Turkey, Budapest, Hungary, February 8–9, 2013.

Juncos, Anna E. "The EU's Post-Conflict Intervention in Bosnia and Herzegovina: (re)Integrating the Balkans and/or (re)Inventing the EU?." *Southeast European Politics* 6, no. 2 (2005): 88–108.

Kaldor, Mary. "In Defense of New Wars." *Stability* 2, no. 1 (2013): 1–16.

———. *New and Old Wars: Organised Violence in a Global Era*. Cambridge: Polity, 1999.

Kalyvas, Stathis N., and Nicholas Sambanis. "Bosnia's Civil War: Origins and Violence Dynamics." In *Understanding Civil War: Evidence and Analysis*, edited by Paul Collier and Nicholas Sambanis, 191–229. Washington, DC: World Bank, 2005.

Keohane, Daniel. "EUFOR Althea (Bosnia and Herzegovina)." In *European Security and Defence Policy, The First 10 Years (1999–2009)*, edited by Giovanni Grevi, Damien Helly and Daniel Keohane, 211–220. Paris: European Union, 2009.

Kernic, Franz. "The Soldier and the Task: Austria's Experience of Preparing Peacekeepers." *International Peacekeeping* 6, no. 3 (1999): 113–128.

Knauer, Jannik. *EUFOR Althea: Appraisal and Future Perspectives of the EU's Former Flagship Operation in Bosnia and Herzegovina*. College of Europe, Department of EU International Relations and Diplomacy Studies, 2011. https://www.coleurope.eu/system/files_force/research-paper/edp_7_2011_knauer.pdf?download=1.

Knezovic, Sandro. "Scanning EUFOR-Operation Althea and a Possible Croatian Role in It." *Croatian International Relations Review* 40, no. 41 (2005): 125–131.

Kolb, Alice, and David A. Kolb. *Bibliography of Research on Experiential Learning Theory and the Learning Style Inventory*. Department of Organizational Behavior, Weatherhead School of Management. Cleveland, OH: Case Western Reserve University, 1999.

Kolb, David. A. *Experiential Learning: Experience as the Source of Learning and Development*. Englewood Cliffs, NJ: Prentice Hall, 1984.

Kühne, Winrich. "Peace Support Operations: How to Make Them Succeed." *Internationale Politik und Gesellschaft* 4 (1999): 358–367.

Marques, Joan. "Understanding the Strength of Gentleness: Soft-Skilled Leadership on the Rise." *Journal of Business Ethics* 116 (2012): 163–171.

Miller, Laura L. "Do Soldiers Hate Peacekeeping? The Case of Preventive Diplomacy Operations in Macedonia." *Armed Forces and Society* 23, no. 3 (1997): 415–450.

Moskos, Charles. *Peace Soldiers: The Sociology of a United Nations Military Force*. Chicago: University of Chicago Press, 1976.

Perrin, Mark W., Robert Eskridge, and Daniel Burghart. *Army Peacekeepers: Warriors with Special Skills*. Washington, DC: National War College, 2001.

Pierce, Linda G. *Barriers to Adaptability in a Multinational Team*. Paper presented at the Human Factors and Ergonomics Society 46th Annual Meeting, Baltimore, MD, September 30–October 4, 2002.

Ramajaran, Lakshimi, Katerina Bezrukova, Karen A. Jehn, Martin Euwema, and Nicolien Kop. "Relationship between Peacekeepers and NGO Workers: The Role of Training and Conflict Management Styles in International Peacekeeping." *International Journal of Conflict Management* 15, no. 2 (1990): 167–191.

Raver, Jana L., Mark G. Ehrhart, and Ingrid C. Chadwick. "The Emergence of Team Helping Norms: Foundations within Members' Attributes and Behavior." *Journal of Organizational Behavior* 33 (2012): 616–637.

Robles, Marcel M. "Executive Perceptions of the Top 10 Soft Skills Needed in Today's Workplace." *Business Communication Quarterly* 75, no. 4 (2012): 453–465.

Sigri, Unsal, and Ufuk Basar. "An Analysis of Assessment of Peacekeeping Operations." *Korean Journal of Defense Analysis* 26, no. 3 (2014): 389–406.

Stanley, Chua Hon Kiat. "Psychological Dimensions of Peacekeeping: The Role of the Organization." *Journal of the Singapore Armed Forces* 29, no. 2 (2003). http://www.mindef.gov.sg/safti/pointer/back/journals/2003/Vo129_2/1.htm.

Tranca, Oana, and Richard Garon. *Fight It or Freeze It: Which Generation of Peacekeeping Operations Is More Apt to Solve Conflicts*. Paper presented at 49th ISA Annual Convention, San Francisco, CA, March 25–30, 2007.

United Nations. "2005 World Summit Outcome." Resolution adopted by the General Assembly 60/1. 2005, Sixtieth session Agenda items 46 and 120, October 24, 2005.

United Nations Department of Peacekeeping Operations. *UN Stress Management Booklet*. New York: United Nations, 1995.

United Nations Institute for Training and Research. *Peacekeeping Training Programme*. http://www.unitar.org/ptp/.

Ülgen, Hayri, and Kadri Mirze. *İşletmelerde Stratejik Yönetim*. Istanbul: BETA Basım Yayım Dağıtım A.Ş., 2014.

Woehrel, Steven. "Bosnia: Current Issues and U.S. Policy." *Current Politics and Economics of Europe* 22, no. 3 (2011): 255–273.

Yanakiev, Yantsislav. "Educating Adaptable Military Leaders and Training of Teams for Coalition Operations." In *Cultural Challenges in Military Operations*, edited by Cees M. Coops and Tibor Szvircsev Tresch, 203–216. Rome, IL: NATO Defense College, 2007.

5   Personalized Mediations and Interventions in the Ivoirian Conflict

Amy Niang

MEDIATORS CAN BE seen as the carriers of a particular kind of sovereignty given the nature of their intervention and the requirement—manifest in the Ivoirian case—for a capacity for creativity and improvisation. This particular kind of sovereignty is built and deployed, and it is informed by mediators' capacity to tap into different registers of legitimacy and a capacity to (re)interpret the terms of mediation mandates. This chapter examines mediation processes in Côte d'Ivoire between the period of 2002 and 2011. It specifically analyzes the framework that enabled Blaise Compaoré to broker a peace deal in 2007—a decisive moment that paved the way for "postconflict" elections. A characteristic of the Ivoirian conflict is the sheer extent of external intervention(ism) in the various mediations, the conflict resolution strategies, and the elaboration of a working legal and institutional framework to carry and conclude these processes.

This chapter thus examines whether there are ways in which a mediator can and does appropriate the mediation process by giving it a direction it might otherwise not have taken. In our case of interest, the 2002–2011 military and political crisis in Côte d'Ivoire, the personal touch of Compaoré with regard to processes, political and legal, the nature of agreements, actors' conduct, and mediation outcomes point to different possibilities of understanding conflict management and resolution patterns in different African contexts. More importantly for the mediation literature, the phenomenon of an unlikely mediator, as exemplified by Compaoré, provides useful methodological and empirical resources for thinking differently about mediation as an applied science. In fact, if Compaoré's mediation career poses an analytical puzzle to perspectives commonly developed in the literature, this has to do with his counterintuitive and unconventional methods that therefore deserve proper engagement. Compaoré has experienced the political history of West Africa in a continuous, first-person perspective. As such, his vision of stability across the region relies on a certain configuration of power that enables his enduring influence on the region's politics. His approach to the resolution of the Ivoirian conflict thus bore the marker of conservative politics most commonly associated with Félix Houphouët-Boigny, his political mentor, and by extension the muddled political governance model of postcolonial Francophone Africa.

Thabo Mbeki's mediation provides a comparative background to Compaoré's engagement with the Ivoirian conflict as mediator-in-chief. If the Ouagadougou Agreement (2007) was seen as the mechanism that enabled progress in the peace process most decisively, the Pretoria discussions and subsequent agreements constituted a significant framework that paved the way for an inclusive process. Mbeki's engagement in Côte d'Ivoire was a first for a South African president in Francophone Africa. Mbeki's lack of knowledge and expertise on the rest of the continent in general and on Francophone Africa in particular hampered his best efforts, while his anti-imperial narrative worked against an expectation of neutrality attached to an African Union (AU) envoy. Leadership styles between the two mediators differed insofar as one could schematically identify an overly legalist approach to the mediation by Mbeki and perhaps an overly political approach to Compaoré's. However, in both cases, multilevel interactions tend to play out differently—on the one hand across the personal and the political, and on the other hand across the personal, the bilateral, the regional, and the international.

The chapter is framed around three arguments. First, it contends that the Ivoirian crisis mediation offers a unique example of a form of personalization of a conflict resolution process hinged on the multiple and overlapping sovereignties of key actors and institutions including that of mediators. Second, the political economy of conflict management in the Ivoirian case demonstrates how the prominence of self-interest can be a driver in the shifting constitution of orders and norms in mediation processes. Third, the crisis that ensued from the contestations over the 2010 elections and the manner in which it was handled by the international community reveal a growing tendency by the international community to use elections as a mode of conflict resolution on the one hand, and on the other, a certain fixation on processes and procedures that more often than not overshadow deep structural issues that caused the conflict in the first place.

The chapter highlights various problems with internationally mediated agreements, not least the fact that they tend to operate on a logic of their own, to do with supposedly successful diplomatic interventions that culminate in the signing of an agreement on the basis of concessions from participating parties; rarely at this level do those structural issues at the roots of conflicts get properly addressed. In the Ivoirian case specifically, the requirement of enforcement of the democratic norm at the expense of the treatment of deep political, social, economic, and cultural questions meant that elections—pushed to uncertain and implausible levels—became the recognized measure of recovery and legality no matter how these might be contested. In the words of one former mediator, "Thus, in various ways, the events in Côte d'Ivoire could serve as a defining moment in terms of the urgent need to reengineer the system of international relations. They have exposed the reality of the balance of power in the post–Cold War era, and put paid to the fiction that the major powers respect the rule of law in the conduct of international relations, even as defined by the UN Charter, and that, as democrats, they respect the views of the peoples of the world."[1] The electoral outcome eventually had to be enforced through military means after months of standoff during which violence sponsored by supporters of both Alassane Ouattara and Laurent Gbagbo, the two major contenders for the presidency, claimed many lives between the end of 2010 and early 2011. Ultimately, the neutrality of the UN as a peacemaker and arbitrator was heavily questioned in regard to the manner in which the 2010 postelectoral crisis was resolved.

Background to the Ivoirian Conflict

Arguably, the Ivoirian conflict started in September 2002. A mutiny in Bouaké and Abidjan turned into a failed military coup, which in turn became a rebellion that was to last for many years. Marginalized officers from northern Côte d'Ivoire constituted the Patriotic Movement of Côte d'Ivoire (MPCI) and later merged with two further dissident groups, namely the Popular Movement for the Greater West (MPIGO) and the Movement for Peace and Justice (MPJ). They demanded the immediate enforcement of their citizenship rights as fully fledged Ivoirians, not as *Djulas* or "northerners" or "foreigners." They demanded a right to partake in the national project as such and to share in its resources on equal terms with other social groups and categories. In a country de facto divided into North and South, a five-year stalemate ensued that debilitated its human, institutional, agricultural, and other resources.[2]

Despite the extent of the damage inflicted by a draining conflict, Côte d'Ivoire was never a failed state, nor was it a case of an ethnic strife in the sense in which these are commonly understood. There were, however, structural tensions and contradictions that beset Ivoirian politics and society, and these had to do with regional, ethnic, and religious antagonisms fueled by an unequal distribution of citizenship rights, unequal access to productive and land resources and related social exclusions, and large disparities between an impoverished North and a relatively well off South. Socioeconomic disparities and political marginalization were starker in the early 1990s due to the disintegration of the social compact that had enabled peaceful cohabitation and political stability—albeit with limited freedom—under Houphouët-Boigny.

The Houphouët-Boigny legacy informs a paternalist approach to political stability, deployed through an unequivocal model of a strongman leadership. It is embodied in a culture of "dialogue and peace" in its formalized ideology. In reality, however, it was a clever political engineering system that sought to regulate sociopolitical life not just in Côte d'Ivoire but also in its immediate neighborhood in a monopolistic fashion and in a way that supported and sustained elite interests and maintained the political status quo. In the particular case of Burkina Faso, the implications of the tacit agreement between Mossi traditional authorities and Ivoirian political elites and employers enabled the mass migration of Burkinabè workers to southern Côte d'Ivoire as early as in the 1930s and the 1940s, when a portion of Upper Volta was still an integral part of Côte d'Ivoire. The arrangement endured well into postcolonial times as Houphouët-Boigny implemented a generous and enlightened immigration policy that allowed many West Africans to settle in Côte d'Ivoire as workers. In fact, when Compaoré was invited to the Linas-Marcoussis talks in the early days of the Ivoirian crisis, he made it a point to have the issue of land ownership and land redistribution in northern Côte d'Ivoire included in the talks and the final agreement. The inclusion of a land clause was important to Burkina Faso not least because of the internal repercussions and spillovers of the Ivoirian conflict on Burkinabè politics. The return of a considerable number of migrant workers to Burkina Faso put enormous economic and political pressure on the Burkinabè government, so much so that the resolution of the Ivoirian crisis was as much a Burkinabè issue as it was an Ivoirian issue. In fact, one Burkinabè minister openly blamed diaspora Burkinabè from Côte d'Ivoire for the protests and mutinies that have become quite common in recent years in Burkina Faso. The repercussions of the exclusionary policy of *Ivoirité* were to be felt at the level of both access to resources and economic opportunities for West African migrants, particularly Burkinabè laborers, for most of whom the benefits of citizenship were denied in Côte d'Ivoire and restricted back home in Burkina Faso.[3]

Initial Mediations and Interventions

The various mediations initiated by regional and international bodies failed to deliver an adequate and lasting solution to the crisis beyond the very predictable. As the parties dilly-dallied on the means of implementation, it became clear that the real problem lay in the fact that mediated agreements "relied heavily on traditional peace formulas and paid insufficient attention to the underlying issue of citizenship" as a root problem.[4] Typically, mediation efforts in African conflicts, whether initiated by regional bodies or by international organizations, whether led by concerned neighbors, well-intentioned allies, or official envoys dispatched by an organization, seek to restore "peace and stability," therefore a status quo. Rarely are mediation missions meant to effect radical reforms of the kind that can address underlying grievances. Côte d'Ivoire was no exception to this, for the issue of the social and political exclusion of millions of Ivoirians, whose legitimate right to Ivoirian citizenship was under question, was often ancillary to the question of power sharing and political leadership, which were arguably specific to elites on the various sides of the political and military divide.

In the early days of the conflict, concerned neighbors in West Africa rushed to Bouaé and Abidjan to work out some kind of truce between the warring brothers. Abdoulaye Wade of Senegal sent his minister of foreign affairs, Cheikh Tidiane Gadio, who managed to secure the very first ceasefire in October 2002. As the Economic Community of West African States (ECOWAS), AU, and the United Nations (UN) got involved, the round of mediators was in full swing. The result was a raft of agreements signed first in Linas-Marcoussis, then Accra (I, II, III), Pretoria (I and II), and finally Ouagadougou. Accra III gathered a dozen heads of state in a concerted efforts by the UN, the AU, and the ECOWAS to resolve the conflict in July 2004. It was agreed, among other key points, that belligerents would work on implementing previous agreements, notably on disarming their factions, while President Gbagbo committed to clarifying the powers of the prime minister in addition to reforming eligibility requirements for candidacy to the presidency by September 2004.[5]

A problem with external interventions is that they are often informed by a normative outlook that entrenches a common disconnect: while the international community is concerned with the preservation and the restoration of order, that is, the status quo, its strategies are overdetermined by a concern for policy and process, which tends to eclipse the substantive questions that produce animosity in the first place. In the end, Ivoirians saw in the various agreements political strategies meant to advance the interests of specific actors and rarely those of the people in the name of whom they were being brokered.

Thabo Mbeki: Advancing a Pan-African Agenda

Recognizing the failure of Accra III, in fact of the dead end that previous agreements had led to, the AU initiated a new series of talks in Pretoria in April 2005 among Ivoirian leaders under the mediation of Mbeki. Between 2002 and 2007, many mediators were called in, from former Ghanaian president John Kufuor to the former Senegalese president Wade to regional and international institutions including ECOWAS, AU, and UN. Compaoré stepped in as mediator in a context whereby the South African mediation was under heavy fire stemming from members of the Ivoirian opposition. The latter accused the South African mediator of partiality and bias in managing the Ivoirian conflict. They accused Mbeki "of reinforcing the divide between the protagonists instead of bringing them together."[6] Mbeki was criticized for conceding tremendous prerogatives to the presidential camp in the interpretation and implementation of the Pretoria Agreements. This was the view of those, such as Henri Konan Bédié, who had at first praised his unique mediation qualities. Bédié thought that Mbeki "[was] a real mediator endowed with the spirit of arbitrage, creative and imaginative."[7]

A bone of contention throughout the crisis had been the candidacy of Alassane Ouattara for the Ivoirian presidency made unconstitutional by Article 35 of the 2000 Ivoirian Constitution reviewed under Bédié and passed by the July 2000 referendum during the reign of General Robert Guei. Houphouët-Boigny's model of patrimonial management of social diversity produced political stability, engineered and artificially maintained through clientelist politics.[8] However, the institutionalization of Ivoirité under Bédié was a catalytic moment in the confrontational politics that characterized the post-Houphouët-Boigny period. Ivoirité was a revisionist conception of indigenous citizenship promoted by Bédié and his supporters. The ideology provided a strategic and rhetorical argument against the candidacy of Ouattara, then depicted as "the Burkinabè" who had presidential ambitions over Côte d'Ivoire.[9] Article 35 of the 2000 Constitution stipulated that a candidate to the Ivoirian presidency had to be born in Côte d'Ivoire from Ivoirian parents and should not have renounced his or her Ivoirian citizenship. Rather than amending Article 35, Gbagbo was allowed instead to use Article 48 of the constitution to carry out reforms stipulated by the Pretoria Agreements but adamantly opposed by an Ivoirian parliament intent on resisting what it perceived as neocolonial interventions. Given this context, "Mbeki's emerging doctrine of a proactive and assertive African policy underwritten by the determination to reverse the spectre of civil wars" found an adequate laboratory in the Ivoirian conflict.[10] In fact, South Africa's underdeveloped geopolitical and geostrategic understanding of African conflicts arguably worked against Mbeki's capacity to win the trust of all stakeholders. Moreover, a key component of Mbeki's active diplomacy was to take unilateral initiatives in order to fulfill what he perceived as South Africa's role as both continent leader and interlocutor on issues of security and economic development. His methods were inevitably deemed too personalized to be viable. Ironically, Compaoré was no less personal in his approach to the Ivoirian conflict. In fact, it can be argued that his personal knowledge and stakes in the outcome of the crisis were determining factors not only in Gbagbo's "invitation" for his mediation of the *dialogue direct* but also in shaping the form and content of the Ouagadougou Peace Accord. The only difference was that whereas Mbeki was seen as overtly sympathetic to Gbagbo's account of the crisis (i.e., a neoimperial assault on African sovereignty), Compaoré was also seen as deeply partial in favor, if not actively in support, of the Ivoirian rebellion.

Contrary to Compaoré, whose participation in the Ivoirian peace process was underpinned by specific material and political interests, Mbeki's engagement was informed primarily by an ideological commitment to an African liberation perspective. His detractors sought to impress the idea that the economic fallouts of a South African political penetration in Côte d'Ivoire were an underlying motivation given that the period of his involvement coincided with the expansion of South African companies in West Africa, not just in Côte d'Ivoire but also in Nigeria and Ghana.

Given his position as an outsider of regional politics, Mbeki's partial successes that culminated in the signing of the Pretoria Accords were the result of an exercise in persuasion subject as much to the volatile nature of partisan politics under conflict dispensation as it was to the mediator's personal relations with key stakeholders. In that sense, I. William Zartman is right to point to the importance of persuasion as the overarching strategy of mediation for African mediators, especially when they are having to deal with peers as their interlocutors in a facilitation situation. As Zartman notes, "The African mediator's primary weapon is persuasion, which reinforces the personal nature of the task and reflects the need for the perception of a mutually hurting stalemate. The mediator's main leverage lies in his ability to help his brothers out of the bind into which their conflict has led them."[11] If there hasn't been much research on direct mediatory exchanges among heads of state to permit a detailed analysis, available evidence indicates that theirs tend to be an exercise of pure persuasion.

A major weakness of Mbeki's mediation—despite a real desire for South Africa to be seen to be more involved on the continent—was a lack of knowledge and a limited capacity to understand politics in West Africa, especially in Francophone Africa. South Africa's long isolation from the continent remains a handicap that gets in the way of the country's ambition to become a regional leader.[12] Successive South African governments have not invested in the intellectual and institutional resources that can allow it to engage the continent on an informed basis. Given these limitations, Mbeki's approach toward the Ivoirian situation was meant to be practical and pragmatic; this entailed relying on independent lawyers to adjudicate on specific legal and institutional points where parties to the conflict were not in agreement. Mbeki also relied on a "38 person strong Military Advisory and Monitoring Team to Cote d'Ivoire to assist Ivorian demobilisation and reintegration efforts regarding the rebels."[13] However, Mbeki's position on the question of the referendum was heavily criticized as a narrow legalistic interpretation of an eminently political problem. The "crisis of interpretation" in reality hinged on previous commitments whose enforcement had seriously been vitiated by political strategizing on both sides of the conflict. Mbeki's engagement was also weakened by rivalries among prominent African heads of state. For instance, Olesegun Obasanjo, as AU chair, appointed Mbeki as mediator in November 2004 but was soon seen to be actively undermining the latter on account of mounting tensions around the conflicting ambitions of

Nigeria and South Africa over continental representation in a putative reformed UN Security Council.[14]

Mbeki's neocolonial rhetoric, his Afro-centeredness, his legalistic approach to conflict resolution, his sympathy toward Gbagbo, and hence aversion to old French-Ivoirian policies were many elements that ended up muddying his engagement in the process. Criticisms grew on Mbeki's mediation style and positions, not only from the rebels, who viewed his apparent closeness to Gbagbo as problematic, but also from West African peers, especially from competitor-mediators such as Wade of Senegal, and from France, who took a jaundiced view of a powerful African state's interference in the politics of one of the most important elements of its *chasse-gardée* (sphere of influence) in Francophone Africa—despite the fact that Mbeki was an AU envoy. Amid these criticisms, Mbeki stepped down as mediator in 2006. Difference in leadership styles between Mbeki and Compaoré mattered relatively less than is often thought. In fact, the context, conditions, and terms of involvement of the two leaders differed markedly. Whatever the value of the moral frame that motivated South Africa's engagement in Côte d'Ivoire, in the end it was compromised by many externalities and overlapping interventionisms.

At any rate, the Pretoria Agreements (2005) were pivotal in two fundamental ways. First, they sidelined—the proper term might in fact be *suspended*—the Ivoirian Constitution in order to enable all disqualified candidates to take part in the scheduled elections in a context whereby divergent interpretations of the constitution were at the heart of the political crisis. Second—and this was going to be a highly significant factor in the postelectoral negotiations—it was decided that the elections were going to be certified by the UN.

The Compaoré "System" at Work in the Ivoirian Conflict

Compaoré, like many others who came to power unconstitutionally through a bloody coup d'état, had subsequently succeeded in making himself look like a decent, civil, and "democratic" president. The absence of entrenched protocols of power in the early stages of a political rule more often than not perpetuate a culture of violence and unaccountability.[15] Despite the tremendous moral capital he has accumulated over the years as a peace broker, Compaoré has not succeeded in shaking off the suspicion that he has not entirely abandoned the commissioning of acts of violence in his methods of rule and personal expansion. In recent years, he has relentlessly sought to preserve a status of *médiateur incontournable* (indispensable mediator) in regional conflicts. The accumulated political capital has been tremendously crucial in his political survival in Burkinabè politics. There is a key paradox in that for many African analysts, his mediations have by and large been unsuccessful if one appreciates "success" as the capacity of the mediation to prevent an armed conflict or the resurgence of violence. But one would perhaps need to distinguish the mediation process and outcome from the process of implementation itself, for the Ouagadougou Accord was hailed at the time as a resounding success.

A common perception of Compaoré is that of an arsonist who used his country as a support base for a plethora of rebel groups that have attempted to destabilize the region writ large. Thus, according to his detractors, he stirs up trouble only to come back to help resolve it.[16] Compaoré's reputation as a troublemaker extends beyond the confines of West Africa.[17] In fact, it would be plausible to speak of a "before" and an "after" in Compaoré's prolific career.[18] As a troublemaker, he has been associated with Charles Taylor in Liberia and Sierra Leone, with Jonas Savimbi in Angola, with Daouda Malam Wanke in Niger against Ibrahim Bare Mainassara, in Chad with Idriss Debi, in the Central African Republic (CAR) with François Bozizé Yangouvonda, and with dissident groups in Guinea against the Lansana Conté regime before becoming a big brother to the leaders of the Forces Nouvelles (FN), especially Guillaume Soro. Given this political past, his career as mediator seemed like a usurpation of sorts.

The turbulent period described above was succeeded by a career transition characterized by Compaoré's commitment to achieving a twin objective, one personal and the other political. On the one hand, Compaoré sought to reinvent himself into a decent chap well established in the conventions of representative democracy and civil rule. On the other hand, he sought to turn Burkina Faso into an active and useful player to contend with in the West African diplomatic scene. A first landmark opportunity arose in 1993 during the Togolese political crisis followed by a series of successful mediations with Tuareg and militant groups in the Sahel in various missions to free hostages. Despite lingering doubts as to his motivations in undertaking mediation missions, it is clear that he has been able to manage a convincing reconversion into a peacemaker. When it comes to the Ivoirian conflict, Compaoré's interests in the resolution of the crisis, at least his vision of the type of ideal resolution, reflected an alignment of his own personal interests with those of FN. More than in any other mediation mission, his mediation strategies were to be mobilized to their fullest in supporting a political outcome that would not only work for Ivoirian stakeholders but also confirm him as a seasoned and well-rounded political mediator.

Compaoré's well-versed skills as a mediator had been put to effective use more than half a dozen times in the West African region and elsewhere on the continent. He has tremendously contributed to the practice of mediation as a specialized and distinct discipline in African regional politics and diplomacy. He is a man of initiative and political deftness, as well as an experienced strategist. Yet, despite his established influence on a number of peace processes across the region, is it possible to speak of a *Compaoré System* that stands out as a recipe for de-escalation, détente, and even conflict resolution? If there is indeed any system to contend with, it has to be conceived as a model supported by three distinct pillars. First, Compaoré draws from a rich political capital forged over a quarter century of regional politics that makes him something of a repository of the region's political history. Second, he draws on alliances, extended networks, and unconventional private procedures that are effectively mobilized whenever he is called on to mediate. Third, he relies on external legitimacy conferred by seniority but also by his willingness to advance external French, Libyan (under the late Muammar Gaddafi), and United States interests in the region. A fourth element of the strategy that is not documented in the mediation literature pertains to Compaoré's use of highly skilled personal appointees, often his foreign ministers but also a number of advisors, as backstoppers.[19] The example of Djibril Bassolé is worth mentioning. Bassolé was a police officer who emerged as one of Compaoré's most trusted men. He played a crucial role first from 1993 to 1995 during the Togolese crisis, then again as an appointee in 1990 to 1995 in the context of negotiations between the Tuareg and the Nigerien government. Since then he has served as deputy minister (1999–2000), then minister of security (2000–2007) before becoming minister of foreign affairs twice (2007–2008 and 2011–2014). Bassolé has been involved in virtually every mediation mission led by the Burkinabè president.[20] In fact, he became a mediator in his own right when he was appointed a joint mediator by the UN and the AU in Darfur (2008–2011).

The deployment of this type of human resource embeds a practice of personalization in the Compaoré System, which brings two notable advantages. First, the accumulated experiences of backstoppers buttress the capital of trust for the principal mediator. Second, an appearance of distance is cultivated, and it gives the word of the principal mediator the increased quality of an informed and well-thought-out position. In the Ivoirian case, this meant that by the time a stakeholder meeting took place, background work had already been achieved by local cadres and the facilitator's team so as to smooth rough edges.[21] More often than not, Compaoré is able to reframe mandates and reinterpret the terms of his mission according to specific dispositions, especially where his personal stakes are involved. Critics argue that he often is both the arsonist and firefighter in the conflicts he is called on to help resolve. One commentator, for instance, notes that, given this reputation, "he is, at first glance, an unlikely peacemaker: a former protégé of Colonel Gaddafi, who seized power in a bloody coup 25 years ago and has been accused of stoking Africa's brutal civil wars."[22] In fact, if Compaoré was quick to put forward pragmatism over loyalty following the fall of Gaddafi in 2011, evidence of a strong Libyan presence and investments in the country still abound. If Gaddafi's portrait no longer hangs over the hall of the Libya hotel, the latter forms part of many investments that include a conference center, a shopping mall, and residential units in the neighborhood of Ouaga 2000, the Burkina Commercial Bank (former Libyan Bank of Development), and many loans and gifts (e.g., the Libya Cultural Centre, the Monument to the Martyrs).[23] The late Gaddafi received an honorary doctorate from the University of Ouagadougou, and a main thoroughfare of the capital city of Burkina has been named after him, the Boulevard Muammar-el Kaddhafi.

What amounts to the Compaoré System is a meticulous approach to mediation that relies on resource persons and a thorough knowledge of the political context as well as key stakeholders capable of influencing internal dynamics. In addition to Bassolé, there is Salif Diallo, now ambassador; Gilbert Diendéré, the head of the president's security guard; a Malian adviser, Lamine Sow; and a Mauritanian adviser, Mustapha Chafi.[24] The latter was instrumental as a go-between with Nigerian Tuareg and the government and more importantly in the various negotiations for the release of hostages in the Sahel detained by Al-Qaeda in the Islamic Maghreb (AQIM) and other groups.[25] On the other hand, a team of advance men (i.e., *démarcheurs* [deal makers], infiltrators, informants, and various *hommes-de main* [henchmen])—most of them unknown to the wider public and working in the shadow—make up the apparatus that provides support to Compaoré's intervention strategies. In the Ivoirian case, a small and well-structured team made up the Office of the Facilitator, headed by Boureima Badini, a prominent lawyer and politician.

Contrary to Mbeki, for whom the anti-imperial rhetoric provided an ideological hook in gaining the trust of Ivoirian political actors, Compaoré was seen as pretty much the man of the West, a defender of French ambition to preserve the ideological architecture of la Françafrique even while speaking the language of transparency and relations between "equals."[26] Françafrique is often likened to a family-like network run by doyens (notably the late Houphouët-Boigny and Omar Bongo, Abdou Diouf, and Compaoré) and junior political figures on the continent and in French political and media circles. It is characterized by institutional, semi-institutional, and obscure forms and practices, annual get-togethers (the Franco-African summit), elite protocols, and an extended network of mediators and intermediaries. Its tentacles extend into politics, business, and the military. It has development aid and the political image of incumbent presidents as its terrain of predilection for shady economic and political deals. Françafrique thus became a conservative framework and the sphere of enaction of anachronistic and neocolonial types of relations in lieu of normalized and transparent relations among autonomous entities. The outward manifestations are French military bases, the use of the CFA franc pegged to the euro by eight African countries, and numerous French businesses, consultants, and advisers. The other side, often decried in the media and by civil society groups, is associated with secrets and dirty practices that have supported the rule of dictators and human rights violators throughout the past decades. Françafrique is also associated with the pillage and predatory exploitation of African economic resources by French and African political and economic elites, capital flight, corruption, mercenary expeditions, devastating wars (Democratic Republic of Congo, Biafra, Côte d'Ivoire), election rigging, constitutional manipulation, and more.[27] The Gbagbo camp was particularly distrustful toward Compaoré, who constituted, in their eyes, a major ideological obstacle to a second African independence from France.

Despite the uneasy position of the Burkinabè president, Compaoré's involvement in the resolution of the Ivoirian conflict was inevitable. There were officially over 2.5 million Burkinabè living in Côte d'Ivoire at the time of the conflict in 2001–2002. The Burkinabè president could therefore in no way be indifferent to the political situation of its intimate neighbor, given the manner it affected the welfare of Burkinabè nationals. Moreover, as a landlocked country that depended on the port of Abidjan for its imports, Burkina Faso had a vested interest in the resumption of normal economic activities in Côte d'Ivoire. For Ivoirians, their motivations were certainly different, but they made Compaoré the ideal mediator. Incidentally, "Compaoré also happened to be the acting president of ECOWAS so that it was 'natural' that he should attempt to mediate between the different parties."[28] As such, an invitation through the official channels of the ECOWAS made Compaoré's involvement less problematic. Officially, President Gbagbo submitted a request to the rotating president of the ECOWAS on January 23, 2007, in order to "facilitate direct dialogue between former belligerent to the armed conflict of Côte d'Ivoire" in accordance with UN Security Council resolutions 1633 (2005) and 1721 (2006).[29] In reality, with the help of his close collaborators such as Chafi, Compaoré could act as both a personal and an ECOWAS mediator, and he could rely on a range of both official and unofficial channels to carry his mission. If in theory there wasn't much difference in the objectives of the Compaoré mission from those of previous ECOWAS or the UN missions, the tensions between the various heads of state that had been involved before him had a negative influence on the peace process. When Compaoré took over, his mission could be carried unimpeded by potentially competing interpretations or interests.

The Ouagadougou Accord: A Roadmap Out of a Crisis

If the Pretoria talks were crucial in that they provided an opportunity for an African solution to an African problem, the Ouagadougou talks were seen as even more important in that they provided a platform for a "West African solution to a West African problem."[30] This conviction was particularly strong in the view of Compaoré's permanent representative in Côte d'Ivoire, Boureima Badini, who contends that "[my] mission was made easy by the fact that I was accepted.

If I can draw a parallel with a UN representative who does not have the same culture, the same vision of things, he would have been less successful. As far as I'm concerned, I knew, I lived their [Ivoirian protagonists] struggles, I shared meals with them, I shared their experience. I was impartial and positive in my mission, in order to build trust."[31] To a certain extent, the choice and mandate of the permanent representative of the Office of the Facilitator translated the extent of Compaoré's commitment; he knew that the facilitator was in it for the longest haul. Badini's job was to build a trust relationship with all disputants and stakeholders. This mission entailed getting to grips with the endemic causes of the conflict and a sufficient understanding of cultural and political dispositions of the protagonists. This data-mining and knowledge-building process was crucial for developing an appropriate mechanism for concerted consultation, but also for the subsequent implementation phase of the peace agreement.

The very nomination of a team, by Compaoré, that is entirely devoted to the nitty-gritty of the negotiation was one of his key strategies. The deployment of the Compaoré System in Côte d'Ivoire was supported by an institutional apparatus and a network of resource individuals, in other words people who reported back directly to the mediator. In addition to the high-profile and close collaborators such as Bassolé and Chafi who were involved at most strategic junctures in the process, a second level of hommes-de-main makes up a local structure in the country of intervention; these are often recruited among long-term friendships in the army and the administration.[32] The Office of the Facilitator sat on the Comité d'evaluation et d'accompagnement (CEA) (Evaluation and Monitoring Committee), which was tasked with the monitoring of the implementation process. This office was, in a way, the articulation of a convergence of external interests and internal dynamics. It reported back to the facilitator as well as the key stakeholders, and it was frequently consulted by foreign representations and UN agencies. Thus, as an operations office, the facilitator's office had the task of securing adherence beyond persuasion; it was able to appropriate and reinterpret its mandate according to the vagaries of Ivoirian politics and the many delays that hampered the implementation process. Its mission was a delicate one given the highly polarized and precarious nature of local politics. As can be expected under such circumstances, the office got entangled in recriminating politics and was often the target of violence, particularly as the results of the elections were not to the liking of all actors.[33] However, Compaoré's ability to navigate carefully in the labyrinth of identity politics, to lend an ear to constant charges of bad faith from both parties, and to allow time for the peace process to consolidate did eventually pay off.

Thus, when all resources seemed to have been exhausted at the subregional, continental, and international levels, the choice of Compaoré as the facilitator of direct talks appeared as the very last resort in rehabilitating a broken peace process. For Gbagbo and his allies, to invite Compaoré as mediator expressed a need "to go back to the roots of the conflict."[34] Such a move was also dictated by a requirement of acknowledgment of Gbagbo's "second war of independence" and his well-honed rhetorical characterization of the Ivoirian rebellion as a foreign attack on Ivoirian sovereignty.[35] The hostility between the two countries built up throughout the years leading to the 2007 detente. It culminated in a formal complaint laid by Burkina Faso to the AU's Peace and Security Council on account of an Ivoirian violation of its air space.

It is common knowledge that Compaoré heavily sponsored FN and gave them safe haven in Burkina Faso. The many villas in the new district of Ouaga 2000 that belong to members of FN rebellion are testimony to the ease with which the rebels were able to conduct their business unimpeded in Burkina Faso. Compaoré is said to have been involved in the "the planning, the organization, the provision of weapons and the funding of the Mouvement Patriotique de Côte d'Ivoire (MPCI) that later became the Forces Nouvelles."[36] Therefore for many, Compaoré was more than a financier and was in fact the political sponsor of the rebellion. For Gbagbo in particular, the Ivoirian crisis was first and foremost "a bilateral problem between Côte d'Ivoire and Burkina" if not a foreign terrorist attack, and as such the conflict could only ever be resolved through bilateral diplomacy.[37] A meeting in Abuja in December 2006 provided an opportunity to Désiré Tagro, then Gbagbo's interior minister, to approach Burkinabè officials with a suggestion that their president put his experience to good use by facilitating direct talks between warring parties. This was arguably Gbagbo's extension of an invitation to Compaoré to get involved. One can understand Gbagbo's reluctance to getting Compaoré involved even though a pragmatic logic may have dictated him to keep an enemy friend even closer by officially inviting him to be a stakeholder in the peace process. Already in 2001, Gbagbo had accused Burkinabè agents of being part of an attempt to stage a coup on January 7, 2001, an incident that sparked a series of violent attacks against Burkinabè nationals and that spurred mass flight into Burkina Faso.[38] On the other hand, Compaoré was never a passive actor in the process, even when he was not involved as a mediator. In the political economy of the Ivoirian conflict resolution, his was very much in a position of *demandeur* (solicitor, requester), in other words that of a proactive, willing actor.[39]

Gbagbo's decision to invite Compaoré to facilitate the direct talks is an interesting move that undermines common arguments in the mediation literature about the imperative of impartiality in negotiation processes. In fact, it demonstrates that the policy stand on impartiality is rather untenable as it does not sufficiently problematize the intersection of intent and interests with regard to the various stakeholders involved in any negotiation. Neither does it look too critically at the link between the need for leverage and the nature of relations between stakeholders. The modalities of attribution of mediation mandate are, for instance, far from straightforward. In the case of Compaoré, there was an added political significance. More than any previous mediator, Compaoré's *entrée en jeu* (entry as a new actor) marked a significant ideological departure on one hand and a methodological experiment on another. He did not just appear out of nowhere. His shadow had all along obscured the various transactions for peace. The Ouagadougou talks gave real meaning to an idea of direct talks in a way that translated the converging motivations of actors involved.

The establishment of an Office of the Facilitator tasked with enabling "the realization of the objectives contained in the agreement" and headed by a special representative, Badini, was crucial to the maintenance of close contact with the main stakeholders and to a methodical follow-up of the implementation process.[40] The work of the mediator was far from achieved with the signing of the Ouagadougou Accord. It was carried throughout the following years, up to the time when it was deemed appropriate to organize the presidential election in 2010. The special representative was appointed between March 2007 and May 2012 and operated like an after-sales service whose role was twofold. He was to bring the two main signatory parties, the presidential camp and FN, to agree on a consensual interpretation for the Ouagadougou Accord and commit to implementing its clauses. Given that the Ouagadougou Accord was the last of a long list of peace agreements, implementation was to determine the extent of success or failure. In addition, he was to seek creative ways of including other political parties and civil society organizations in the peace process, hence the establishment of the Comité d'évaluation et d'accompagnement.[41]

Formal negotiations lasted roughly a month, between February 5 and March 3, 2007, although important behind-the-scene talks and dealings paved the way to the actual meetings in Ouagadougou. The specificity of the Ouagadougou Accord in relation to previous meetings and agreements owed much to the personality of Compaoré but also to the factors and circumstances that have repeatedly thwarted advances gained in the implantation of key points of agreements, namely, the identification process, the demobilization and reinsertion of rebel armies into the national army, the organization of inclusive elections, and the question of land. In fact, Compaoré stepped in as mediator at a time of great crisis fatigue; the national economy was on the verge of paralysis, and ordinary Ivoirians were starting to show signs of imminent revolt against warring parties. There was also the fear that the conflict would drag on for many more years with debilitating consequences. Compaoré took up his mandate in a context whereby successive mediators had been caught in instrumentalization strategies, often becoming either collateral damage or involuntary protagonists in a merciless struggle. From the very beginning indeed, the Ivoirian crisis was mired in its own intractability; many conflict resolution strategies had been exhausted at all levels of institutional representation, regional (ECOWAS), continental (AU), and international (UN, the Organisation Internationale de la Francophonie, Sant' Egidio). Furthermore, the failure of regional organizations in the face of the parties' intransigence called for a different mediation formula that was result-driven rather than the successive inclusive frameworks marred by lengthy procedures.

Ways of Mediating: Interlocutor, Facilitator, and Formulator

Compaoré's intervention in the Ivoirian conflict can be conceptualized within changing mediation practices, especially in a global context whereby mediation processes have become increasingly politicized. Thinking about mediation in terms of intervention is conceptually useful, especially as the political crisis had made Côte d'Ivoire a zone of intensive multilevel interventions. In fact, from the date of expiration of the presidential mandate of Gbagbo in 2005, Côte d'Ivoire was placed under UN tutelage, and so to speak on a drip, as the overlapping jurisdiction and applicability of its national constitution and the effects of various UN Security Council resolutions exercised conflicting forms and levels of interference and political determinations. This followed a persistent pattern of French interventionism in Ivoirian internal affairs—the Linas-Marcoussis Agreement, for instance, catalyzed anti-French sentiment in Côte d'Ivoire. Under such a context, Compaoré's intervention, although received with mixed views given the Burkinabè president's position as both actor and arbitrator in addition to being a man of the West, elicited less animosity than could have been expected. Despite the constraints, Compaoré's mediation was successful.

First, Gbagbo's contention that the Ivoirian political crisis was a bilateral problem between Côte d'Ivoire and Burkina Faso was not entirely unfounded. For while Compaoré's involvement was informed by a cost-benefit analysis, the potential gains for the rebellion in the outcome of the negotiations equally served his interests as their mentor and possibly sponsor of the rebellion.

Second, as a facilitator, Compaoré was to bring the rebels to the negotiation table and make them amenable to the terms of compromise that required them to be co-responsible. This was a change of mindset from a rebellion mentality to a more conventional and democratic posture. The mediation crucially allowed Compaoré to reassert and consolidate his leading role in the region through sheer political feat. He not only managed to convince rebels to take a positive stance toward negotiation but also succeeded in convincing Gbagbo, a man who had always seen him as a dangerous manipulator, to agree to a set of pragmatic arrangements to do with identification, demobilization, and organization of open elections. Throughout the process, Compaoré had to tread on delicate ground, given the manner in which personal political interests and mediation objectives were intertwined.

Third, Compaoré operated at times as a formulator. He exerted considerable influence on the rebels' political vision, given their dependence on him as a sponsor and on Burkina Faso for the material existence of the rebellion. The formulator aspect of Compaoré's role was already salient during the Linas-Marcoussis talks in 2003, therefore even before he became the official mediator in 2006–2007. In flagging the question of land early on in the process, Compaoré sought to initiate a multilevel approach to a question that concerned both Côte d'Ivoire and Burkina, given the important Burkinabè population working in the agricultural sector in Côte d'Ivoire. On this issue, the personal and the national intersected in a striking manner. Compaoré also had every reason to work toward a political resolution that conceded power and resources to the rebels. A return on investment for him would also translate into economic benefits for Burkina Faso.[42] The Ouagadougou Accord was also a sort of rebound from the infamous Linas-Marcoussis agreement. Many saw in some of Compaoré strategies French remote-piloting and influence.

A Peculiar Kind of Sovereignty

For Compaoré to successfully negotiate the Ouagadougou Accord, he had to deploy the skills of an experienced mediator, but he also had to rely on his political resources in both Côte d'Ivoire and the extended networks woven over the years across the region. One cannot underestimate the extent of political knowledge and network at the disposal of someone many have come to regard as a godfather figure in West African politics. Trust was obviously a nagging issue, and its operationalization a recurrent dilemma for a facilitator already saddled with a controversial reputation. On one hand, his detractors affirm that "his allies always win" as if his very mediation was part of a well-designed and carefully thought out plan that stretched the logic of violent conflicts into nonviolent but equally coercive means.[43] But such statements are not always helpful, given that they are often meant to endow his mediation career with a special status. Nonetheless, Compaoré proved to be a persuasive mediator, for his facilitation enabled a relatively peaceful transition toward presidential elections in 2010. His mission as facilitator did not end with the signing of the agreement. There were countless meetings with the Cadre Permanent de Concertation (Permanent Consultation Framework), made up of the four key figures of the political conflict, namely: the then incumbent Gbagbo of the Front Populaire Ivoirien (FPI), Soro representing the FN, Ouattara of the Rassemblement des Républicains (RDR), Bédié representing Parti Démocratique de Côte d'Ivoire (PDCI), and the CEA tasked with the monitoring of the implementation of the agreement as a permanent framework for the consolidation of national cohesion.[44] In many ways, Ouagadougou became a hub of deliberation on Ivoirian politics as it now became easy for nighttime visitors to openly seek the advice of the official facilitator. In fact, Hotel Laico (for Libyan African Investment Co., or formerly the Libya Hotel), a five-star hotel built with Libyan investment, has come to be something of a vibrant hangout for West African politicians, a role previously played by the palace of Yamassoukouro under Houphouët-Boigny. Compaoré's role went beyond balancing shifting power among Ivoirian adversaries. It also consisted of ensuring that the terms of the agreement informed different approaches to building trust and the adequate conditions for healthier partisan politics. The transfer of ownership operated in the very conception of the parameters of the Ouagadougou Accord as opposed to previous peace agreements.

If the Accra and Pretoria peace agreements were to an extent merely mechanisms of implementation of the Linas-Marcoussis agreement, the Ouagadougou Accord enabled a face-to-face dialogue between the different protagonists with limited external interference.[45] The previous mediations were aimed at, rather predictably, a typical transitional cohabitation (bicephalism). But Compaoré in a way achieved what others could secure only temporarily, that is, a diplomatic neutralization of the main adversaries—the Gbagbo camp and FN.[46] First, he convinced Soro to recognize Gbagbo as president even if his electoral mandate had expired in October 2005 and he owed the extension of his mandate to a UN resolution. The leader of the FN along with the unarmed Ivoirian opposition leaders had rejected Gbagbo as a resolution president rather than a constitutional president. Second, the two parties were more willing after the Ouagadougou Accord not only to be more committed to a power-sharing arrangement, but also to oversee the very implementation of identification, demobilization, and reintegration as part of national reconstruction. How Compaoré managed to succeed where his predecessors had failed is a question open to many interpretations.[47] If often "[the] creation of leverage for effective mediation could be the result of remunerative, normative, and coercive bases of power, touted in a manner to discourage warfare," in the Ivoirian case one could safely argue that Compaoré's commitment to working alongside the main protagonists for a concerted solution to the crisis—even if this was to elicit frustration from a number of stakeholders—was as much a political necessity as it was the enactment of a particular capacity to innovate while fitting.[48] Crisis fatigue combined with the erosion of popular support for continuous confrontation certainly had something to do with that.

Compaoré's style is a meticulously deployed approach to conflict resolution, one that prioritizes a practice of dialogue that integrates the parameters of the political conflict. If many mediators tend to shy away from the risk of being sucked into often muddy domestic politics, Compaoré tends to model his approach to the contours of the political landscape. In fact, as the Ouagadougou negotiations proceeded, a particular ideological confrontation was taking place between Gbagbo and Compaoré as ultimately the key protagonists in a long-drawn-out battle over political compromise and the strained assertion of different kinds of legitimacy.

The question of personalization of the mediation process, on the form and content of key texts and conclusions, was most apparent in the Linas-Marcoussis (2003) and Ouagadougou (2007) peace agreements. In fact, despite Compaoré's being only a guest to the talks, his participation in Linas-Marcoussis was pivotal. He was instrumental in the inclusion of a special clause on land tenure reform. The land question, so crucial to Burkina Faso, given the large proportion of its citizens living in Côte d'Ivoire, is as much an internal problem to Burkina Faso as it is to Côte d'Ivoire. In fact, the massive return of Burkinabè migrants from Côte d'Ivoire had resulted in much pressure on land claims and subsequent political incidents that threatened to destabilize the Compaoré regime (protest vote, urban riots, etc.).[49] Despite giving signs of wide consultation of regional institutions and key and peripheral players (namely the ECOWAS and AU), Compaoré mostly acted alone. He relied on a small but diligent team and network to run his mission. His minister of foreign affairs, Bassolé, was a key player throughout.

The example of Compaoré's approach to the Ivoirian mediation is useful in reframing the conceptual underpinning of the position and responsibilities of a mediator. Contrary to common practices, Compaoré's understanding of political reform and peaceful transition in Côte d'Ivoire was transformative rather than conservative, and it was inscribed in a long-term strategy that kept him involved and depended on beyond the signing of the Ouagadougou Accord. His approach was a stark contrast to Mbeki's insistence on supporting the legitimate authority (i.e., elected) of Côte d'Ivoire. Compaoré's personalized method was thus apparent in his capacity to deviate from the original logic of the mediation. From what some of the actors that had been involved in the mediation process are willing to concede, it would seem that the two main parties were willing to rely on the continued arbitration of the facilitator to keep each other accountable with regard to implementation on the basis of terms of the agreement. Compaoré's political vision of a post-Ouagadougou framework was to be partly exercised through subsequent engagement. The facilitator in person or through his permanent representative was a sitting member of both the Cadre Permanent de Concertation and the CEA. It was expected, and agreed, that Compaoré would arbitrate in case of divergence on the interpretation of the accord within the two committees.

Pecuniary benefits were not the only incentive or motivation for the various candidates to mediation.[50] There was always something morally gratifying, for any president, in resolving a conflict. The mediation process was stalled several times because of rivalries and squabbles over regional leadership between Wade on the one hand and presidents Gnassingbé Eyadema, Olusegun Obasanjo, and Omar Bongo on the other. This denoted a first level of personalization, whereby regional political actors with competing ambitions and interests vied for prominence and legitimacy in leading the peace talks. The petty competition was all the more detrimental as it stalled the peace process at the onset. A second level of personalization was obvious in the overlapping of interest and mandate in the case of Compaoré. Conventional peace mediation assumes that the interest of actors and mandates should not counter key principles of successful mediation, namely the requirement of neutrality and impartiality. This chapter argues that the Burkinabè mediation was relatively successful precisely because the concern for neutrality and impartiality stopped being an overarching principle once Compaoré, largely perceived as a party to the conflict, was called on to facilitate the dialogue direct. There is thus a need to reconceptualize the element of bias in mediation. Bias is not always nor necessarily an impediment to a proper mediation, as has generally been argued in the literature. Rather, it is something that can be factored into resolution models in a constructive manner. As Kwesi Aning contends, "When international peace negotiations become part of national politics, they become a possible means for political struggle over different economic and political goals involving domestic, regional and international actors with particular interests in the outcome of a given conflict situation."[51] Evidence from the Ivoirian case points to an important fact that a mediation process is never an autonomous and impartial matter but rather the partial translation of distinct ambitions and interests and sometimes serious tensions between domestic and international politics. The Ivoirian conflict resolution ultimately is a classic example whereby neighbors are called to mediate conflicts. Here, the science of mediation as the deployment of well-structured strategies and methods is put to the test as rational and tested models reach their limits.

The 2010 Presidential Election and Postelectoral Crisis

In a way, the 2015 elections in Nigeria—for a large part being organized under rather uncertain security and political conditions because of the destabilizing action of Boko Haram—are a reminder of the 2010 Ivoirian elections. If the two cases are relatively different on account of the type of political crisis under question, an important dilemma of both is whether organizing elections under conditions of political uncertainty, territorial divide, and intermittent violence is an appropriate thing to do. In Côte d'Ivoire, the organization of the election, stressed in each one of the various agreements, was to be the culmination of a series of conditions and reforms to do with disarmament and integration of rebel groups and militias, territorial reunification, the return of government adminis-tration in all parts of the country, and a sensible level of security that would allow people to vote peacefully without any form of intimidation.

The very terms of the various agreements and the mechanisms of imple-mentation of the most recent one, the Ouagadougou Accord, point to a recurrent problem with peace processes mediated by the international community. The lat-ter has increasingly been using elections as a means to resolving political con-flicts. If the imperative of expediency does prompt compromises capable of pro-viding temporary respite, election is often likely to jeopardize the possibility of durable peaceful conditions. In the Ivoirian case, the various interventions of the international community in the end allowed the organization of elections. These were neither free nor fair, given the security context and the fact that many po-tential voters could not vote in ideal conditions or at all. The postelectoral situa-tion was fraught with extremely destabilizing violence that momentarily plunged the country back to a situation similar to that of the early 2000s. For one thing, "the internationally mediated peace agreements weighted heavily on power shar-ing, ceasefire, and election modalities at the expense of creating a mechanism to resolve the citizenship issue."[52] In fact, there was nothing particularly creative or different about this approach to conflict resolution. What happened instead was a common formula often administered to conflict situations on the continent, that is to say a quick-fixing that satisfies the mandate of envoys and the international community. This much was reiterated in Mbeki's retrospective deliberation on the outcome on the Ivoirian elections: "the international community insisted that what Cote d'Ivoire required to end its crisis was to hold democratic elec-tions, even though the conditions did not exist to conduct such elections. Though they knew that this proposition was fundamentally wrong, the Ivoirians could not withstand the international pressure to hold elections."[53] He added that "the objective reality is that the Ivorian presidential elections should not have been held when they were held. It was perfectly foreseeable that they would further entrench the very conflict it was suggested they would end."[54]

A normative innovation with potential significant future implications was the issue of UN certification of the election result. As a UN-certified election, the 2010 Ivoirian presidential election is an example of the extent to which external interventions and determinations can interfere with domestic processes. For the African continent more generally, it confirmed just how internationalized Afri-can domestic politics have become. In an unprecedented move, the international community rejected the election results approved by the Ivoirian Constitutional Council (CC) in favor of those issued by the Independent Electoral Commis-sion (IEC). In a postelectoral context woefully strained by divergent apprecia-tions of issues of constitutionality, legality, and legitimacy, the apparent bias of the United Nations Mission in Côte d'Ivoire (UNOCI) in favor of presidential candidate Ouattara further tainted the image of the international community in Côte d'Ivoire. More critically, the fact that three arrest mandates would be issued against the Gbagbo camp and none against the Ouattara camp, and that Gbagbo himself would end up at the International Criminal Court, made many in Côte d'Ivoire and in Africa in general see the latter as equally politicized and therefore biased as the international community.

The results of the 2010 presidential election were contested, with both the Gbagbo and Ouattara sides claiming victory. The armies backing the two candidates thus entered into a conflict committing many atrocities in the process. In fact, Ouattara was sworn in as the new Ivoirian president only after a six-month stalemate (November 2010–May 2011). In the end, election results had to be enforced militarily by the FN with the military backing of France and UNOCI, which both acted on the basis of a liberal interpretation of UN Security Council resolution 1975 and outside a frame of impartiality. However, the question of the political and social integration of deeply divided communities remains a conundrum. Ouattara has since had to face tremendous hostility from the near half of the Ivoirian population that did not vote for him and that feel relatively disenfranchised under his rule. In the early days of the postelectoral stalemate, ECOWAS, France, the UN through Secretary-General Ban Ki-Moon, and the special representative of the secretary-general, Choi Young-jin, recognized Ouattara as the winner of the 2010 presidential election, a view that was formalized in UN Security Council resolution 1962 voted on December 20, 2010. The resolution had the unprecedented effect of nullifying the view of the Constitutional Council of Côte d'Ivoire that presumably acted on the basis of sovereign constitutionally.[55]

As South Africa, Angola, Uganda, and Equatorial Guinea questioned the legitimacy of the international community's right to declare the winner of contested elections, Mbeki was dispatched once again by AU in order to negotiate a way out of the deadlock. He was to be followed by a dozen other envoys. The situation had, however, deteriorated this time around to a point of no return. Upon consulting the various parties involved, Mbeki declared, "You will not have peace without democracy, and neither democracy without peace."[56] His was a minority view that expressed anxieties around the disconnection between the orientation of shuttle diplomacy and the various negotiations on the one hand, and the situation on the ground on the other. On both sides of the conflict, people were getting summarily executed or burned alive, some were being arrested, militias were attacking the neighborhoods of political adversaries using heavy weapons, roadblocks were being set, and protestors were being attacked by security forces. In addition, neither party seems too keen to disarm for fear or expectation of a reignition of violence.[57] Despite the enormous resources invested in organizing the election, it is marred by unprecedented levels and forms of violence.

Many observers have pointed out that the UN mission in Côte d'Ivoire has increasingly become reluctant to publicly criticize the Ouattara camp even though the wartime militias that supported him have not fully been disarmed or reintegrated. Moreover, some of those that are believed to be responsible for some of the atrocities in the 2002–2003 period and in the postelectoral period are now occupying important political posts in the Ouattara government. In fact, it has been revealed that the UN Security Council buried the report of an international investigation commission that provided names of perpetrators and sponsors of violence within the ranks of Ouattara's government and army who were never investigated.[58]

Conclusions

An appreciation of mediation processes from the trajectories of Compaoré and Mbeki points to the evolving principles, norms, and practices of mediation diplomacy from a set of standardized models and strategies of conflict resolution to a personalized enterprise whereby the mediator injects a dose of personal sovereignty. The efficacy of mediation missions often relies on a balanced combination of contingency and context, both of which can be superseded or overwritten by particular personal approaches that tend to confirm one key principle: that nothing is random about these processes. Compaoré had the stature of a pivotal actor in West African politics, but a compromised political past tainted his credibility. However, Compaoré did not enter the fray of the Ivoirian mediation process as a complete stranger. His ambiguous position as neighbor, actor, stakeholder, and facilitator accorded him key insights that were fully deployed in his task to persuade the parties to the conflict of the opportunity of peace rather than the continuation of a draining and costly war. On the other hand, Mbeki was largely seen at first as holding the promise of liberation and the restoration of legitimate Ivoirian institutions opposite of an international community beleaguered against a "democratically elected" president. In the end, his idea of a negotiated peaceful solution did not win the day but carried the strength of a possible alternative.

The degree of personalization of the negotiation process meant that the facilitator's agenda heavily shaped the conditions and the outcome of the talks. If, in the end, both the Pretoria and the Ouagadougou peace agreements merely became scripts for the management of a temporary and artificially maintained stability, this was in keeping with an increasing tendency for actors involved in peace processes, at the national, regional, and international levels, to rely on the organization of elections as the goal of mediation and an ultimate enforcement strategy.

The question therefore is: where did peace mediations in Côte d'Ivoire go wrong? There are possibly two general and one specific answers. First, the policy and politics of civil protection enshrined in the doctrine of responsibility to protect (R2P) that presided over the international community's engagement in Côte d'Ivoire—NATO's military intrusion in Libya is another striking case—is deeply problematic given the dissonance between intent and means.[59] Second, a continuous concern, among mediators and regional organizations, with process and legal frameworks as a measure of success meant that underlying tensions and hostilities were merely superficially suppressed. Finally, the good guys versus villains approach taken by the international community was effective in ousting an obstinate Gbagbo out of power. However, the narrow focus on elections has seriously jeopardized the treatment of structural issues in a long-term perspective, and the possibility of national reconciliation.

Notes

1. Mbeki, "What the World Got Wrong in Cote d'Ivoire."
2. For further references on the Ivoirian conflict and political crisis see among others Marshall-Fratani, "The War of 'Who Is Who,'" 9–43; Bah, "Democracy and Civil War," 597; Banégas "Côte d'Ivoire," 535–552; Akokpari, "'You Don't Belong Here,'" 88–105; Dozon, "La Côte d'Ivoire entre Démocratie, Nationalisme et Ethnonationalisme," 45–62.
3. Haut Commissariat des Nations Unies aux Droits de l'Homme, *Rapport de la Commission*; Human Rights Watch, *Le Nouveau Racisme*.
4. Bah, "Democracy and Civil War," 597.
5. Ibid., 608.
6. Akindes, "South African Mediation in the Ivorian Crisis," 143.
7. Bédié interview with RFI.
8. Akindes, *Racines des Crises Socio-politiques en Côte d'Ivoire et Sens de l'Histoire*.
9. See Amando Cutolo for an insightful analysis of the intersection of Ivoirité, modernity, liberalism, and citizenship in Cote d'Ivoire: Cutolo, "Modernity, Autochthony and the Ivorian Nation," 527–552. Ivoirité became a poisonous ideology that legitimated extant views that some Ivorians were more Ivorian than others and were therefore more entitled to exclusive political and socioeconomic rights.
10. Khadiagala, "South Africa's Role in Conflict Resolution in the Democratic Republic of the Congo (DRC)," 71.
11. Zartman, "Inter-African Negotiations and Reforming Political Order," 222.
12. Vines, "South Africa's Politics of Peace and Security in Africa," 53–63, 54.
13. Ibid., 56.
14. Adebajo, "The Bicycle Strategy of South Africa's Bilateral Relations in Africa," 121–136.
15. Ellis and Haar, "Religion and Politics in Sub-Saharan Africa," 175–201, 197. Needless to say therefore, from troublemaker to *monsieur bons-offices*, and from putschist to peacemaker, his has been a tumultuous and eventful trajectory. Just how a man with such a tortuous record could become a respected senior mediator on the continent is a question that puzzles many an observer. In a turbulent West African region marked by shaky "pluralist democracies" at grips with the scourge of military coups and sudden violent changes, his greatest achievement has been his ability to put himself forward as a mentor, and be recognized as a wise man, like Houphouët-Boigny. Just like his mentor, his record as a stabilizer in Burkina Faso—the

country that experienced no less than seven coups between 1966 and 1987 and that has been relatively peaceful since then—places him in a most ideal place to facilitate dialogues, broker peace agreements, and preach regional stability to preserve the status quo rather than promote democracy or human rights.

16. In the sarcastic words of one observer: "Vous voyez, c'est l'histoire du petit de la classe qui veut se donner des airs de grand. Son pays n'est pas le plus riche de la région, mais il a voulu en faire une place incontournable. Pour cela, il captait les rébellions, cela lui permettait, après, de se mettre en valeur et de s'imposer comme négociateur" ["You see, this is precisely the story of the kid who is last in the classroom and who likes to put on airs. His country is not the richest in the region, yet he wanted to turn it into a hub. To achieve this goal, he used to capture rebellions, which allowed him to enhance his standing and then impose himself as negotiator."]; see Kpatindé interview with RFI, October 31, 2014.

17. Most of these rebels were suspected of having a pied-à-terre in Ouagadougou.

18. In the limited and carefully staged interviews he has granted on the question of his mediation activities, Compaoré speaks of a moral mission as a Christian and a concerned neighbor devoted to building peace in the region. There is something of a self-styled persona that emerges from his narrative; there is also something relentless about the manner in which he has undergone a redemptive transformation from a turbulent activist to a senior advisor. In the many interventions in mainstream media and different fora, Compaoré has succeeded in deflecting recurrent questions about his ambiguous positions in mediation missions, tending to displace the question of his political activism to the terrain of the much-abhorred "Françafrique," whereas in reality the transactions of a mediator weighed more heavily at times on the political balance than external pressures.

19. I owe this insight to an anonymous reviewer.

20. See Pomper, "Les Hommes de l'Ombre"; see also Pomper, "Compaoré: Profession Médiateur."

21. Interview with Boureima Badini, Ouagadougou, January 2013.

22. Freeman, "Meet President Blaise Compaoré of Burkina Faso."

23. Glez, "Compaoré, le Chouchou Émancipé de Kadhafi." The Libyan Arab Foreign Bank (LAFB) owned 50 percent of the Burkina Commercial Bank.

24. Glez, "Compaoré, le Chouchou Émancipé de Kadhafi."

25. Hugeux, "Sahel."

26. Jafré, "Le Burkina Faso, Pilier de la 'Françafrique.'"

27. La Françafrique has endured despite a changing economic environment that has brought new partners with no colonial ties with Africa. See Wyss, "The Gendarme Stays in Africa," 81–111.

28. Interview with PD, March 2013.

29. Parti Démocratique de la Côte d'Ivoire-Rassemblement Démocratique Africain, *Dialogue Direct*; UN, *Déclaration du Président du Conseil de Sécurité des Nations Unies*.

30. Interview with Boureima Badini, Ouagadougou, January 2013.

31. Ibid.

32. International Crisis Group, *Burkina Faso*, 23.

33. Members of the office are said to also have benefited from the mission. The daughter of the permanent representative was for instance awarded mining concessions in Ivory Coast.

34. Interview with A. Arnold, Abidjan, January 2013.

35. Banégas, "Côte d'Ivoire," 197–251.

36. International Crisis Group, "Cote d'Ivoire," 5.

37. Interview with a Burkinabè journalist, Ouagadougou, January 7, 2013 (most of my interviewees, especially Burkinabè journalists, wished to remain anonymous; even if there is

relative freedom of speech in Burkina, many think that one still has to be careful about what one says in public). During the years 2001 and 2002, there were many attempts to ease tensions between the two countries following a series of incidents as well as hostile declarations on both sides on their neighbors' design to destabilize them.

38. United Nations, *Report of the General Secretary on Ivory Coast.*

39. Interview with UNOCI official, Abidjan, January 2013.

40. Also Office of the Special Representative; interview, Burkinabè journalist, Ouagadougou, January 2013.

41. Interview with Boureima Badini, Ouagadougou, January 2013.

42. During the conflict, the rebellion used Burkina Faso to export resources such as cocoa. In fact, the vice president of the National Association of Farmers Organisations of Cote d'Ivoire (ANOPACI) accused Burkina Faso and Mali of exporting cocoa illegally, for neither country was a producer; see "Burkina Faso, Mali Accused of Exporting Ivorian Cocoa."

43. Interview with A. Arnold, Abidjan, January 2013.

44. Pépé, "Blaise Compaoré Arrive Aujourd'hui a Yamassoukouro."

45. Interview with Burkinabè official, Ouagadougou, January 2013.

46. See ICG, "Cote d'Ivoire."

47. The idea that the Ouagadougou agreement was a success is obviously open to debate. If nothing, the disastrous 2010 elections, the results of which had to be militarily enforced in order to oust Gbagbo, prove that the mediation merely consolidated a standoff and a semblance of stability so that elections could be organized as an ultimate instrument of conflict resolution.

48. Aning, "Healer of Hegemon," 57.

49. One Burkinabè minister accused the Diaspora of being behind riots and mutinies in BF in 2011. BC and Gbagbo (April 2011) both had their power threatened of destabilization (BC ran from his presidential palace).

50. Although in the case of Compaoré, the accumulated gains of the various missions are probably quite substantial.

51. Aning, "Healer or Hegemon," 60.

52. Bah, "Democracy and Civil War," 599.

53. Mbeki, "What the World Got Wrong."

54. Ibid.

55. Bellamy and Williams, "The New Politics of Protection," 832.

56. Radio France Internationale, "ECOWAS Meets on Côte d'Ivoire as Mbeki Mediation Fails to Deliver."

57. Wells, "Cote d'Ivoire."

58. Ibid.; Mbeki has also contended that "the international community has assiduously suppressed proper appreciation of various explosive allegations which, rightly or wrongly, have informed and will continue to inform the views of the Gbagbo-supporting population in southern Cote d'Ivoire—and much of Francophone Africa!" Mbeki, "What the World Got Wrong."

59. International Commission on Intervention and State Sovereignty, *The Responsibility to Protect.*

References

Adebajo, Adekeye. "The Bicycle Strategy of South Africa's Bilateral Relations in Africa." *South African Journal of International Affairs* 15, no. 2 (2008): 121–136.

Akindes, Francis. *Racines des Crises Socio-politiques en Côte d'Ivoire et Sens de l'Histoire.* Paper presented at the conference on Identity, Security, and the Negotiation of National Belonging in West Africa: Reflections on the Crisis in Côte d'Ivoire, CODESRIA and the Nordic Africa Institute, Dakar, SN, May 15–16, 2003.

———. "South African Mediation in the Ivorian Crisis." In *Africa's Peacemaker? Lessons from South African Conflict Mediation*, edited by Kurt Shillinger, 113–152. Johannesburg, ZA: Fanele, 2009.

Akokpari, John. "You Don't Belong Here": Citizenship, the State and Africa's Conflicts: Reflections on Ivory Coast," In *The Roots of African Conflicts: The Causes and Costs*, edited by Alfred Nhema and Tiyambe Zeleza, 88–105. Oxford: James Currey, 2008.

Aning, Kwesi. "Healer of Hegemon: Assessing Perceptions of South Africa's Role and Motivation in African Mediation." In *Africa's Peacemaker? Lessons from South African Conflict Mediation*, edited by Kurt Shillinger, 57. Johannesburg: Fanele, 2009.

Bah, Abu Bakarr. "Democracy and Civil War: Citizenship and Peacemaking in Cote d'Ivoire." *African Affairs*, 109, no. 437 (2010): 597–615.

Banégas, Richard. "Côte d'Ivoire: Patriotism, Ethnonationalism and other African Modes of Self-writing." *African Affairs* 105, no. 421 (2006): 535–552.

———, "Côte d'Ivoire: Une Guerre de la Seconde Indépendance? Refonder la Coopération Française sur les Brisées du Legs Colonial." *Fonds d'Analyse des Sociétés Politques* 2 (2006): 197–251.

Bellamy, Alex J., and Paul D. Williams, "The New Politics of Protection? Cote d'Ivoire, Libya and the Responsibility to Protect." *International Affairs*, 87, no. 4 (2011): 825–850.

"Burkina Faso, Mali Accused of Exporting Ivorian Cocoa," *Panapress*, June 3, 2004. http://www.panapress.com/Burkina-Faso,-Mali-accused-of-exporting-ivorian-cocoa-12-548213-33-lang2-index.html.

Cutolo, Amando. "Modernity, Autochthony and the Ivorian Nation: The End of a Century in Côte d'Ivoire." *Africa* 80, no. 4 (2010): 527–552.

Dozon, Jean-Pierre. "La Côte d'Ivoire entre Démocratie, Nationalisme et Ethnonationalisme." *Politique Africaine* 78 (2000): 45–62.

Ellis, Stephen, and Gerrie ter Haar. "Religion and Politics in Sub-Saharan Africa." *Journal of Modern African Studies* 36, no. 2 (1998): 175–201.

Fratani, Ruth-Marshall. "The War of 'Who is Who': Autochthony, Nationalism, and Citizenship in the Ivoirian Crisis." *African Studies Review* 49, no. 2 (2006): 9–43.

Freeman, Colin, "Meet President Blaise Compaoré of Burkina Faso—The Man Who Could Help Solve Africa's al-Qaeda Crisis." *Telegraph*, November 17, 2012. http://www.telegraph.co.uk/news/worldnews/africaandindianocean/mali/9680574/Meet-President-Blaise-Compaore-of-Burkina-Faso-the-man-who-could-help-solve-Africas-al-Qaeda-crisis.html.

Glez, Damien. "Compaoré, le Chouchou Émancipé de Kadhafi." *SlateAfrique.com*, June 16, 2011. http://www.slateafrique.com/2657/burkina-faso-compaore-le-chouchou-emancipe-de-kadhafi.

Haut Commissariat des Nations Unies aux Droits de l'Homme. *Rapport de la Commission d'Enquête sur les Évènements Liés à la Marche Prévue*, March 25, 2004, Abidjan.

Hugeux, Vincent. "Sahel: Les Secrets d'un Sauveur d'Otages." *L'Express*, March 10, 2013.

Human Rights Watch. *Le Nouveau Racisme, la Manipulation Politique de l'Ethnicité en Côte d'Ivoire*. Report 13.6, August 2001.

International Crisis Group. "Burkina Faso: Avec ou Sans Compaoré, le Temps des Incertitudes." *Rapport Afrique* no. 205 (July 2013): 1–55. http://www.crisisgroup.org/~/media/Files/africa/west-africa/burkina-faso/205-burkina-faso-avec-ou-sans-compaore-le-temps-des-incertitudes.pdf.

———. "Cote d'Ivoire: Faut-il Croire à l'Accord de Ouagadougou." *Rapport Afrique* no. 127 (June 2007): 1–31. http://www.crisisgroup.org/~/media/Files/africa/west-africa/cote-divoire/French%20translations/Cote%20dIvoire%20Can%20the%20Ouagadougou%20Agreement%20Bring%20Peace%20French.ashx.

International Commission on Intervention and State Sovereignty. *The Responsibility to Protect: Report of the International Commission on Intervention and State Sovereignty*. Ottawa: International Development Research Centre, 2001.

Jafré, Bruno. "Le Burkina Faso, Pilier de la 'Françafrique.'" *Le Monde Diplomatique*, January 2010.

Khadiagala, Gilbert. "South Africa's Role in Conflict Resolution in the Democratic Republic of the Congo (DRC)." In *Africa's Peacemaker? Lessons from South African Conflict Mediation*, edited by Kurt Shillinger, 67–80. Johannesburg: Fanele, 2009.

Mbeki, Thabo. "What the World Got Wrong in Cote d'Ivoire." *Foreign Policy*, April 29, 2011.

Parti Démocratique de la Côte d'Ivoire-Rassemblement Démocratique Africain. *Dialogue Direct: Accord Politique de Ouagadougou*. March 2007. http://www.securitycouncilreport.org/atf/cf/%7B65BFCF9B-6D27-4E9C-8CD3-CF6E4FF96FF9%7D/Cote%20d'Ivoire%20S2007144.pdf.

Pépé, Michèle. "Blaise Compaoré Arrive Aujourd'hui a Yamassoukouro." *Fraternité Matin*, March 8, 2008.

Pomper, Fabienne. "Compaoré: Profession Médiateur." *Jeune Afrique*, November 30, 2011.

———. "Les Hommes de l'Ombre." *Jeune Afrique*, November 30, 2009.

Radio France Internationale. "ECOWAS Meets on Côte d'Ivoire as Mbeki Mediation Fails to Deliver." Broadcast December 7, 2010.

UN. "Déclaration du Président du Conseil de Sécurité des Nations Unies." S/2007/144, March 27, 2007.

———. *Report of the General Secretary on Ivory Coast*. S/100/374, March 26, 2003.

Vines, Alex. "South Africa's Politics of Peace and Security in Africa." *South African Journal of International Affairs* 17, no. 1 (2010): 53–63.

Wells, Matt. "Cote d'Ivoire: l'Impunité d'Aujourd'hui est le Crime de Demain." *Jeune Afrique*, May 8, 2014.

Wyss, Marco. "The Gendarme Stays in Africa: France's Military Role in Côte d'Ivoire." *African Conflict and Peacebuilding Review* 3, no. 1 (2013): 81–111.

Zartman, I. William. "Inter-African Negotiations and Reforming Political Order." In *Africa in World Politics: Reforming Political Order*, edited by Donald Rothchild and John W. Harbeson, 222. Boulder, CO: Westview Press, 2009.

6 African Agency in New Humanitarianism and Responsible Governance

Abu Bakarr Bah

SINCE THE END of the Cold War, Africa has been plagued by new forms of civil wars emblematic of what have been referred to as new wars.[1] Africa's new wars, such as the civil wars in Rwanda, Liberia, Sierra Leone, Côte d'Ivoire, Democratic Republic of Congo (DRC), and Central African Republic (CAR), increasingly became devoid of meaningful social justice causes and took the form of violence that targets civilians and thrives on perpetual anarchy and pillage.[2] More recently, Africa's new wars have taken the form of terrorism in countries such as Somalia, Kenya, Nigeria, and Libya.[3] Africa's new wars have led to tremendous human suffering and further threatened regional and international security. The gross human security and terrorism threats of Africa's new wars have led to growing external concerns over security in Africa. However, external interests in African security are multilayered and contentious. Indeed, humanitarian concerns over human rights violations, refugee formation, and dire threats to human security that teeter on genocide and large-scale massacre are part of the concerns that increase interest in African new wars.[4] While these concerns have triggered benevolent military interventions in countries such as Sierra Leone and Liberia, efforts to promote regime change based on Western security and political interests in countries such as Libya, Sudan, and Côte d'Ivoire have increased African concerns about the excesses of global liberal governance under the doctrine of responsibility to protect (R2P) and the global War on Terror.[5] This twin reality of genuine concerns about humanitarian tragedies and the fear of Western interventions and neocolonialism imbued in the doctrine of global liberal governance have propelled African countries and the African Union (AU) to adopt new security and governance frameworks that exert African agency in addressing security and governance challenges in the continent and thwart external attempts to infuse Western security and governance priorities in Africa.

Africa's new security and governance strategy is embodied in the African Peace and Security Architecture (APSA) and various mechanisms to promote democracy and good governance, most notably the New Partnership for Africa's Development (NEPAD) and the African Charter on Democracy, Elections and Governance (ACDEG). APSA, NEPAD, and ACDEG emerged at a time of growing and complicated violent political conflicts in Africa and a renewed continental and global interest in security and liberal governance. This global push for democracy and new sense of humanitarianism, which challenge orthodox notions of sovereignty and security, are key elements of global liberal governance.[6] APSA, NEPAD, and ACDEG raise important questions about African agency and the capacities of African states to participate in the application of the new humanitarianism and the global liberal governance doctrines that have become cornerstones of contemporary security and development policies in Africa.

This chapter examines the security and political context within which APSA and other African governance mechanisms emerged and the contemporary challenges of their application. While the chapter discusses relevant aspects of NEPAD and ACDEG, it is primarily focused on APSA, which is the core African security mechanism. In particular, the chapter examines the interconnections between the AU's doctrine of nonindifference and the effort to assert African agency in the application of new humanitarianism and global liberal governance in African security and governance issues. Moreover, it examines the synergy between the doctrine of nonindifference to human security and the AU's effort to promote responsible governance and democracy.

This chapter argues that the development of APSA and other AU good governance and democracy promotion instruments is driven not only by the genuine need to promote human security, democracy, and good governance in African countries, but also by the strategic desire of African leaders to assert African agency in African affairs and thereby thwart the application of Western global liberal governance in Africa. The chapter builds on Cyril Obi's critique of post–Cold War AU governance instruments. For Obi, the central problem with AU governance and security mechanisms is that they "largely reflect neoliberal perspectives and elitist interests that hardly reflect African realities and lack the capacity to transform the socioeconomic conditions of the majority of African people."[7] While Obi sees African governance mechanisms more as failures because they are anchored in a neoliberal perspective that is exploited by the elite and delivers nothing for the masses, I contend that AU mechanisms are designed not only to enhance human security and good governance in Africa but more importantly to assert African agency. Though the AU mechanisms are a failure for the African masses, they are a partial success in containing the application of global liberal governance in Africa and are beneficial for African political leaders. AU governance mechanisms allow African leaders to champion human security, democracy, and good governance in other African countries, while undermining those same principles in their own country. In that sense, I agree with Obi that "AU's performance is partly linked to the contradictions between the nature of the state and ruling elites on the continent, and to the ways that these define dominant forms of political power that tend to manipulate and undermine any real attempts at compliance with universalist principles of democracy" and human security.[8] In sum, the AU notion of nonindifference, which is central to APSA, NEPAD, and ACDEG, is simultaneously a moral virtue, a useful policy frame for peace and development, and a stratagem against global liberal governance. Nonindifference gives African leaders a moral claim to agency and the tools to exert agency in Africa.

APSA was born out of the transformation of the Organization of African Unity (OAU) into the AU. The AU Constitutive Act of 2000 established seventeen key institutions covering a wide range of security, governance, and development issues.[9] In particular, the act shifted from the extant OAU policy of noninterference in the affairs of member states to a covenant of nonindifference to issues of human security and governance in Africa. It charged the AU with the responsibility to protect people in situations of war crimes, crimes against humanity, and genocide. In collaboration with the continent's Regional Economic Communities (RECs),[10] the AU established the Peace and Security Council (PSC) to actualize the new security doctrine of nonindifference in dealing with security, humanitarian, and governance crises in Africa. The protocol establishing the PSC entered into force on December 26, 2003.[11] Since the establishment of the PSC, several other institutions have been set up by the AU to promote security and deal with conflict through the doctrine of nonindifference. These include the Continental Early Warning System (CEWS), the Military Staff Committee (MSC), the African Standby Force (ASF), the Panel of the Wise (PoW), and the African Peace Fund (APF). Collectively, the PSC and these other institutions form the APSA.

In line with the spirit of the AU Constitutive Act of 2000, African leaders established NEPAD in 2001. NEPAD seeks to be "a radically new intervention, spearheaded by African leaders, to address critical challenges facing the continent: poverty, development and Africa's marginalisation internationally."[12] The AU Constitutive act recognized that bad governance was at the center of Africa's security challenges and devised numerous instruments aimed at promoting free and fair elections and good governance.[13] As such, a key issue for NEPAD is economic and corporate governance. NEPAD acknowledges that "the delivery of high quality programmes and projects to promote Africa's development and regional integration can only be realised in an environment that permits good economic and corporate governance."[14] NEPAD focuses on enhancing management, procurement processes, and accountability, and creating transparent government policies. The cornerstone of NEPAD's Economic and Corporate Governance program is the African Peer Review Mechanism (APRM).[15] The APRM was to monitor the conduct of African governments in four critical areas: democracy and political governance, economic governance, corporate governance, and socioeconomic development. The underlying theme of all the areas is the promotion of a democratic and accountable system of governance and a transparent and ethical leadership that benefits the people. The review process itself is conducted by three organs of the APRM, namely: the Country Review Mission Team, the Panel of Eminent Persons, and the Committee of Participating Heads of State and Government. Though the effectiveness of NEPAD has been questioned, its existence underscores the growing recognition of the need for people-centered liberalism in African economic development.[16]

ACDEG, which was adopted in January 2007 in Ethiopia, is an expansion of the Lome Declaration adopted by the OAU in 2000.[17] Like the Lome Declaration, ACDEG sought to eliminate unconstitutional changes of government through coups and use of arms and undue manipulation of laws and constitutions to prolong a government's stay in power beyond its mandate. The ultimate goal of ACDEG is to inculcate multiparty democracy, peaceful transfer of power, and good governance, which would lead to the entrenchment of "the universal values and principles of democracy and respect for human rights" throughout Africa.[18]

The adoption of the doctrine of nonindifference in African security and humanitarian affairs under APSA and the effort to enforce good governance and democracy through NEPAD and ACDEG points to significant efforts by African leaders to appropriate the language of human security, democracy, and good governance and assert African agency in the application of global liberal governance in Africa. Both the human security values espoused in APSA and the good governance and democracy principles promoted by NEPAD and ACDEG are rooted in the doctrine of nonindifference entrenched in the AU Constitutive Act of 2000. However, nonindifference was simultaneously driven by a genuine humanitarian concern for the plight of the African masses and a pragmatic stratagem by African leaders to contain Western interference in African political and security matters. Thus, the effort to build political and military institutions to actualize the doctrine of nonindifference raises important questions about the effort to assert African agency and ownership over the continent's security and the effort of African countries to localize and partake in global liberal governance. If APSA, NEPAD, and ACDEG are successful, the doctrine of nonindifference would mark a significant change in the debate about legitimacy, sovereignty, and neoimperialism in Africa. Moreover, it would lay a model for African collaboration and humanitarianism that can be channeled to wider issues of governance and human development in Africa beyond civil war situations. However, these AU mechanisms have been only minimally successful in enhancing human security, democracy, and good governance in Africa.

Agency, Good Governance, and New Humanitarianism

African civil wars have been largely linked to bad governance.[19] The shift to nonindifference occurred at the same time as the AU and other international actors have been pushing for democracy and good governance as a way to promote human security and human development. The AU has made democracy, transparency, and accountability the cornerstones of governance and adopted a zero-tolerance policy for military coups.[20] In essence, the AU's notion of nonindifference rests on both democracy and good governance within countries and collective responsibility for peace and security within Africa. However, democracy, good governance, and human security can be understood only in light of broader international doctrines and policies relating to security and democratic governance in Africa and beyond. As Obi rightly noted, it is "important to raise questions about the state of the discourse on African democracy, and its ties, if any, to policy and practical actions at the national, regional, and continental levels."[21]

The establishment of APSA and NEPAD are both efforts to enhance human security and assert African agency in African security and political matters. If APSA and NEPAD are successful, their key legacy would be shifting the debate on African security and political matters from the neoimperialistic tendencies of the application of military humanitarianism (i.e., R2P and the War on Terror) in Africa to one that makes Africa a real partner in the application of global liberal governance. African agency implies that African states are the drivers of intervention policies in Africa and have the central role in authorizing international interventions and the operation of humanitarian and antiterrorism military activities in the continent. Any external military intervention would have to be based on a request by the AU.[22] Moreover, African leaders would be the ones defining what democracy and good governance mean and assessing their implementation in Africa. Craig Calhoun defines *agency* as the ability to engage in autonomous social action and operate independently of the constraints posed by extant social structure.[23] Given the history of foreign interventions in African security matters, the assertion of African agency needs to be viewed from both a historical and a contemporary lens. Mustafa Emirbayer and Ann Mische provide a historically grounded notion of agency that sees agency as "the temporally constructed engagement by actors of different structural environments—the temporal-relational contexts of action—which, through the interplay of habit, imagination, and judgment, both reproduces and transforms those structures in interactive response to the problems posed by changing historical situations."[24] In this sense, African agency in its security, humanitarian, and political affairs calls for understanding of the past and present security policies and governance frameworks, the interconnections between African security and global security, and the way African countries are transforming the security architecture of Africa and implementing democracy in the continent.

The APSA is rooted in the ethics of collective responsibility and nonindifference, which have been evoked in the AU's policies on continental security and governance matters within member countries. The doctrine of nonindifference relates to both African security crises and the problems of governance that often lead to violent conflicts. While the PSC mandate of nonindifference to security crises is explicit, the AU's policies of nonindifference toward problems of governance are a bit more subtle, yet equally important. The AU's policies on governance are more explicitly spelled out in its strategic framework for pan-African socioeconomic development, namely, NEPAD. NEPAD, which was established in 2001, rests on the AU's belief that African economic and social development hinges on good governance. One of NEPAD's core goals is "strengthening the capacity of member states to ensure good corporate governance and management of development programmes."[25] The AU's insistence on good governance dovetails with wider international policies toward democracy and governance in Africa.

The push for good governance in Africa was first spearheaded by the IMF and the World Bank during the wave of democratic transitions of the 1990s.[26] In 1996, the IMF identified "promoting good governance in all its aspects, including by ensuring the rule of law, improving the efficiency and accountability of the public sector, and tackling corruption, as essential elements of a framework within which economies can prosper."[27] This infusion of neoliberal economic policies with insistence on democracy and the rule of law became the hallmark of the Western challenge to African leaders to govern in a way that enhances freedom and economic development.[28] The AU appropriated the good governance discourse through NEPAD. NEPAD has been focused on enhancing management, procurement processes, and accountability and creating transparent government policies. The cornerstone of NEPAD's good governance policy is the APRM, which is rooted in the doctrine of nonindifference. As the AU states, the APRM "is a mutually agreed instrument voluntarily acceded to by the Member States of the AU as an African self-monitoring mechanism. The APRM is a bold, unique and innovative approach designed and implemented by Africans for Africa." The APRM's mandate "is to encourage conformity in regard to political, economic and corporate governance values, codes and standards, among African countries and the objectives in socioeconomic development within the New Partnership for Africa's Development."[29]

This emphasis on African ownership of the African security and development agenda first emerged during the decolonization period and the effort to promote African development through the development paradigm anchored in one-party political regimes and state-centered economic policies during the immediate post-independence period.[30] As Claude Ake points out, however, "The ideology of development itself became a problem for development because of the conflict between its manifest and latent functions. The conflict is apparent in the actions of African leaders who proclaimed the need for development and made development the new ideology without necessarily translating it into a program of social transformation. They did so not because they were uninterested in societal transformation but because their minds were absorbed in the struggle for power and survival."[31] The failure of the previous African efforts to promote peace and human development were hampered by the authoritarian political systems of African countries and the Cold War, which resulted in proxy ideological and military warfare in Africa. The new effort to take ownership of African security and governance issues emerged in a post–Cold War environment, characterized by new wars and entrenchment of the doctrine of global liberal governance.

The AU's doctrine of nonindifference, in both its security and governance forms, dovetails with the notion of new humanitarianism imbued in global liberal governance.[32] New humanitarianism is a radical outgrowth of the extant post–Cold War international humanitarian intervention policies for dealing with the security challenges of new wars.[33] Robert Johansen distinguishes narrowly defined humanitarian interventions from interventions motivated by concerns about human rights violations or collective security.[34] However, the critical question has always been how to respond to new wars, which the international community has been unable to prevent or address. As the International Commission on Intervention and State Sovereignty (ICISS) notes, "Millions of human beings remain at the mercy of civil wars, insurgencies, state repression and state collapse. . . . What is at stake here is not making the world safe for big powers, or trampling over the sovereign rights of small ones, but delivering practical protection for ordinary people, at risk of their lives, because their states are unwilling or unable to protect them."[35] The reality of new wars, in both their orthodox and terrorism warfare variants, has necessitated the adoption of the doctrine of R2P and the War on Terror. As a result, new humanitarianism has inevitably developed a military component.

Skepticism about international humanitarian intervention is not based on rejection of the moral imperative to protect vulnerable populations. Rather, it is rooted in the uneasiness about violations of sovereignty and reinforcement of the vestiges of colonialism.[36] Conversely, proponents of humanitarian intervention question traditional notions of sovereignty that privilege state sovereignty over the natural rights of citizens.[37] They distinguish state security from human security and disaggregate state sovereignty from popular sovereignty.[38] The decoupling of the security interests of the state and its power elite from the human rights and safety of the citizenry has undercut traditional notions of state sovereignty and redefined sovereignty as a responsibility to protect.[39] Thus, when states are unable to protect their citizens, they are expected to seek and accept international humanitarian help. This expanded notion of humanitarian intervention is essentially new humanitarianism. New humanitarianism, which demands the restoration of human security, promotion of democracy, and support for human development, is actualized through global liberal governance.[40]

The AU has appropriated new humanitarianism through its doctrine of nonindifference to civil wars and major threats to human security and materialized it through APSA, NEPAD, and ACDEG. The AU's doctrine of nonindifference is a radical departure from the OAU's principal focus on resisting foreign aggression and asserting the sovereignty of African states. According to article II of the OAU Charter, the purpose of the OAU was: "a) to promote the unity and solidarity of the African States; b) to coordinate and intensify their cooperation and efforts to achieve a better life for the peoples of Africa; c) to defend their sovereignty, their territorial integrity and independence; d) to eradicate all forms of colonialism from Africa; and e) to promote international cooperation, having due regard to the Charter of the United Nations and the Universal Declaration of Human Rights."[41] This OAU anticolonialism mission was buttressed with seven principles of the OAU that assert

- the sovereign equality of all Member States;
- non-interference in the internal affairs of States;
- respect for the sovereignty and territorial integrity of each State and for its inalienable right to independent existence;
- peaceful settlement of disputes by negotiation, mediation, conciliation or arbitration;
- unreserved condemnation, in all its forms, of political assassination as well as of subversive activities on the part of neighbouring States or any other State;
- absolute dedication to the total emancipation of the African territories which are still dependent;
- affirmation of a policy of non-alignment with regard to all blocs.[42]

While the AU maintains the commitment to "defend the sovereignty, territorial integrity and independence of its Member States" as envisioned under the OAU Charter, the AU Constitutive Act makes no explicit reference to colonialism and leaves out the key OAU objective "to eradicate all forms of colonialism from Africa." Instead of focusing on colonialism and state sovereignty, the AU Constitutive Act identified new objectives relating to the internal economic, social, and political threats to African security and development, which are in line with the tenets of global liberal governance. These new objectives are to be addressed through a principle based on collective African responsibility and nonindifference to African problems, which will be authentically African and at the same time congruent with global liberal governance.[43] In particular, the new objectives stated in article 3 of the AU Constitutive Act, include to

- accelerate the political and socio-economic integration of the continent;
- promote peace, security, and stability on the continent;
- promote democratic principles and institutions, popular participation and good governance;
- establish the necessary conditions which enable the continent to play its rightful role in the global economy and in international negotiations;
- promote sustainable development at the economic, social and cultural levels as well as the integration of African economies;
- promote co-operation in all fields of human activity to raise the living standards of African peoples;
- coordinate and harmonize the policies between the existing and future Regional Economic Communities for the gradual attainment of the objectives of the Union;
- advance the development of the continent by promoting research in all fields, in particular in science and technology;
- work with relevant international partners in the eradication of preventable diseases and the promotion of good health on the continent.[44]

The new emphasis on social and economic development, technology, democracy, internal stability, and regional and international cooperation was buttressed with principles based on shared African responsibility and nonindifference to problems in any part of the continent. These principles, outlined in article 4 of the AU Constitutive Act, include

- establishment of a common defence policy for the African Continent;
- the right of the Union to intervene in a Member State pursuant to a decision of the Assembly in respect of grave circumstances, namely: war crimes, genocide and crimes against humanity;
- the right of Member States to request intervention from the Union in order to restore peace and security;
- promotion of self-reliance within the framework of the Union;
- respect for democratic principles, human rights, the rule of law and good governance;
- promotion of social justice to ensure balanced economic development;
- respect for the sanctity of human life, condemnation and rejection of impunity and political assassination, acts of terrorism and subversive activities;
- condemnation and rejection of unconstitutional changes of governments.[45]

The principle of nonindifference is the AU's version of the doctrine of R2P, which emerged through the UN at the end of the genocides in Bosnia and Rwanda and became a centerpiece of new humanitarianism and global liberal governance.[46] By asserting "the right of the Union to intervene in a Member State pursuant to a decision of the Assembly in respect of grave circumstances, namely: war crimes, genocide and crimes against humanity" in article 4 of the AU Constitute Act, the AU clearly appropriates new humanitarianism and asserts itself as the principal enforcer of global liberal governance in Africa. In line with new humanitarianism, the AU also takes a human security and human development approach to African security. The AU's objectives and principles on social and economic development and the promotion of democracy and good governance fit well into the neoliberal and sustainable human development notions of governance and economic development. By prohibiting unconstitutional changes of government, insisting on democratic elections and human rights, and emphasizing social justice and economic development, the AU appropriates the discourses of liberalism and human development in a way that fits into the people-centered liberalism imbued in global liberal governance.[47] The AU materialized its vision of nonindifference by establishing APSA as a common defense policy and creating NEPAD as the mechanism for realizing good governance and human development. In line with ACDEG, the AU established the Democracy and Electoral Assistance Unit to help countries organize multiparty elections, observe elections, and attest to the democratic qualities of elections.[48] The AU has also adopted a policy of expelling countries that have had an unconstitutional change of government (i.e., coups) until the country holds an election and constitutionally installs a government.[49]

All of these AU mechanisms represent a clear departure from the OAU's approach to African security and an affirmation of Africa's effort to take ownership of African security and governance issues in a way that is aligned with global liberal governance but also thwarts external application of global liberal governance in Africa. Though the AU has moved from the language of colonialism, African concern over Western interference in Africa and the prioritization of Western security and economic interests in African remain major concerns for African leaders. However, instead of taking a frontal assault on neoimperialism as the OAU did in its charter, the AU has appropriated Western principles and interests in a way that seeks to transform them and impact their application in Africa. Clearly, AU leaders understand that outright resistance to Western security interests and desires to mold African politics and economies would not be successful given the weak military and economic positions of African countries. While the OAU had the advantage of seeking alternative superpower allies during the Cold War, the AU has very little alternative to Western neoliberalism in the post–Cold War period. As such, maintaining good relations with Western powers has become even more important for African political leaders. What seems to be a more realistic strategy to resisting the imposition of Western security and political priorities in Africa is adaptation and cooptation. AU leaders realize that for African countries to be viable actors in the continent's security and political affairs, African security and governance policies must adapt to the post–Cold War era and accept the tenets of global liberal governance. In reality, African agency is more in the form of Emirbayer and Mische's notion of agency as an effort to reproduce and transform structures of domination,[50] instead of Calhoun's idea of agency as the capacity for autonomous social action operating independently of the constraints posed by extant social structure.[51]

Elements of the APSA and Their Application to African Global Liberal Governance

The core of APSA is the PSC, which is vested with political powers. The PSC is responsible for the overall promotion of peace, security, and stability in the continent. It is empowered to engage in preventive diplomacy and manage Africa's political and military response to security and humanitarian crises.[52] In particular, the PSC was established in order to

a. promote peace, security and stability in Africa, in order to guarantee the protection and preservation of life and property, the well-being of the African people and their environment, as well as the creation of conditions conducive to sustainable development;

b. anticipate and prevent conflicts. In circumstances where conflicts have occurred, the Peace and Security Council shall have the responsibility to undertake peace-making and peacebuilding functions for the resolution of these conflicts;

c. promote and implement peace-building and post-conflict reconstruction activities to consolidate peace and prevent the resurgence of violence;

d. co-ordinate and harmonize continental efforts in the prevention and combating of international terrorism in all its aspects;

e. develop a common defence policy for the Union, in accordance with article 4(d) of the Constitutive Act;

f. promote and encourage democratic practices, good governance and the rule of law, protect human rights and fundamental freedoms, respect for the sanctity of human life and international humanitarian law, as part of efforts for preventing conflicts.[53]

The PSC is composed of fifteen members, elected by the AU Executive Council on a regional basis (three from Central Africa, three from East Africa, two from North Africa, three from Southern Africa, and four from West Africa).

PoW is essentially an unconventional political body. It operates through diplomacy and application of what is considered African traditional wisdom in peacebuilding and conflict resolution.[54] Article 11 of the protocol establishing the PSC called for a five-person panel of "highly respected African personalities from various segments of society who have made outstanding contributions to the cause of peace, security and development on the continent" with a task "to support the efforts of the PSC and those of the Chairperson of the Commission, particularly in the area of conflict prevention."[55] The first panel was set up in December 2007. Members serve for a term of three years, which can be renewed once. Some of the people who have been appointed to the panel include Ahmed Ben Bella of Algeria, Salim Ahmed Salim of Tanzania, Mary Chinery Hesse of Ghana, and Kenneth Kaunda of Zambia.

PoW is empowered to "undertake such action deemed appropriate to support the efforts of the PSC and those of the Chairperson of the Commission for the prevention of conflicts."[56] The mandate of PoW is largely to advise and provide moral and political support to the PSC and AU on matters of general conflict prevention and the application of justice and reconciliation in countries undergoing war. PoW was to pay special attention to the situation of women and children in armed conflicts. In addition, members of the panel were to use their moral, political, and social capital and leadership skills to do conflict mediation and broker peace agreements between warring parties. PoW absorbs the language of gender and child rights, which is highly valued by Western partners, but also provides a channel for the AU to circumvent legalistic approaches to resolving conflict by focusing on perceived traditional African wisdom of conflict resolution based on consensus building.

APSA also includes a technical component to help mitigate conflicts by anticipating conflict situations and providing timely information on evolving violent conflicts based on specifically developed indicators. Article 12 of the protocol establishing the PSC calls for the establishment of CEWS.[57] CEWS is responsible for collecting and analyzing data and providing decision makers with timely and relevant information. It is empowered to work with other international agencies, including the UN, NGOs, and research centers and academic institutions. In reality, CEWS is also a way to attract financial and technical support from Western powers vested in the War on Terror. The data, findings, and recommendations of CEWS are to be made available to the PSC and the other bodies of APSA, which should help them address potential conflicts and threats to peace and security in Africa. In particular, CEWS consists of an observation and monitoring center (i.e., "the Situation Room") located at the Conflict Management Division of the AU. The center is responsible for data collection and analysis. CEWS also includes the observation and monitoring units of the Regional Mechanisms for Conflict Prevention, Management, and Resolution. These regional units collect and process data within their areas and transmit them to the Situation Room.

APSA also has military components. The protocol establishing the PSC called for the establishment of the MSC and the ASF.[58] The MSC was established to advise the PSC on military and security issues in its effort to promote and maintain peace and security in the continent. The MSC held its first meeting in October 2004 in the midst of the Darfur crisis. The MSC was to be composed of senior military officers from PSC member countries, which were expected to send defense attachés to the AU. In addition to the meetings of the senior military officers in the MSC, the chiefs of defense staff of PSC member countries were also expected to hold regular meetings to discuss matters assigned to them by the PSC. In addition to advising the PSC, the MSC was charged with acting as liaison between the PSC and the chiefs of staff of PSC member states and ensuring proper harmony between the AU's conflict prevention and resolution policies and actions and the security mechanisms of the RECs. The MSC would also help with the development of the early warning systems and coordination with ASF missions. In principle, the establishment of the MSC should position African political and military leaders well to shape the execution of military humanitarianism in Africa. AU military command headquarters would be the places where Western military officers fighting terrorism or delivering humanitarian assistance would be hosted and potentially swayed by their African counterparts.

The framework for the ASF was established in March 2005.[59] The ASF was to be deployed with the authorization of the RECs and the AU. In addition, the AU was to seek UN Security Council authorization in support of ASF deployment. Like the other APSA mechanism, the ASF was to save Western powers the need to deploy troops in Africa. With the development of the ASF, the AU can deploy troops to do the work of global liberal governance under firm African political and military command. All that the AU would need from Western powers is technical and financial support for the ASF. For Western powers, this would work well in places where Western political or economic interests are minimal.[60] The ASF was to be trained according to a standardized doctrine that is consistent with that of the UN (such as the UN Multinational Peacekeeping Handbook), and complemented by African specificity. The ASF would comprise five regional standby units, namely, Eastern Africa Standby Force, Northern Standby Brigade, Economic Community of West African States (ECOWAS) Standby, Central African Standby Brigade, and Southern Africa Standby Brigade. ASF is to be a multinational and multidisciplinary force with military, police, and civilian components. The force units are to be held on standby in their countries of origin, ready to be deployed as needed, using a system of on-call lists.[61] The ASF was to be supported by a system of AU Military Logistical Bases (AMLD), consisting of the AU Military Logistical Depot and regional logistical bases, which should facilitate rapid deployment and mission sustainability.

The ASF Policy Framework requires the establishment of a fifteen-person Planning Elements (PLANELMs) at the AU headquarters and at each of the RECs/regional headquarters. The PLANELMs would act as the fulltime planning headquarters for ASF. Each REC would maintain a mission-headquarter-level management capability in the form of a brigade headquarters. The ASF was to be furnished with "an appropriate Africa-wide interoperable C^3IS integrated infrastructure, linking deployed units with mission HQs, as well as with the AU, PLANELMs and Regions/RECs."[62]

APSA requires a significant amount of resources, especially for the ASF. As such, APSA includes the APF, which was established in 2004. While the fund has received significant pledges, the fund is far below what is required to fully support APSA, especially the critical ASF. Corinna Jentzsch provides a detailed analysis of the funding mechanism for AU peacekeeping and peacebuilding efforts. As she pointed out, "Inadequate financial, material, and logistical resources support for peace operations in Africa is a major challenge. This problem has made the African Union (AU) and its member states dependent on the international community, especially in times of major crisis."[63] Most of the dependency has been on the EU, which principally supports the APF through the African Peace Facility, and on the UN and NATO for technical and logistical assistance.[64]

The combination of dependency and African effort to assert agency in its security and governance matters has produced a form of hybrid paternalism. As Thomas Kwasi Tieku and Tanzeel F. Hakak argue, hybrid paternalism has rendered

> the relationship between AU and UN . . . inherently symbiotic and codependent. On one side, the AU not only shares the UN's Africa peacekeeping role, but it sometimes serves as a scapegoat for shortcomings in some of the UN's operations on the African continent. . . . In addition, the UNSC has a partner it can use to gain consent to intervene in all the states in Africa (except Morocco). On the other end of the spectrum, the UN provides AU with financial, technical, and human resources it often needs to fulfill its mandate. The UN also gives the AU a global voice and an international platform.[65]

While hybrid paternalism sees the AU's effort to partake in global liberal governance as beneficial for African states, albeit partially, Edward Ansah Akuffo's analysis of the cooperation between the AU and NATO shows that Africa's interests can be easily ignored in the application of global liberal governance in Africa. As Akuffo pointed out, "The different approaches adopted by the AU and NATO with regard to the Libyan crisis created a clash of positions as well as a clash of leadership. The differences between the AU and NATO appear to be deeply rooted in NATO's abandonment of the principle of AU request."[66]

The situation in Libya shows the limits of African agency in the application of global liberal governance in Africa in cases that are strategically paramount for Western security, political, or economic interests. However, other cases of conflict show the possibilities for African agency in the application of global liberal governance in the continent. Western technical and financial assistance has enabled the AU to develop APSA and undertake its own peacekeeping and peacebuilding missions and thereby exert African agency in the application of global liberal governance in Africa. Through its strategy of adaptation and cooptation, the AU has politely developed an African global liberal governance. Since the conception of APSA in the AU Constitutive Act of 2000, various elements of APSA have been established. The PSC and PoW have been engaged in peace mediation efforts, though success is minimal. The AU has also deployed several ASF missions. These include the Multinational Force of the Economic and Monetary Community of Central Africa (FOMUC), AU Mission in Burundi (AMIB), AU Mission in Sudan (AMIS), AU Mission in Somalia (AMISOM), AU Mission for Support to the Elections in Comoros (AMISEC), and African-Led International Support Mission in Mali (AFISMA).

AMIB, which is considered to be a fairly successful AU peacekeeping mission, was primarily mandated to supervise, observe, monitor, and verify the implementation of the ceasefire and the Arusha Agreement in Burundi. A key part of its work was implementation of Burundi's disarmament, demobilization, and reintegration program. AMIB was mainly supported by South Africa, which provided around half of the 3,335 soldiers deployed under AMIB. AMIB, which was deployed from 2003 to 2004, cost over $100 million. In 2004, the mission was handed to the UN. Similarly, AMISEC was able to help promote stability during the 2006 election crisis in Comoros. As in Burundi, South Africa was the main contributor to AMISEC, which was a very small mission. As the violence surrounding elections intensified, AMISEC was replaced with the AU Electoral and Security Assistance Mission (MAES) in May 2007. At the peak of the Comoros crisis in March 2009, the AU deployed around 1,350 troops. MAES ended in October 2008 after Comoros was fairly stabilized.

While the AU has been able to stabilize Burundi and Comoros, which are small countries with relatively less intensive civil wars, other cases involving big countries have proved to be very difficult for the ASF and the entirety of APSA. In Sudan, AMIS has been largely unsuccessful. It was developed in 2004 to end violence and protect civilians in Darfur; however, violence against civilians continued at an alarming level. AMIS began with 150 troops and increased to only 7,000 by mid-2005. AMIS was to be replaced by a UN peacekeeping mission, which Sudan rejected. AMIS was replaced by a hybrid UN-AU mission into Darfur to replace the previous AU-led mission in 2007. Somalia has been one major test for the ASF in part because the AU has deployed a significantly large force in Somalia and major neighboring countries, especially Kenya and Ethiopia, are vested in stability in the country. AMISOM was deployed in January 2007 to replace and subsume the Inter-Governmental Authority on Development (IGAD) Peace Support Mission to Somalia (IGASOM). AMISOM's mandate is to conduct peace support operations to stabilize the country and create conditions for the conduct of humanitarian activities. Moreover, it is supposed to support the Somali Federal Government as it prepares the country for a referendum on the national constitution and a general election by 2016. AMISOM has fully deployed its authorized 21,586 soldiers and 540 police officers. The troops are drawn from countries such as Uganda, Burundi, Djibouti, Sierra Leone, Kenya, and Ethiopia under the ASF. AMISIOM has received significant financial and logistical support from the UN and Western powers in large part because of the connections between the Somali civil war and terrorism warfare. In particular, the EU has been providing funds for troop allowances and other mission expenses through the APF. While AU success in Somalia is still an open question, CAR shows the general weakness of APSA. The recent breakdown of law and order and the near-genocide situation shows APSA's failure to deliver on early warning and preventive diplomacy. Moreover, it has been unable to deploy a strong peacekeeping force in CAR.

From a purely security perspective, the effectiveness of APSA as a whole has been minimal, as evident in the number of unresolved violent conflicts in Africa. In terms of applications, the ASF is one of the most critical and challenging parts of APSA. This is in part because it requires significant resources but also because it provides real capability for the AU to actualize its policy of nonindifference. It is clear from the spate of conflicts and humanitarian crises in the continent (Mali, CAR, South Sudan, etc.) that the conflict prevention dimension of APSA has been insufficient. Thus, the ASF is even more important in dealing with old and new crises. As I have pointed out, however, APSA is more than a security framework. It is also a strategic political framework to thwart Western domination over African affairs and a means of asserting African agency in the application of global liberal governance in Africa. Given the growing collaboration between African and Western powers in African security issues, it is possible to see Africa's new security framework and doctrine of nonindifference as successful adaptation and cooptation of global liberal governance. African countries have been collaborating with NATO, the UN, the EU, France, and United States in security crises in countries such as Côte d'Ivoire, Mali, Nigeria, and Somalia. In all of these cases, African political and military leaders are key participants in the application of global liberal governance in Africa.

Conclusions

The doctrine of nonindifference and its related mechanisms (APSA, NEPAD, ACDEG, etc.) are important developments in the African security and governance architecture. They not only tap into contemporary global security and political realities and principles, but they also offer a new way of asserting African agency in African political and security matters. In theory, nonindifference should be an unproblematic approach to enhancing democracy, good governance, and human security in Africa. Equally, it is a wise strategy for thwarting neoimperialism and asserting African agency. The real problem of the doctrine of nonindifference is the gap between stated AU principles on democracy, good governance, and human security at the continental level on the one hand and the application of similar policies by individual African leaders in their own country.

The irony of nonindifference is that African leaders who have championed good governance, democracy, and peace in other African countries often engage in activities that undermine those same principles in their own countries. Hence, the AU doctrine of nondifference is applied primarily toward African neighbors instead of the compatriots at home. Some of the African leaders sent to Côte d'Ivoire in 2010 to convince Laurent Gbagbo to respect the election results and step down from the presidency would later engage in actions that undermine democracy and promote political violence in their own countries. One of the most ironic cases is that of Abdoulaye Wade in Senegal, who was a fervent champion of NEPAD and democracy. Despite his image as the elder statesman of African good governance, peace, and democracy, Wade undermined democracy in Senegal by trying to illegally extend his stay in power and by creating a system of political patronage in favor of his son. Wade was eventually forced by a popular uprising to vacate the presidency after the end of his constitutional term in 2012. Other notorious cases include those of Nigerian presidents General Ibrahim Babangida and General Sani Abacha. Babangida and Abacha were fervent promoters of the international interventions in Liberia and Sierra Leone to promote human security and democracy in those two countries. Ironically, Babangida and Abacha were two of the most brutal dictators in Nigeria. Both of them brutally suppressed the restoration of multiparty democracy in Nigeria. Even in South Africa, Thabo Mbeki's policies on peace and good governance in Africa did not match his domestic record. As one of the architects of the AU and APSA, Muammar Gaddafi responded to the Arab Spring in a way that was a grave contradiction to the values of human security and democracy espoused in the AU Constitutive Act. This disconnection between the application of the doctrine of nonindifference at the continental level and the clear violations of democracy and good governance principles at home buttresses the view that nonindifference is mostly a stratagem against global liberal governance rather than a benevolent principle of self-empowerment and promotion of peace, democracy, and good governance in Africa. What seems to be emerging from the doctrine of nonindifference is an African global liberal governance that has co-opted Western policies in order to thwart the application of global liberal governance in Africa by Western powers.

Notes

1. Kaldor, *New and Old Wars*.
2. Reno. *Warlord Politics and African States*; Bah, "State Decay and Civil War," 199–216.
3. Cilliers, "Terrorism and Africa," 91–103; Abrahamsen, "A Breeding Ground for Terrorists?" 677–684.

4. Cohen and Deng, *Masses in Flight*; Duffield, *Global Governance and the New Wars*.

5. ICISS, *The Responsibility to Protect*, 11; UN, "2005 World Summit Outcome"; Akuffo, "The Politics of Interregional Cooperation," 108–128; Bah, "Democracy and Civil War," 597–615.

6. Bah, "The Contours of New Humanitarianism," 2–26; Duffield, *Global Governance and the New Wars*.

7. Obi, "The African Union and the Prevention of Democratic Reversal in Africa," 62.

8. Ibid., 66.

9. African Union, *Constitutive Act of the African Union*.

10. Arab Maghreb Union (UMA); Common Market for Eastern and Southern Africa (COMESA); Community of Sahel-Saharan States (CEN-SAD); East African Community (EAC); Economic Community of Central African States (ECCAS); Economic Community of West African States (ECOWAS); Intergovernmental Authority on Development (IGAD); and Southern African Development Community (SADC).

11. African Union, *Protocol Relating to the Establishment of the Peace and Security Council of the African Union*.

12. New Partnership for Africa's Development, "About."

13. Obi, "The AU and the Prevention of Democratic Reversal in Africa."

14. New Partnership for Africa's Development, "Thematic Areas."

15. New Partnership for Africa's Development, "African Peer Review Mechanism."

16. Bah, "People-Centered Liberalism"; Chabal, "The Quest for Good Government and Development in Africa," 447–462; Ukeje, "Rethinking Africa's Security in the Age of Uncertain Globalization."

17. Organization of African Unity, *Lomé Declaration of July 2000*.

18. African Union, *African Charter on Democracy, Elections and Governance*.

19. Bah, "State Decay," 71–89.

20. Organization of African Unity, *Decisions Adopted by the Sixty-Sixth Ordinary Session of the Council of Ministers*.

21. Obi, "The AU and the Prevention of Democratic Reversal in Africa," 80.

22. Akuffo, "The Politics of Interregional Cooperation."

23. Calhoun, *Dictionary of the Social Sciences*.

24. Emirbayer and Mische, "What Is Agency?," 970.

25. NEPAD, "Economic and Corporate Governance."

26. Bah, "People-Centered Liberalism."

27. IMF, *Communiqué of the Interim Committee of the Board of Governors of the International Monetary Fund*.

28. Bah, "People-Centered Liberalism"; Bratton and Van de Walle, *Democratic Experiments in Africa*.

29. African Union, "Mission."

30. Ake, *Democracy and Development in Africa*; Edozie, "Pan-African Security and Pax Africana," 38–59.

31. Ake, *Democracy and Development in Africa*.

32. Bah, "The Contours of New Humanitarianism."

33. Duffield, *Global Governance and the New Wars*; Schümer, *New Humanitarianism*; Bah, "The Contours of New Humanitarianism."

34. Johansen, "Limits and Opportunities in Humanitarian Intervention," 61.

35. ICISS, *The Responsibility to Protect*, 11.

36. Hoffmann, Johansen, Sterba, and Väyrynen, *The Ethics and Politics of Humanitarian Intervention*, 61; Ayoob, "Third World Perspective on Humanitarian Intervention and International Administration," 99–118; Crawford, *Argument and Change in World Politics*.

37. Hoffmann, *The Ethics and Politics of Humanitarian Intervention*; Nardin, "The Moral Basis of Humanitarian Intervention," 57–70; Weiss, *Humanitarian Intervention*.

38. Annan, "Two Concepts of Sovereignty," 49–50; Commission on Human Security, *Human Security Now*.

39. Cohen, *Masses in Flight*; Annan, "Two Concepts of Sovereignty"; ICISS, *The Responsibility to Protect*.

40. Bah, "The Contours of New Humanitarianism."

41. Organization of African Unity, *Charter of the Organization of African Unity*.

42. OAU, *OAU Charter*.

43. AU, *Constitutive Act of the AU*.

44. Ibid.

45. Ibid.

46. Tieku and Hakak, "A Curious Case of Hybrid Paternalism," 129–156; Bah, "The Contours of New Humanitarianism"; Duffield, *Global Governance and the New Wars*.

47. Duffield, *Global Governance and the New Wars*; Bah, "People-Centered Liberalism."

48. African Union, "Our Mandate."

49. Obi, "The AU and the Prevention of Democratic Reversal in Africa"; AU, *African Charter on Democracy*.

50. Emirbayer, "What Is Agency?"

51. Calhoun, *Dictionary of the Social Sciences*.

52. AU, *Protocol*.

53. Ibid.

54. Bolaji, "Adapting Traditional Peacemaking Principles to Contemporary Conflicts," 183–204.

55. African Union, "Panel of the Wise (PoW)."

56. AU, *Protocol*.

57. Ibid.

58. Ibid.

59. African Union, Experts' Meeting on the Relationship between the AU and the Regional Mechanisms for Conflict Prevention, Management and Resolution.

60. Tieku, "A Curious Case of Hybrid Paternalism"; Akuffo, "The Politics of Interregional Cooperation."

61. Cilliers and Malan, "Progress with the African Standby Force."

62. AU, Experts' Meeting.

63. Jentzsch. "Opportunities and Challenges to Financing African Union Peace Operations," 87.

64. European Commission, *African Peace Facility Annual Report 2013*; Akuffo, "The Politics of Interregional Cooperation"; Tieku, "A Curious Case of Hybrid Paternalism."

65. Tieku, "A Curious Case of Hybrid Paternalism," 131.

66. Akuffo, "The Politics of Interregional Cooperation," 109.

References

Abrahamsen, Rita. "A Breeding Ground for Terrorists? Africa & Britain's 'War on Terrorism.'" *Review of African Political Economy* 31, no. 102 (2004): 677–684.

African Union. *African Charter on Democracy, Elections and Governance*. Addis Ababa, ET: January 30, 2007.

———. "Mission." *African Peer Review Mechanism*. http://www.aprm-au.org/mission.

———. *Constitutive Act of the African Union. Adopted by the Thirty-Sixth Ordinary Session of the Assembly of Heads of State and Government*. Lome, TG: July 11, 2000. http://www.au.int/en /sites/default/files/ConstitutiveAct_EN.pdf.

———. "Our Mandate." *Democracy and Electoral Assistance Unit*. http://www.au-elections.org.

———. Experts' Meeting on the Relationship between the AU and the Regional Mechanisms for Conflict Prevention, Management and Resolution. Roadmap for the Operationalization of the African Standby Force. EXP/AU-RECs/ASF/4(I). Addis Ababa, ET, March 22–23, 2005.

———. "Panel of the Wise (PoW)." *African Union Peace and Security*. http://www.peaceau.org/en /page/29-panel-of-the-wise-pow.

———. *Protocol Relating to the Establishment of the Peace and Security Council of the African Union. Adopted by the 1st Ordinary Session of the Assembly of the African Union*. Durban, ZA: July 9, 2002. http://www.au.int/en/sites/default/files/Protocol_peace_and_security.pdf.

Ake, Claude. *Democracy and Development in Africa*. Ibadan, Nigeria: Spectrum Books, 2001.

Akuffo, Edward Ansah. "The Politics of Interregional Cooperation: The Impact of NATO's Intervention in Libya on Its Relations with the African Union." *African Conflict and Peacebuilding Review* 4, no. 2 (2014).

Annan, Kofi. "Two Concepts of Sovereignty." *Economist*, September 16, 1999. http://www .economist.com/node/324795.

Ayoob, Mohammed. "Third World Perspective on Humanitarian Intervention and International Administration." *Global Governance* 10 (2004): 99–118.

Bah, Abu Bakarr. "The Contours of New Humanitarianism: War and Peacebuilding in Sierra Leone." *Africa Today* 60, no. 1 (2013): 2–26.

———. "Democracy and Civil War: Citizenship and Peacemaking in Côte d'Ivoire." *African Affairs* 109, no. 437 (2010): 597–615.

———. "People-Centered Liberalism: An Alternative Approach to International State-Building in Sierra Leone and Liberia." *Critical Sociology* (2015): 1–19. doi:10.1177/0896920515583538. http://crs.sagepub.com/content/early/2015/05/04/0896920515583538.full.pdf+html.

———. "State Decay and Civil War: A Discourse on Power in Sierra Leone." *Critical Sociology* 37, no. 2 (2011): 199–216.

———. "State Decay: A Conceptual Frame of Failing and Failed States in West Africa." *International Journal of Politics, Culture, and Society* 25, no. 1–3 (2012): 71–89.

Bolaji, Kehinde A. "Adapting Traditional Peacemaking Principles to Contemporary Conflicts: The ECOWAS Conflict Prevention Framework." *African Conflict and Peacebuilding Review* 1, no. 2 (2011): 183–204.

Bratton, Michael, and Nicholas Van de Walle. *Democratic Experiments in Africa: Regime Transitions in Comparative Perspective*. Cambridge: Cambridge University Press, 1997.

Calhoun, Craig, ed. *Dictionary of the Social Sciences*. New York: Oxford University Press, 2002.

Chabal, Patrick. "The Quest for Good Government and Development in Africa: Is NEPAD the Answer?" *International Affairs* 78 (July, 2002): 447–462.

Cilliers, Jakkie. "Terrorism and Africa." *African Security Studies* 12, no. 4 (2003): 91–103.

Cilliers, Jakkie, and Mark Malan. "Progress with the African Standby Force." *Institute for Security Studies* 98 (May 2005). http://dspace.cigilibrary.org/jspui/bitstream/123456789/31227/1 /PAPER98.pdf?1.

Cohen, Roberta, and Francis Mading Deng. *Masses in Flight: The Global Crisis of Internal Displacement*. Washington, DC: Brookings Institution Press, 2012.

Commission on Human Security. *Human Security Now*. New York: United Nations, 2003.

Crawford, Neta. *Argument and Change in World Politics: Ethics, Decolonization, and Humanitarian Intervention.* Cambridge: Cambridge University Press, 2002.

Duffield, Mark. *Global Governance and the New Wars: The Merging of Development and Security.* London: Zed Books, 2001.

Edozie, Rita Kiki. "Pan-African Security and Pax Africana: Navigating Global Hierarchies." *African Conflict and Peacebuilding Review* 4, no. 2 (2014): 38–59.

Emirbayer, Mustafa, and Ann Mische. "What Is Agency?" *American Journal of Sociology* 103, no. 4 (1998): 962–1023.

European Commission. *African Peace Facility Annual Report 2013.* http://www.europarl.europa.eu /meetdocs/2014_2019/documents/dpap/dv/apf_web_/apf_web_en.pdf.

Hoffmann, Stanley, Robert C. Johansen, James P. Sterba, and Raimo Väyrynen. *The Ethics and Politics of Humanitarian Intervention.* South Bend, IN: University of Notre Dame Press, 1996.

ICISS. *The Responsibility to Protect: Report of the International Commission on Intervention and State Sovereignty.* Ottawa: International Development Research Centre, 2001.

IMF. *Communiqué of the Interim Committee of the Board of Governors of the International Monetary Fund.* Press Release Number 96/49, September 29, 1996.

Jentzch, Corinna. "Opportunities and Challenges to Financing African Union Peace Operations." *African Conflict and Peacebuilding Review* 4, no. 2 (2014): 86–107.

Johansen, Robert C. "Limits and Opportunities in Humanitarian Intervention." In *The Ethics and Politics of Humanitarian Intervention*, edited by Stanley Hoffmann, Robert C. Johansen, James P. Sterba, and Raimo Väyrynen, 61. South Bend, IN: University of Notre Dame Press, 1996.

Kaldor, Mary. *New and Old Wars: Organised Violence in a Global Era.* Cambridge: Polity, 1999.

Nardin, Terry. "The Moral Basis of Humanitarian Intervention." *Ethics and International Affairs* 16 (2002): 57–70.

New Partnership for Africa's Development. "About." http://www.nepad.org/about.

———. "African Peer Review Mechanism." http://www.nepad.org/economicandcorporate governance/african-peer-review-mechanism/about.

———. "Thematic Areas; Economic and Corporate Governance; Overview." http://www.nepad.org /economicandcorporategovernance.

Obi, Cyril. "The African Union and the Prevention of Democratic Reversal in Africa: Navigating the Gaps." *African Conflict and Peacebuilding Review* 4, no. 2 (2014): 60–85.

Organization of African Unity. *Charter of the Organization of African Unity.* http://www.refworld .org/docid/3ae6b36024.html.

———. *Decisions Adopted by the Sixty-Sixth Ordinary Session of the Council of Ministers*, CM/Dec. 330–363 (LXVI), Harare, ZM, May 28–31, 1997.

———. *Lomé Declaration of July 2000 on the Framework for an OAU Response to Unconstitutional Changes of Government.* http://www2.ohchr.org/english/law/compilation_democracy /lomedec.htm.

Reno, William. *Warlord Politics and African States.* Boulder, CO: Lynne Rienner, 1999.

Schümer, Tanja. *New Humanitarianism: Britain and Sierra Leone, 1997–2003.* New York: Palgrave Macmillan, 2008.

Tieku, Thomas Kwasi, and Tanzeel F. Hakak. "A Curious Case of Hybrid Paternalism: Conceptualizing the Relationship between the UN and AU on Peace and Security." *African Conflict and Peacebuilding Review* 4, no. 2 (2014): 129–156.

Ukeje, Charles. "Rethinking Africa's Security in the Age of Uncertain Globalisation: NEPAD and Human Security in the 21st Century." Paper submitted to the 11th CODESRIA General Assembly, Maputo, Mozambique, 6–10 December, 2005. http://www.codesria.org/IMG/pdf /ukeje.pdf.

UN. "2005 World Summit Outcome." Resolution adopted by the General Assembly 60/1. 2005, Sixtieth session Agenda items 46 and 120, October 24, 2005.

Weiss, Thomas. *Humanitarian Intervention: Ideas in Action.* Cambridge: Polity Press, 2007.

7 Regime Change

Neoliberal State Building and Its Collapse on Iraqi Society

Deniz Gökalp

Colonies must be obtained or planted, in order that no useful corner of the world may be overlooked or left unused.

Woodrow Wilson, cited in William Loren Katz

We will actively work to bring the hope of democracy, development, free markets, and free trade to every corner of the world.

George W. Bush, *The National Security Strategy of the United States of America*

A liberated Iraq can show the power of freedom to transform that vital region, by bringing hope and progress into the lives of millions

George W. Bush, the *Guardian*

THE SCHOLARSHIP ON modern state building has been founded on the works of the classical names that focused on the emergence of the Western liberal democratic nation-states.[1] Since then, social scientists have explored the spread of the European state as the dominant and legitimate state model around the world through the rise of an international system based on imperialism and colonial expansions. The scholarship has presented enough evidence demonstrating how different the histories of the Western states are from each other (i.e., a standard state model doesn't exist) and how challenging it is to replicate the Western experiences with the state building in the context of the Arab Middle East.[2] However, there is not a coherent sociological literature on state building in the Arab Middle East with a critical articulation of the impact of foreign interventions on the processes of state building and the disruptions and reconstructions of those processes at the expense of people and societies. One important historical factor determining the trajectory of modern state building everywhere is the legacy of colonialism, though each society has inherited a different set of assets or liabilities depending on their status in colonial relations. The Netherlands, a country poor in natural resources, financed its state-building process for centuries with assets expropriated from the colonies. In contrast, Iraq, a country rich in natural resources, suffered, even after independence from the United Kingdom, the consequences of the direct and indirect British control that legalized theft of its natural resources essential to financing the state building and national consolidation of state institutions.

European colonizers demarcated the international borders in the Arab Middle East and gained militarized control in the region, brutally oppressing local anti-imperialist resistance.[3] However, as opposed to the stereotypes about Middle Eastern states as artificial entities and the Middle East as a geography where there has never been a culture of democracy, modern state, and civil society, most Middle Eastern countries have had histories of ethnosectarian tolerance, dynamic political cultures, and diverse civil associations and political parties. Two of the most troubled Middle Eastern countries today, Iraq and Syria, managed to build modern state institutions and even experimented with democracy after independence from their European colonizers.[4] Based on the same logic of artificiality, one of the most artificial nation-states in the Middle East would be Israel. Indeed, the impossibility of replicating the Western models of state building in the Arab Middle East has had less to do with the innate differences in social, cultural, and political structures and more to do with complex repercussions that international interventions (colonial occupations, mandate agreements, economic sanctions and/or direct control of economic resources, foreign-supported military coups, crippling the attempts to practice democracy, etc.) introduced into the processes of state building since the collapse of the Ottoman Empire. Iraq has been through all kinds of foreign intrusion since the 1920s.[5]

The British never gave up on influencing the domestic politics in Iraq to control the army, land, resources, and foreign relations and never trusted that the people of Iraq could govern the Iraqi state whose borders had been manipulated for the British interests.[6] However, it has also been surprisingly challenging for the United Kingdom, and later the United States, to dominate Iraqi politics and control its oil given the anti-imperialist resistance of the Arab nationalists, communists, and pan-Arabists, as well as the consolidation of the stubborn Ba'ath regime after the 1970s. The Ba'ath party government under Saddam Hussein would soon start acting recklessly to pursue a madcap political agenda across Iraq's internationally recognized borders, attacking the territories of other sovereign states and engaging in politics that undermined the national interests of the foreign powers in the oil-rich Arabian Gulf. According to William Polk, the

Ba'ath regime headed by Saddam Hussein had done things that only states like the United States, United Kingdom, or Israel could get away with: mass murder, assassination of dissidents, and invasion of other people's lands.[7] Ironically enough, it was the foreign creditors, including the members of the G-8 and the Paris Club, that provided Saddam Hussein with generous "odious" loans that he used to finance his war against Iran and "activities that, often to the lenders' knowledge were against the interests of the Iraqi people."[8]

An important strand of recent research highlights the legacy of British colonialism to explain the state failure in Iraq and/or propose scenarios regarding the future of Iraq after the 2003 invasion. Toby Dodge provides an analysis of the British mandatory period in Iraq, and he holds the incompetent British policy toward Iraq during the early stages of the state-building process and British ignorance about Iraqi society responsible for the creation of structural deficiencies within Iraqi state institutions and the consolidation of tribal hierarchies in Iraqi society. Saddam Hussein employed strategies similar to those of the earlier British rule to control and manipulate ethnic, social, and class divides in Iraq, especially during the 1990s when there were harsh United Nation (UN) sanctions on Iraq that caused economic crisis, large-scale impoverishment, and popular contention in the country.[9] Consequently, Iraqi state institutions became weak and corrupt during the 1990s. Finally, US neoliberal reconstruction efforts, unable to save the Iraqi state from a complete collapse, have resulted in the rise of authoritarianism. The precarious state system that was hastily designed by Americans based on false neoliberal and neoconservative ideological assumptions has started to be abused by despotic Iraqi politicians like the former prime minister Nouri al-Maliki through informal networks of family, tribe, patronage, coercion, and corruption.[10]

In their highly debatable book published a year after the invasion in 2004, Liam Anderson and Gareth Stansfield argue that it was impossible to keep Iraq in unity after the occupation, given its highly politicized culture based on ethnic and sectarian divisions that were products of social manipulations and the arbitrary use of violence during the British mandatory period. Assuming that ethnic and sectarian identities corresponded to irreconcilable political divisions and neglecting the complex articulation of those identities in social, political, and geographical terms in Iraq, Anderson and Stansfield propose a policy agenda defending an immediate "managed partition" of Iraq before the country falls into a bloody civil war.[11] Their prediction of a sectarian bloodshed unless a peaceful managed partition was implemented has turned into a self-fulfilling prophecy under the ill-managed US-led political agenda based on the assumption that the *muhassasa* system (ethnosectarian power sharing in the government) was the only legitimate and reasonable political option for Iraq.

Though there is useful sociological research on Latin America, Africa, and Central Asia, we have to mainly rely on historians, political scientists, and anthropologists to make sense of the legacy of colonialism and imperialism as well as their new forms of disruptions and destructions in the aftermath of the Cold War in the Middle East. Inspired by Georgi Derluguian's groundbreaking sociological analysis on the Caucasus, this chapter contends that market globalization and neoliberal penetration have turned into a "major structural condition for the perpetuation of ethnic [and sectarian] conflicts" in Iraq as a direct result of the crumbling of state structures and authority during the occupation.[12] As Derluguian points out, "The anger of threatened and dispossessed groups . . . [has turned] towards competing groups."[13] Derluguian uses the Weberian notion of neopatrimonialism to define the privatization of state offices and corrupt patronage practices based on mafia-style familial social relations during and after the collapse of communism and transition to democracy. He states that "occasional bouts of political violence . . . occur mainly in the form of mafia-style assassinations and rebellions by subordinate or threatened neopatrimonial 'clans' and communities of patronage."[14] He further argues:

> Just as the CIA in the eighties helped to create in Afghanistan and across the Middle East new fundamentalist movements and clandestine networks that soon acquired an autonomous dynamic, the inchoate and violent political struggles in Chechnya of the nineties gave rise to a public religious discourse which often had unexpected ramifications. In the language of sociology, this added a new layer of causality to contemporary processes. But religion did not become a potent force in itself—to claim that would be a reification, as if religion were indeed a self-propellant phenomenon. Rather, Islam became a means of political and moral legitimation, a channel to the resources of Middle Eastern political circles, and the source of a discourse that gradually replaced a discredited nationalism. If religion became a hotly contested field, it was because different personalities and the armed formations behind them now claimed Islam for their own purposes.[15]

Guillermo O'Donnell uses the term *brown areas* as a metaphor to define the neofeudalized regions beset with chronic violence in the Latin America where "ineffective states coexist with autonomous, also territorially based, spheres of power. States become ostensibly unable to enact effective regulations of social life across their territories and their stratification systems. Provinces or districts peripheral to the national center . . . create (or reinforce) systems of local power which tend to reach extremes of violent, personalistic rule—patrimonial, even sultanistic—open to all sorts of violent and arbitrary practices."[16] Accordingly, in a country like Iraq where the state apparatus alongside the army and public institutions was dismantled to exterminate the old regime and impose a crude neoliberal ideology through a military invasion, violence tends to erupt because of the vacuum of the state authority and public institutions.

Highlighting the complications associated with the internationally designed and implemented efforts of state building and democracy promotion in Iraq, Medani argues that "the U.S. invasion and occupation has given rise to a 'state-building' process that is in the reverse of the process by which modern states were built. In particular, the present pattern of corruption, clientelism and rent seeking has led to a simultaneous erosion of the tax revenue base and political legitimacy."[17] Iraq has been turned into a tax haven for foreign investment with one of the most favorable tax laws in the world. The new Iraqi state is not only institutionally incompetent to ensure security and rule of law, and assert its legitimacy domestically and internationally, but it is also incapable of overseeing the economy and collecting taxes in the face of neoliberal encroachment over the laws and institutions. This lack of capacity to oversee and regulate economic activities is even worse in the case of informal activities of international, regional, and local entrepreneurs operating in Iraq. Medani argues:

> Absent formal bureaucratic and military institutions, in Iraq, as in other failed and collapsed states, violence substitutes for formal political mobilization. Under U.S. occupation, however, violence is mainly directed against civil authorities and civilians and not the occupying army. The aim is similar to violence associated with state-building efforts elsewhere—to capture territory through political control . . . and to eliminate or expel foreign as well as domestic political rivals. That this violence is increasingly based on regional or religious identities is primarily because this offers a sense of security in a context where formal ideologies are absent, and unregulated markets require social regulation.[18]

This chapter aims to contribute to the scholarly and policy discourse on state failure, social collapse, and political violence in the face of neoliberal reconstruction through military occupation. It addresses the postinvasion state-building process in Iraq, arguing that the so-called state-building process is a series of misguided international efforts based on a crude neoliberal ideology to regulate the war(s) in Iraq, as well as to normalize the tragic impact on Iraqi society of the complete dismantling of the Iraqi state and state institutions. The research is based on fieldwork conducted in northern Iraq in 2014. Meetings with government officials, representatives of UN entities, activists, academics, journalists, and students were held in Erbil and Sulaymaniyah in January, May, and June of 2014. In addition, observational data regarding urban transformation, social diversity, economic change, population displacement, social inequalities, and contentious politics were collected. Due to security issues, traveling to Baghdad was not an option, and the interviews with Baghdad-based individuals were conducted in Erbil through Skype.[19]

From State Building to Breakdown

The American invasion of Iraq in 2003 was a war against the Iraqi state. The invasion crushed Iraqi social and political institutions, as well as the Iraqi army, to smithereens and created a huge vacuum of power and insecurity, leaving the civilian Iraqis at the mercy of various militant groups and radical movements. The Iraqi state was indeed quite resilient and managed to survive an eight-year-long war with Iran in the 1980s, the Gulf War in 1991, and thirteen years of international embargo in the 1990s without turning into a failed state. Iraq was an independent sovereign state with full-fledged modern institutions, ruled by an oppressive authoritarian party (i.e., Ba'ath) government until its social and economic infrastructure was destroyed by the US-pushed UN sanctions to weaken the Iraqi state in the 1990s.[20] Not surprisingly, Iraq was among the rogue states identified by President George W. Bush in *The National Security Strategy of the United States* (2002) because it was an anomaly of decolonization like the other rogue states.[21]

Rogue states are anarchical or "states that simply refused to be coerced."[22] The invasion of Iraq in 2003 was a continuation of what was left unfinished in Iraq by the end of the Gulf War in 1991: regime change. Regime change is part of the global trend of neoliberal reconstruction and disciplining of the divergent states of former colonies, such as Iraq, Somalia, Yemen, former Yugoslavia, and Afghanistan. In Anna Agathangelou's words: "Beginning with a series of reconstruction wars in Europe (i.e. Yugoslavia) and then the Gulf War in 1991, we have seen the unleashing of armies . . . on those 'anarchical' sites and sovereigns, ecologies and bodies to secure infinite access . . . to oil, people and the whole of Asia itself."[23]

The implications of regime change in former Yugoslavia in the 1990s, for instance, had been disastrous (and in Europe as a whole because political violence always spills over national borders as asylum seekers, victims of war, trafficked humans, etc.), and one would expect the powerful global actors to have learned lessons from the tragic consequences of the externally imposed neoliberal reconstruction of the states in Eastern Europe and Central Asia. Indeed, based on Bush's and Condoleezza Rice's earlier statements against using US troops for state building, the invasion of Iraq had been perceived by observers as a venture with "a heritage in over 20 years of neoliberal policy towards the post-colonial world" that "was born of the Washington consensus developed in the 1980s" but was "a limited exercise in regime change and then state reform" rather than an adventure aiming at the annihilation of the Iraqi state.[24]

Though there were originally conflicting views in Washington regarding what kind of role to play in the reconstruction of the new Iraq after the invasion, the one requiring the most radical agenda, a deeply invasive neoliberal intrusion into the Iraqi state and society, came to dominate the nature of the United States involvement in Iraq starting from the early months of the invasion.[25] The neoliberal reconstruction imposed on Iraq, and also intended to be carried on in the rest of the Middle East in the near future, was by no means limited to the sphere of the economy. Borrowing from Wendy Brown, "in order to comprehend neoliberalism's political and cultural effects, it must be conceived of as more than a set of free market economic policies that dismantle welfare states and privatize public services in the North, make wreckage of efforts at democratic sovereignty or economic self-direction in the South, and intensify income disparities everywhere. Certainly neoliberalism comprises these effects, but as a political rationality, it also involves a specific and consequential organization of the social, the subject, and the state."[26] As also observed by Agathangelou, "U.S. neoliberalism as proposed by Milton Freedman and the Chicago School values 'creative destruction' and rejects the separation of social and economic activity."[27] In the same vein, the complete dismantling of the political, social, and military structures shortly after the invasion due to the United States' distrust of the institutions of the Ba'ath regime as well as the Iraqis within these structures revealed a much more comprehensive neoconservative agenda beyond a limited reform program.

The dominant view about Iraqis in Washington circles was based on an orientalist assumption that had its roots in the British imperial bigotry toward Iraq in the 1920s. Upon the withdrawal of the Ottoman administration from Iraq following World War I, the British expected Iraqis to be docile and grateful to the United Kingdom and to agree with the oppressive and exploitative terms of the British mandatory agenda that would include the installation of a non-Iraqi royal family (Hashimite dynasty originally from Mecca) as the head of the state. In opposition to the orientalist reading of Iraqi society by the British, Iraqis demonstrated decisive, and often unified, anti-imperialist resistance until the revolution of 1958. The Americans had a similar false expectation of appreciation from Iraqis for destroying everything that was associated with the earlier regime and turning them into liberated subjects of American entrepreneurship. Just as the British imperialists, Americans presumed that "the Iraqi population would welcome an American presence and be hungry for all that the U.S. could bring to Iraq."[28]

During the three years following the US-led invasion, and right after the circus-like 2005 elections staged for the international public, it was clear that Iraq was on the verge of becoming a failed state. Embodied in the defunct Greater Middle East Initiative (GMEI), the Washington circles had a misguided neoimperialist and neoliberal expectation that "Iraq would be the start of a much larger project to restructure the Middle East. A democratic, liberal and capitalist Iraqi republic would, by its example, serve as a catalyst for the dramatic reshaping of politics across the region."[29] Instead, Iraq has become the prime example of a social, economic, political, and humanitarian disaster created by the internationally sponsored regime change and state reconstruction efforts in the era of military neoliberalism.

Rebuilding Iraq and Redesigning Social Hierarchies: Beyond Ethnosectarian Enmities

There are various arguments regarding the actual aims of the United States for declaring war on Iraq, including, among many others, the ones highlighting the United States' ambitions to create a pro-American (and pro-Israeli) regime in Iraq as a bulwark against the much-hated regional enemy (i.e., Iran), to enhance the scope of its influence in the oil-rich Arabian Gulf against the growing economic power of China in the world, and to restructure Iraqi economy as a free market tax haven for foreign businesses. The radical agenda initiated by Paul Bremer and embraced by the American administration required the destruction of the older state institutions, including the Iraqi army and public institutions associated with the former Ba'ath regime, and the restructuring of the entire Iraqi state from scratch to achieve the United States' aims that are still disputed more than a decade after the invasion. Other than turning Iraq into an open market for corporate pillaging of the Iraqi national assets that the neoconservatives in the United States administration had aspired to since the 1990s, none of the other goals mentioned by United States policy makers (i.e., building a democratic, liberal, prosperous Iraq; eradicating terrorism in the world; making the world a safer place, etc.) has been achieved yet. Peter Galbraith, an American diplomat who has been a fervent supporter of the war on Iraq and a beneficiary of Iraqi oil owing to his special relationship with the Iraqi Kurdish leadership, expressed his frustration with the handling of the so-called state building by the American administration as follows:

> I never imagined that the Bush administration would manage the post-invasion period as incompetently as it did. I never thought that we would enter Baghdad without a plan to secure any of the city's public institutions. I never imagined that the administration would assume it had no responsibility for law and order. I never imagined that the Bush administration would turn the management of the occupation over to political cronies while pushing aside qualified professionals. I never thought that the administration would have been unable to spend any significant part of the reconstruction funds for a full 18 months after taking over the country. I had grave doubts about the extraordinary breadth of the Pentagon's ambition in the early period when they were talking about a Germany or Japan-type occupation in which we make Iraq into a model democracy. If we had managed the post war with a coherent strategy and a modicum of competence, I don't think we would be in the mess that we are in now.[30]

The irony of the postinvasion era in Iraq is twofold. First, US policy makers dismantled the Iraqi state completely and in distrust paralyzed the sectors of Iraqi society that were willing to work for reconstruction. However, United States policy makers were not ready for (or were not interested in or did not know how to administer) state building in the way sociological studies would suggest.[31] Second, the so-called reforms and laws in the name of state building were indicating a systematic "state-building in reverse."[32] The process of destruction of the Iraqi state and its precarious reconstruction under the supervision of the Americans and the United Nations Assistance Mission in Iraq (UNAMI) has been indeed quite consistent in itself and exactly in line with neoliberal aspirations. Despite the increased necessity for security domestically and at the borders of the country after the fall of the Ba'ath regime, the Iraqi army has been reduced to a small, private, and ineffective army in the name of strengthening civilian control over politics, when in fact American security concerns had priority over the security of civilian Iraqis. The Iraqi army has been privatized as generals became investors and corruption became institutionalized through the first efforts of the Americans to weaken the Iraqi army on the grounds to empower civilian authority.[33]

After the fall of the Ba'ath regime, about 450,000 public-sector employees were expelled from their jobs in the name of creating a more efficient and smaller public sector when, in fact, the expulsions were a part of the efforts to exterminate the old regime and privatize the public offices and institutions in the name of liberalism without any regard to social repercussions. This action ended up causing a drastic increase in unemployment, the collapse of the state infrastructure and public sector, and frustration with the occupation even among the Iraqis who had welcome the Americans. Millions of Iraqis have been affected by unemployment and denied participation in the so-called state building and internationally designed reconstruction. They have been relegated to the margins of the society to reinvent new livelihoods, social identities, and political affiliations. According to conservative statistics, the unemployment rate increased to 60 percent after the invasion in 2003, and women have been affected disproportionately as they were more likely to be employed in the public sector destroyed by the American reforms. Also, religious groups, sectarian associations, and conservative political parties started gaining constituency among the dispossessed Iraqis at the expense of forming nonpartisan allegiances and secular trust relations in the newly emerging Iraqi civil society organizations and state institutions.[34] It is not surprising that sectarianism, conservatism, and Islamist radicalism started to dominate mainstream politics and society in Arab and Kurdish Iraq since 2003. In the words of Nadje Al-Ali and Nicola Pratt, "The reconstruction process has undermined capacity building within Iraqi institutions and has enabled the spread of corruption. Meanwhile, the failure of the reconstruction process has fueled violence, the spread of conservative social agendas, and the rise of Islamist parties—all with negative consequences for women."[35] Millions of dollars and significant international expertise have been channeled to create an NGO culture in the name of capacity building for civil society when, in fact, millions of unemployed public sector professionals, workers, peasants, displaced families, homeless, disabled, and other victims of structural violence (i.e., the majority of Iraqi society) have been systematically prevented from organizing independently outside the highly depoliticized NGO sector disconnected from the social realities of the masses.[36]

The American invasion has been the final stage of an internationally organized crime against the people of Iraq following the imposition of the UN sanctions throughout the 1990s that created a humanitarian disaster with tragic consequences for the most vulnerable sectors of Iraqi society.[37] According to the most conservative statistics, hundreds of thousands of Iraqis have been killed by the coalition forces in Iraq, millions of Iraqis have died because of war-related causes, and more than four million Iraqis have been displaced internally and internationally; while the casualties of the foreign nations have been recorded diligently, Iraqi casualties are always estimates.[38] Iraqis internally displaced have mostly sought refuge in Iraqi Kurdistan, reminding the Kurds in their regional safe haven that there is political upheaval in Iraq that they are still a part of, and encouraging the opportunistic Kurdish regional government to pursue aggressive demographic engineering in multiethnic provinces under *peshmerga* (Kurdish armed forces in Iraqi Kurdistan) control, given the obvious incapacities of the central government in Baghdad.[39]

The United States government has not been the only actor assuming the role of restructuring and rebuilding Iraq. On September 16, 2004, former UN secretary-general Kofi Annan told the BBC that the Anglo-American invasion of Iraq was illegal by international law. Despite that kind of awareness at the top of the UN about the illegality of the invasion, the occupation has been repackaged by the international community as reconstruction and state building in postconflict Iraq. While the country was being bombed to dust with drone attacks—and this was just the beginning—a supposedly postconflict era had already been opened in rhetoric. It was to be governed by the US-led international actors, and dependable Iraqis were also needed to build a New Iraq from scratch in this so-called postconflict period. About a month after the invasion, on April 21–22, 2003, the Woodrow Wilson International Center for Scholars and the Women Waging Peace Network sponsored by Hunt Alternative Fund organized a forum titled "Winning the Peace: Women's Role in Post-Conflict Iraq" in Washington. The majority of the participants were expatriate Iraqi women (Arab and Kurdish) living in the United States, prominent Kurdish women from the Kurdistan Regional Government (KRG), and women representatives of ethnic and religious minorities of Iraq. Their common denominator was their dislike of the previous

Ba'ath regime, which was the most important characteristic for the organizers of the conference. Indeed, the Iraqi participants had complex constellations of experiences associated with their social class, tribal and political affiliations, ideological stance, and education that the organizers were unlikely to make sense of without proper knowledge about Iraqi history, society, and politics. That would be one of the most critical shortcomings of the foreigners engaged in rebuilding the Iraqi state and society after the occupation: a commitment to identify the pro-American Iraqi friends to work with while being ignorant about the complex histories and identities of those people. In their book *What Kind of Liberation?*, Al-Ali and Pratt conclude, "Indeed our research suggests that the rhetoric was not really about empowering Iraqi women. Instead, Iraqi women represented the objects of a U.S. mission to restore its seriously tarnished superpower identity in the wake of 9/11. The postinvasion reconstruction process has been framed by the trope of 'white men saving brown women from brown men', and this rhetoric has shaped the decisions that have shaped the reality of women's lives in Iraq. Given that the priority of the invasion was U.S. national security, it is unsurprising that the security of ordinary Iraqis was an afterthought."[40]

Against the backdrop of chaos, insecurity, killings, and displacements, hundreds of Iraqi exiles, who had left Iraq during the Ba'ath regime to reside in Western countries, have come back to Iraq to help rebuild their home country under the supervision of US-led international actors. One of them, Iraqi British, expresses her identity crisis in Iraq in her blog as follows: "I realised that no matter how much I try to be one of 'them' I will always be seen as an outsider. . . . Im considered a non Iraqi by my Iraqi colleagues, and am considered a third country national by my U.S. colleagues. . . . Hallelujah. Arent I just lucky. . . . Call me an Alien while youre at it why dont you. So as for now, am an alien, Im a legal alien, am an Iraqi-Brit walking in the Green Zone."[41]

The idea was to involve various international actors in reconstructing Iraqi institutions from scratch, which would include helping Iraqis write a new constitution, reform (i.e., privatize) the security sector, make private contracts with foreign companies to advise Iraqis about how to exploit the national assets for profit, defend human rights against state oppression and women's rights against backward patriarchal Middle Eastern culture, build capacity for civil society, and create free and independent Iraqi media. To this end, for example, the American, German, and Italian governments started providing funds and special training courses to educate Iraqis to work for the new Iraqi media supposedly, to give Iraqi society an independent voice.[42] While the United States has wasted large sums of money to train local pro-American journalists who would cover the elections as part of the democracy show, Germany has taken a less politically motivated stance and provided more systematic and professional support to Iraqi journalists to organize themselves independently.[43] The involvement of various governments and intergovernmental and nongovernmental organizations as well as some formerly exiled Iraqis in the so-called reconstruction process would legitimize the illegal occupation of Iraq and make it look more international than merely American domination. Eligible Iraqis, namely pro-Western, modern, and preferably former exiles, have become students to be educated about how to govern the new Iraq and apprentices watching their masters until they learn how to do things on their own.

When the Iraqi Interim Government (2004–2005) was established to replace the Iraqi Governing Council (2003–2004), its capacity to govern was curtailed to the extent that it was basically unable to govern. In Polk's words, "The power of the new government was to be sharply limited—its armed forces would remain under operational control of the American military; its finances would similarly be overseen by American officials; it would have no authority to amend edicts from the American occupation or even enact new laws; and its key ministries would be dominated by American appointed commissions."[44] The British colonizers in the 1920s did not trust the Iraqis and brought to Iraq Indians to run their mandatory institutions. Similarly, Americans invited exiled Iraqis to work with them to rebuild Iraq after the invasion but have never trusted even those friendly collaborators. A pro-occupation Iraqi exile, Haider Al-Abadi, prime minister since 2014, returned from abroad to work as a minister in the Iraqi Interim Government, expressed his frustration with American distrust in Iraqi decision makers: "If it's a sovereign Iraqi government that can't change laws or make decisions, we haven't gained anything."[45] As a matter of fact, Americans have not had any intention to transfer authority to Iraqis until, they would insist, the Iraqi state was rebuilt as a functioning democracy with its political institutions and ready to be handed over to the Iraqis trusted by the United States.[46] This implies certain processes that would undermine the possibility of any genuine social consensus to the international state building led by the United States in Iraq. Iraqis, both pro-occupation and dissenters, would have no say in the US-dominated politics of the so-called state building that has actually been misguided and failed as expected.

Also, a completely brand new enmity would be introduced to Iraqi society between the Iraqis working with or within the Green Zone (i.e., the international zone in Baghdad housing the foreigners and political and economic entrepreneurs) and the Iraqis left outside of the barbwire heavily armed gates of the Green Zone. Distrust of Americans toward Iraqis has resulted in discriminatory—and often brutal, especially during the early stages of the occupation—attitudes and practices toward the Iraqis who were locally based in Iraq during the Ba'ath regime. The Iraqis who returned from exile after the occupation have been considered anti-Saddam and pro-occupation and favored as associates by the Americans and other foreigners in the country. In turn, a set of complex hierarchies has been introduced by the occupation between the Iraqis formerly exiled in Western countries who were considered as pro-Western, therefore reliable, and the Iraqis formerly exiled in Middle Eastern countries, who were considered as potentially suspicious due to their regional political affiliations. All exile groups, however, were still preferred to the Iraqis who were based in Iraq before the invasion; and the US-funded political parties of Iraqi returnees would be favored over the parties formed by those who had not left Iraq during the Ba'ath regime. A new kind of social division has been created between the Iraqis marginalized by the international actors in charge of rebuilding the new Iraq and the Iraqis incorporated within the so-called state-building and reconstruction process. The United States and the international community in Iraq have concentrated on the electoral politics in the name of democracy and dismantled or ignored the public sector in line with neoliberal thinking.

Most Iraqis, especially in central and southern Iraq, have been urgently in need of security, basic services, and jobs since the first days of the occupation. These war-affected poverty-stricken Iraqis (at least one million of them are currently displaced within Iraq, concentrated in the Kurdistan region of Iraq) have been socially and economically obsolete (i.e., masses in need of humanitarian aid and charity) according to the neoliberal mentality dominant among the international policy makers, if not threats (i.e., potential terrorists) according to the national security interests of the United States. They may be relevant to the post-invasion Iraq only as voters at the ballot boxes, who are necessary to legitimize the presumably democratic new Iraq created by the US-led international community. Nonetheless, a small privileged group of Iraqis have been incorporated into the international agendas of ethnosectarian party politics, private entrepreneurship, and NGO creation. This kind of a division between the Iraqis in the Green Zone (as much a metaphor as a physical separation) and outside it is not about ethnosectarian factions, but about Iraqis' affiliation (or lack of it thereof) with the international actors and foreign businesses operating in Iraq.

The End of Civil Society: Silencing Iraqis

Neoliberal mentality has not been limited to the dismantling of the state and public sector. It has also been dominant in shaping civil society in the new Iraq and redesigning its relationship with the state. Opposition was severely suppressed, and independent civil organizing was not allowed in Iraq during the Ba'ath regime. Trade unions and syndicates were organized by the regime, and therefore under the close scrutiny of the state security apparatus. The media were state-controlled as well. Social grievances against the regime, however, were reduced by the benefits provided by a versatile welfare state that was kept intact until the economy was destroyed by the fiscal crisis and failed economic reforms (i.e., privatization and state capitalism) in the late 1980s and the infamous UN sanctions and international embargo imposed on Iraq throughout the 1990s. There were no NGOs or INGOs operating in Iraq until 2003, with the exception of Iraqi Kurdistan, where the international governmental and nongovernmental organizations started to operate as humanitarian agencies after the Baghdad government lost its control of the region to the Americans in 1991.

In line with the postconflict rhetoric, an international agenda that was earlier used in postconflict Yugoslavia, Rwanda, and Cambodia was introduced "to form independent and professional media organizations." The Iraqi Ministry of Information was dissolved and the Coalition Provisional Authority (CPA) took over the control of the Iraqi media as well as the country. The Rapid Reaction Media Team (RRMT) had been formed before the invasion in 2003 to later form the Iraqi Media Network (IMN) under the CPA authority. The CPA issued Order 314 on June 10, 2003, under the title "Prohibited Media Activity" to prevent the broadcast and publication of news and materials that "incites violence against any individual or group, including racial, ethnic or religious groups and women; incites civil disorders, rioting or damage to property; incites violence against Coalition Forces or CPA personnel." The order was solely used to exterminate opposition and dissidence against the CPA.[47] Sawt Baghdad (Voice of Baghdad-Radio Station), *Sada al-Uma* (The nation's echo, a newspaper), *Al-Hawza al-Natiqa al-Sharifa*, and *Al-Mustaqila* (independent newspaper) were among the media silenced by the CPA because they were critical of the United States invasion and presence in Iraq. US-trained Iraqi media teams, pro-American Iraqi exiles, were hand selected to work for the IMN to run newspapers and "plant storyboards" favorable to the Americans and American invasion, and they were paid good amounts of money on a monthly basis.[48] In line with the muhassasa system imposed on the Iraqi political scene, a divided Iraqi media was engineered based on sectarianism. According to Ahmed Al-Rawi, sectarian divisions were introduced and systematically consolidated in creating the so-called independent Iraqi media that would represent the Shi'i, Sunni, and Kurdish public in the country.[49]

The activities of the IMN to restructure the Iraqi media have been in compliance with the liberal democracy model with a focus on marketization, professionalism, and journalistic autonomy.[50] The so-called ideals of the model have also been applied to the capacity-building efforts in civil society formation in Iraq by the foreign actors since 2003. The impacts of the US-led international occupation on Iraqi society and the role of the international community in (re) designing the state-society relations in Iraq have demonstrated strong neoliberal elements. In many ways, the international actors have reduced civil society building to NGO creation through funding and programs focusing on training, capacity building, and raising awareness about the merits of elections, human rights, and private entrepreneurship. The most conspicuous orientalist assumptions embedded in the discourses of international actors are that Iraqis (1) lack awareness about the merits of universal rights and liberties, (2) lack the knowledge and skills necessary for public participation, (3) must be trained by the internationals to be full-fledged participants of civil society (i.e., NGOs), and that (4) grassroots organizations do not comply with Western standards and therefore must be helped by the internationals to build capacity before they are considered legitimate civil society organizations (i.e., NGOs). An equally salient assumption driving the international efforts in their engagement with Iraqi society is that "private entrepreneurship [i]s a pillar of democracy," which has been criticized by scholars as part of soft occupation efforts to mold Iraqi society based on neoliberal economic disciplining.[51] In the same vein, Al-Ali and Pratt point out, "From our research, we would agree that the U.S. administration seeks to shape Iraqi civil society organizations in support of its foreign policy objectives and that foreign funding has sometimes undermined the building of sustainable Iraqi organizations."[52]

Neoliberal encroachment over the (re)formulated social and political institutions has a direct impact on the public sphere, public discourse, and civil society. In post-2003 Iraq, a depoliticized NGO culture has been created by the international community led by the United States and UN. NGOs have been privileged over other types of civil society organizations and institutionally separated from them through legal reforms. The institutionalized division between NGOs and other civil society organizations has contributed to the marginalization and subjugation of various other sectors of Iraqi society including trade unions, syndicates, professional associations, local voluntary organizations, and ad-hoc self-help grassroots groups. Local NGOs, promoted by their international partners and foreign governments, have been promoted among the local population as important agents of democracy and human rights. One local UN employee, Farah S., expresses her frustration with the American Research Triangle Institute (RTT) and American Development Foundation (ADF) as follows: "International organizations treat the locals like school children who should be trained on 'democracy' and 'human rights'. Their agendas are rhetorical . . . they do not have the capacity to implement. . . . We do not want to hear anything else about democracy and human rights anymore. People need to see action and implementation; when it comes to how to have democracy and practice human rights [in conflict zones] internationals are clueless. . . . [Policy recommendations are] completely out of context and out of touch with reality."[53]

The RTT and ADF, which Farah worked for during the first years of the occupation, came to Iraq as contractors with million-dollar deals ($167.9 million for the RTT) to "initiate democratic dialog" in towns and rural areas. Farah and extant studies see this as a futile effort.[54] The UN has been, however, engaged in more long-term programs and projects, and many professional Iraqis in search for jobs and hoping to see improvement in the circumstances of their people have been willing to work for this organization despite Iraq's painful history with the cruel UN-sanctioned embargo on Iraq in the 1990s. The UN, through establishment of UNAMI and UN Country Team (UNCT), has been the most active international agent in "advancing political dialogue and national reconciliation, assisting in the electoral process . . . and promoting the protection of human rights and judicial and legal reform" in Iraq since 2003.[55] Foreign governments led by United States have also been involved in capacity building for the NGO sector, training for civil society about human and women rights, and institutional reform for democracy. Other participating countries include the United Kingdom, Germany, Norway, and Italy, though some of them have been substantially less active in institution building in Iraq than they have been in Afghanistan. Finally, INGOs, such as the International Center for Not-for-Profit Law (ICNL), have had close relations with the United States State Department and the UN in preparing laws specifically accommodating the NGO sector in Iraq.

Iraq was originally thought of as an experimental case for restructuring the state and its relationship with the society in the Greater Middle East. The invasion of Iraq was not only about Iraq, but arguably the first step in reconfiguring the state-society relations in the region.[56] In line with this original plan, the drafting of a brand-new NGO law was undertaken by the UN Office for Project Services (UNOPS) immediately after the invasion in 2003. UNOPS has partnership with United States agencies, the State Department, and the EU and cooperated with the ICNL and the European Center for Non-Profit Law (ECNL) to draft the new NGO law.[57] The new NGO law was approved by the Iraqi Council of Representatives and the Kurdistan Regional Government in 2010 and 2013 respectively. As the ECNL stated in 2012, "The compact is the first of its kind in the Middle East and is the result of a year of discussions and consultations. It will institutionalize the relationship between public authorities and NGOs and outline the values and principles governing their relationship as well as the mutual responsibilities of the parties." UNOPS and its local partners proudly characterize the new NGO law as the "first and best compact" between parliament, government, and NGOs in the Middle East and argue that it has been designed to open a space free from tiring bureaucracy and unnecessary state surveillance for INGOs and NGOs operating in Iraq. More importantly, as explained by Dana Sofi, "the compact firmly recognizes NGOs as partners to public institutions with an important role to complement the work of the public sector."[58]

In an interview with a Baghdad-based UNOPS representative working for the Civil Society and Reconciliation Programme, the respondent highlighted the importance of civil society training and capacity building and the need to embrace Iraqis from different ethnosectarian groups, expose them to each other, and enable them to develop working relations together.[59] It is ironic that the UN assumes the responsibility to expose Iraqis to multiple ethnosectarian identities and train them to develop working relations with each other without acknowledging that Baghdad has been a cosmopolitan city where different ethnic, religious, and sectarian groups (e.g., Sunni, Shi'i, Christian, Arabs, and Kurds) lived together and intermarried for centuries. This kind of view is an indication of a narrow-minded perception of the sectarian civil war in Baghdad that broke out in 2006 as a result of the misguided politics of the United States. Relating the sectarian violence to the so-called enmities-to-be-reconciled among the Iraqis, as if they were always inherently planted within Iraqi society, is politically motivated and diverts the attention of the international public from the responsibilities of the foreigners in creating the circumstances mainly responsible for the radical politicization of sectarian identities and militarization of the sectarian divisions in Baghdad and in Iraq as a whole after 2003.[60]

International as well as Iraqi feminists have accused the United States several times of trading women's rights for cooperation from the Islamists; and that kind of collaboration with the United States has strengthened the leverage of the Sunni and Shi'i Islamist groups in Iraq.[61] The increasing popularity of the Islamist discourses even within the previously secular political formations has reinforced patriarchy. Both men and women have been subjugated within the complex pyramid of patriarchy, constantly redefined with the introduction of new power relations and power actors into Iraqi society and politics under war circumstances.[62] In the same vein, ethnic, sectarian, and tribal identities have been redefined, reinforced, and institutionalized with the help of the muhassasa system of ethnosectarian power sharing in which there are given quotas for representation of ethnic and sectarian groups in the government. As Fanar Haddad notes, "Today's sectarian tensions are the manifestation of a system that enshrined sectarian identity as a core component of its DNA, thereby elevating sectarian identity, and with it, extant sectarian animosities to prominence. To put it simply, every political system has to have winners and losers but when the system is based on sectarian divisions, political loss and gain will be significantly linked to sectarian identity thereby perpetuating its politicisation."[63] Other forms of political organizations crosscutting ethnic and sectarian identities would have channeled Iraqi demands and grievances associated with social injustices before and after the Ba'ath regime toward political decision making and state-building processes. Large sectors of Iraqi society in poverty and insecurity have been marginalized by the internationally planned projects and internationally financed NGO work, and thereby have been co-opted by the emerging conservative and sectarian groups, organizations, and parties with strong grassroots ties.

The restructuring of Iraqi civil society into NGOs trained by foreigners based on supposedly antagonistic ethnic and sectarian identities has already inhibited the emergence of alternative forms of civil organizing and alternative ways of addressing social, economic, and political concerns crosscutting cultural identities. There are currently about 2,000 NGOs in Baghdad and 1,000 in Erbil that fall under the jurisdiction of the new NGO law. Syndicates and trade unions fall under the jurisdiction of a law going back to the Ba'ath era that restricts their scope of activity severely and bans collective bargaining. Within a few months of the invasion, there were three general labor strikes in Basra. One of the first actions of the CPA was to "announce it would enforce a 1987 law banning unions in public enterprises, where most Iraqis [were] employed. Bremer also added Order 1, banning pronouncements that 'incite civil disorder, rioting or damage to property.' The phrase 'civil disorder' encompasses organizing strikes. It has resulted in the detention of leaders of the Iraqi Federation of Trade Unions and the Iraqi Union of the Unemployed by U.S. authorities several times."[64]

UNOPS argues that issues of labor unions and syndicates are within the mandate of the International Labor Organization (ILO), but ILO has done virtually nothing in terms of legal and institutional reforms to protect the labor rights of working-class and professional Iraqis employed in industries dominated by foreigners since the occupation. The ILO and the other relevant international organizations may be hesitant to support the Iraqi labor grievances in order to not undermine the status of South Asian guest workers and European expats in Iraq. Alternatively, the neoliberal mentality of entrepreneurship embedded in the structures, visions, missions, and functioning of these organizations has very little tolerance for labor rights issues. International actors have been unable or unwilling to defend the labor and other interests of the Iraqis because of the discrepancy between the norms, priorities, and agendas of international actors and the interests of the people suffering on the ground.

Iraq is today a devastated country with insecurity, population displacement, unemployment, and lack of basic services (e.g., electricity, sewage, medicine, schools). Ironically, Iraq is one of the richest countries in the world in terms of natural resources. Before the invasion, it managed to establish modern infrastructure, quality universities, hospitals in the Arab Middle East, advanced industries, and a full-fledged welfare state during the 1970s and 1980s due to enormous oil revenues and the commitment of the repressive Ba'ath regime to economic development and co-optation of dissent.[65] It may be anachronistic to try to replicate the developmentalist state of the 1970s and 1980s in the twenty-first century Iraq. Indeed, a more sophisticated state initiative must be undertaken to heal the wounds of injustices done to Iraqis before and after the fall of the Ba'ath regime and to address the current social collapse. In a war-affected country that has been crushed to smithereens by drone attacks and machine guns and looted by foreign contractors for more than a decade now, most Iraqis do not have homes anymore or safety on the streets and are unable to find jobs, send children to school, and take care of the sick and disabled members of their families.[66] Patchwork initiatives of the UN and foreign governments to train Iraqis on how to set up NGOs is not enough to organize Iraqi civil society to voice the human tragedy and ongoing humanitarian crisis; to make demands in the name of the poor, unemployed, displaced, and homeless victims of the war(s); and to seek social and criminal justice for the survivors and the next generations of Iraqis.

The Curious Case of Iraqi Kurdistan: Parallel State Building

Iraqi Kurdistan has been considered a safe haven and an exceptional economic success story in the era of military neoliberalism in Iraq. Security, according to many Kurds, is the most important asset of Iraqi Kurdistan, before its rich oil resources.[67] Since 2003, the Kurdish Regional Government has promoted Iraqi Kurdistan for business and tourism using the motto: "the other Iraq." The Kurdistan region of Iraq already had de facto autonomy throughout the 1990s as a result of Operation Provide Comfort, launched by the United States on the grounds of protecting the Kurds from the atrocities of Saddam Hussein and facilitating the safe return of the Kurdish refugees to the region. Initial international efforts at state building and institutional reconstruction through international humanitarian intervention in 1991 helped the Kurdish leadership in northern Iraq consolidate a two-party regime and preclude the possibility of being an integral part of a united Iraq after the fall of the Ba'ath regime. The establishment of Kurdish autonomy in northern Iraq in 1991 was the first major US-led international action to institutionalize the separation of Kurdish Iraq from Arab Iraq. As a UN representative noted, a completely separate process of legal reform and institutional restructuring has been taking place in Erbil under the supervision of the international community since 1991.[68]

Despite the semblance of normality, Iraqi Kurdistan remains in despair. There was a civil war between the Kurdistan Democratic Party (KDP) led by Mesud Barzani and the Patriotic Union of Kurdistan (PUK) of Jalal Talabani during most of the 1990s. When Barzani asked Saddam Hussein for help defeating the PUK in 1996, this act of treachery traumatized the Iraqi Kurds and left a painful wound in their national memory that has never healed and keeps reminding Kurds of the bloody history of political competition among the Kurdish parties in Iraqi Kurdistan. There was virtually no hope for peace in Kurdistan until 2003, when American military officers, diplomats, and advisors convinced the KDP and PUK to put aside the past and cooperate to exploit the economic potential in their region and work together toward independence.

The United States' role in protecting the rights of the victims of Saddam Hussein in Iraq has been inconsistent. In contrast to American support for the Kurds, the United States helped Saddam Hussein crush the 1991 Shi'i uprising in southern Iraq. The Kurds of Iraq have been favored by the United States, while the Shi'is of Iraq have been associated with Iran, treated less favorably, and even brutalized in 1991 and 2003. Shi'i Iraqis were glad that Saddam Hussein was finally removed, but they never welcomed the presence of the Americans, as most evident in the Shi'i rebellions against the United States occupation of Iraq. Many Kurds, on the other hand, refer to the 2003 invasion of Iraq as their liberation. The conditional humanitarian aid and limited infrastructure building in Kurdistan during the 1990s was transformed into a more assertive capacity building and institutional restructuring under American supervision in 2003.

As opposed to what happened to the central state in 2003, the earlier institutions in Iraqi Kurdistan and the Kurdish armed forces, peshmerga, have been kept intact and reformed according to the standards and expectations of the United States and the UN. Erbil, the Kurdish capital, has been helped to secure economic and political concessions from Baghdad, and the Kurdish leadership has been made to believe in the likelihood that a safe haven for business in Iraqi Kurdistan could be created, while the rest of the country was in chaos and bloodshed. The leadership of the Kurdish Regional Government, whose autonomy was officially recognized in 2005 by the Iraqi central government, has cooperated with the foreign governments, UN, and oil companies to do business with the rest of the world and gain international sympathy for the Kurdish aspiration to completely secede from Iraq. However, the KDP and PUK have continued to have separate peshmerga forces, which indicates a lack of trust between the two militant Kurdish parties controlling Iraqi Kurdistan and shows that they may be running a two-party government in northern Iraq but are far away from the idea of a unified state apparatus above parties.

The emergence of Islamic State in Syria and the Levant (ISIL) has also presented a golden opportunity for the Kurds to advance their secession goal. During my field research in Erbil, I heard numerous accounts that Arab Iraqis are discouraged from staying in territories whose ownership is disputed between the central government in Baghdad and the regional government in Erbil and instead encouraged to move to Erbil and other key Kurdish cities to dilute the Arab population in disputed areas.[69] This salient population relocation is seen as part of the Kurdish policy to increase the concentration of the Kurds in the disputed territories and dislocate Arabs to the major Kurdish cities where they would become a minority.[70] ISIL's military advances in Iraq have recently made it very convenient for Kurdish peshmerga forces to take over disputed territories on security grounds. The Kurdish Regional Government currently controls large swaths of the disputed territories. Moreover, there are indications that the Kurdish Regional Government plans to hold referendums in those areas without consulting with the central government in Baghdad.[71] The Kurdish Regional Government sees the Iraqi state as a failed state with no legitimacy. With a weak

Iraqi army and an ineffective government in Baghdad, it is easier now for Kurdish leadership to push for more authority and direct control over the territories and the resources (oil, gas, pipelines, etc.) it claims as part of Kurdistan.

Iraqi Kurdistan has been rebuilding itself and getting incorporated into international markets, consumption culture, and global capitalism since 2003. There are increasing numbers of shopping malls with stores carrying international brands and parking lots full of luxurious automobiles in Erbil. Indians and Bangladeshis on construction sites are transforming the facade of the city, building neighborhoods and structures that give visitors an impression that they are in the United Arab Emirates instead of Iraq. University students and young people sitting, chatting, and texting on their smart phones in well-decorated cozy cafes in Erbil and Sulaymaniyah look like they have already moved on to a new world independent from the past and have nothing to do with the rest of their troubled country, while children from Arab Iraq and Syria work and beg on the streets. These are some of the many faces of Iraqi Kurdistan passing through a radical social, economic, and political transformation trapped in a troubled region.

As the two dominant Kurdish political parties have been forced into an uneasy collaboration to convince the international community of the possibility of an independent democratic Kurdistan with safe and open markets, the extremely unequal distribution of economic resources among the social classes has introduced new dynamics of oppression and resentment. Competition for rent disturbs the already torn social fabric of the Kurdistani society that is quite mixed in terms of tribal, ideological, ethnic, and sectarian identities. Iraqi Kurds are frustrated as much with the two-party domination, corruption, censorship, and repression as with the increasing number of desperate displaced people and refugees from Iraq and Syria. Kurdish leadership has a reputation of being militarized, authoritarian, and corrupt. Erbil, the capital of Kurdistan, houses disturbing contrasts in which there are refugee children begging on the streets, their families living in precarious shelters in and outside the city center, while the privileged minority, including the wealthy Kurds, foreigners, and expatriates, drive luxurious cars, dine in five-star hotels protected by private security guards, and indulge themselves in extravagant spending at Western-style shopping malls.

Socially marginalized natives of Iraqi Kurdistan looking for jobs and asking for their share of the economic opportunities available only to a selected group of a privileged minority feel frustrated to the extent that protests targeting guest workers, their employers, and the Kurdish Regional Government take place quite often and are repressed by police violence and threats. Locals often block roads in the industrial towns to protests against the Kurdish Regional Government and foreign companies for preferring to hire workers from India and Bangladesh. The confusion about what to do with Syrian refugees, internally displaced Arabs from the rest of Iraq, and the well-off professional expatriates from Western countries has also been superimposed on Iraqi Kurdistan, articulating further socioeconomic complications for the region. As the Kurdish leadership in the Kurdish Regional Government is trying to push forward a politically motivated agenda in the disputed territories of Iraq, capitalizing on the war circumstances, they are now facing more social, economic, and political challenges within and outside Iraqi Kurdistan.

Conclusions

Recently, Iraq has been under the attack of an uncontrolled militant organization, namely ISIL. In November 2014, President Barack Obama stated, "What we learned from previous engagement in Iraq is that our military is always the best, we can always knock out any threat, but then when we leave that threat comes back."[72] However, it is important to note that there was no Islamist terrorist organization in Iraq before 2003 with the exception of Iraqi Kurdistan, where Americans had interfered in 1991 to create a no-fly zone and inadvertently opened space for Al-Qaeda to organize comfortably away from Saddam Hussein's intolerance toward Islamist radicalism. Numerous reports from various organizations and news outlets have amply documented the political and humanitarian crises resulting from widespread violence targeting civilians in Iraq and Syria in the form of terrorism warfare. Middle Eastern history shows that violence cannot be neatly contained within national borders. Violence kills people, breaks families, spreads fear and hatred, divides communities, and displaces the survivors. Violence capitalizes on fears, insecurities, and marginalization of people and produces wicked circumstances for economic and ideological exploitation that perpetuate violence. Violence is also fueled by the global war industry, which according to investigative journalist Jeremy Scahill is "making a killing off of the killing" in Iraq.[73]

In his groundbreaking world-system analysis of the state failure and ethnic and religious violence in the Caucasus at the end of the Cold War, Derluguian warns us not to expect "an organized class politics" from the dispossessed masses in the world's periphery. Operating under circumstances of uncontrolled market globalization, weak state authority, and privatization of economic activities outside the institutional and legal control of the state, those dispossessed masses are likely to engage "in forms of protest and protection that are classified in today's political discourse as ethnic violence, illicit trafficking, the informal economy, religious fundamentalism, crime, crowd rage, or terrorism. In the coming decades we will no doubt see many different attempts to deal with this rising peripheral disorder. They will be pursued by national governments, capitalist multinational groups, international social movements, and perhaps other actors whom we can barely imagine today."[74] Derluguian's words resonate well with the ongoing War on Terror and terrorism warfare in Iraq and beyond.

The initial goal of the United States administration in 2003 in rhetoric was to rebuild the Iraqi state into a model liberal democratic state for the rest of the Middle East. The current situation in Iraq and the region at large is opposite of what has been promised to the international public as well as Iraqis. The scholarship on Iraq should take a critical stance to dismantle the tendency of simplistic blame placed on sectarianism, religious fundamentalism, terrorism warfare, and the stereotypical violent nature of Arab society. There is ample evidence in the social science literature that points to structural circumstances associated with neoliberalism, market globalization, military intervention, and institutional collapse for state failure in Iraq and the growing political violence against civilians in the Middle East.

Notes

1. Moore, *Social Origins of Dictatorship and Democracy*; Skocpol, *States and Social Revolutions*; Flora, Kuhnle, and Urwin, *State Formation, Nation-Building, and Mass Politics in Europe*; Tilly, *Coercion, Capital, and European States*; Tilly, *European Revolutions*.
2. See for example, Charrad, *States and Women's Rights*.
3. Tripp, *A History of Iraq*; Fisk, *The Great War for Civilisation*; Said, *Imperial Continuity*.
4. Danforth, "Stop Blaming Colonial Borders for the Middle East's Problems." For Iraq see Hadid, *Iraq's Democratic Moment*.
5. Polk, *Understanding Iraq*; Tripp, *A History of Iraq*; Marr, *The Modern History of Iraq*; Hadid, *Iraq's Democratic Moment*.
6. Polk, *Understanding Iraq*; Tripp, *A History of Iraq*; Marr, *The Modern History of Iraq*.
7. Polk, *Understanding Iraq*.
8. Alexander, "The Paris Club, the Washington Consensus and the Baghdad Cake," 32.
9. Dodge, "Iraqi Transitions," 705–721; Dodge, "Iraq," 187–200; Dodge, "Coming Face to Face with Bloody Reality," 253–275; Dodge, "State and Society in Iraq Ten Years after Regime Change," 241–257.
10. Dodge, "Coming Face to Face with Bloody Reality"; Dodge, "State and Society in Iraq Ten Years after Regime Change."
11. Anderson and Stansfield, *The Future of Iraq*.
12. Derluguian, *Bourdieu's Secret Admirer in the Caucasus*, 317.
13. Ibid., 318.
14. Ibid., 16.
15. Ibid., 41.
16. O'Donnell, *On the State, Democratization and Some Conceptual Problems*.
17. Medani, "State Building in Reverse," 35.
18. Ibid.
19. To protect privacy of the key informants, pseudonyms are used instead of the real names of the individuals. A random capital letter has been assigned as surname for each pseudonym.
20. Pison-Hindawi, *Vingt ans dans l'ombre du Chapitre VII*.

21. United States National Security Council, "The National Security Strategy of the United States of America."

22. Dodge, "Iraqi Transitions: From Regime Change to State Collapse," 706.

23. Agathangelou, "Bodies of Desire, Terror and the War in Eurasia," 718n124.

24. Dodge, "Iraqi Transitions," 707.

25. Tripp, *A History of Iraq*.

26. Brown, "American Nightmare," 694.

27. Agathangelou, "Bodies of Desire, Terror and the War in Eurasia," 707.

28. Tripp, *A History of Iraq*, 547.

29. Ibid.

30. Toal, "A Conversation with Peter Galbraith about Iraq and State Building," 175.

31. Dodge, "Iraqi Transitions."

32. Medani, "State Building in Reverse."

33. Cockburn, "Iraq's 50,000 'Ghost Soldiers' Analysis."

34. Al-Ali and Pratt, *What Kind of Liberation?* 72–75.

35. Ibid., 85.

36. Zangana, "Colonial Feminists from Washington to Baghdad"; Zangana, "The Three Cyclops of Empire Building"; Medani, *State Building in Reverse*.

37. For interviews with the U.S. policy makers, UN representatives, and Iraqis about the legality and legitimacy of the UN-sanctioned international embargo on Iraq in the 1990s, see Pilger, *Paying the Price*.

38. United Nations Office of the Coordination of Humanitarian Affairs, "Iraq Strategic Response Plan."

39. Krajeski and Meyer, *From "the Other Iraq" to Kurdistan*.

40. Al-Ali, *What Kind of Liberation?*, 85.

41. Campbell, "A True Iraqi," 330.

42. Al Rawi, "The US Influence in Shaping Iraq's Sectarian Media," 374–391.

43. Interview: Cihan K. (pseudonym), journalist, Iraq, May 28, 2014.

44. Polk, *Understanding Iraq*.

45. Ibid., 183.

46. Tripp, "The United States and State-Building in Iraq," 548.

47. Al Rawi, "The US Influence in Shaping Iraq's Sectarian Media," 375.

48. Ibid., 383.

49. Ibid.

50. Relly, Zanger, and Fahmy, "News Media Landscape in a Fragile State," 473.

51. Al-Ali, *What Kind of Liberation?* 60; Zangana, "Colonial Feminists from Washington to Baghdad"; Zangana," The Three Cyclops of Empire Building"; Mojab, "Women's NGOs under Conditions of Occupation and War."

52. Al-Ali, *What Kind of Liberation?* 67.

53. Interview: Farah S. (pseudonym), UNDP employee, Iraq, May 29, 2014.

54. Medani, "State Building in Reverse," 31.

55. United Nations American Mothers Incorporated, *Mandate*.

56. Wittes, *The New U.S. Proposal for a Greater Middle East Initiative*; Ottaway and Carothers, *The Greater Middle East Initiative*.

57. Interview: Adam B. (pseudonym), UNOPS employee, Iraq, May 29, 2014; interview: Hawar D. (pseudonym), former MP, Iraq, May 26, 2014.

58. United Nations Iraq, *New Cooperation Policy between Public Authorities and NGOs Adopted in Kurdistan Region of Iraq*.

59. Interview: Adam B. (pseudonym), UNOPS employee, Iraq, May 29, 2014.

60. Ismael and Ismael, "Whither Iraq?," 609–629; Zangana, "Wailing in Iraq," 41–58.
61. Susskind, "Promising Democracy, Imposing Theocracy."
62. Jones, "Humiliation and Masculine Crisis in Iraq," 70–73.
63. Haddad, "Iraq in 2012."
64. Medani, "State Building in Reverse," 30.
65. Tripp, *A History of Iraq*; Marr, *The Modern History of Iraq*.
66. United Nations Office of the Coordination of Humanitarian Affairs, "Iraq Strategic Response Plan."
67. Gökalp, *The New War in Iraq*; Gökalp, "Institutional Restructuring, Social Change and Gender in Iraqi Kurdistan."
68. Interview: Adam B. (pseudonym), UNOPS employee, Iraq, May 29, 2014.
69. Gökalp, *The New War in Iraq*; Gökalp, "Institutional Restructuring."
70. Krajeski, "From 'the Other Iraq' to Kurdistan"; Krajeski and Meyer, "ISIS Tests Kurdish Bid for Independence."
71. Hussein and Bakir, "Iraq's Crisis and the KRG."
72. Roberts, "Obama Confident US Troop Surge in Iraq Will Put Coalition on Offensive."
73. Scahill, "We Created the Very Threat that We Claim to Be Fighting."
74. Derluguian, *Bourdieu's Secret Admirer in the Caucasus*, 322.

References

Agathangelou, Anna M. "Bodies of Desire, Terror and the War in Eurasia: Impolite Disruptions of (Neo)Liberal Internationalism, Neoconservatism and the 'New' Imperium." *Millennium: Journal of International Studies* 38, no. 3 (2010): 693–722.

Al-Ali, Nadje, and Nicola Pratt. *What Kind of Liberation? Women and the Occupation of Iraq*. Berkley: University of California Press, 2009.

Alexander, Justin. "The Paris Club, the Washington Consensus and the Baghdad Cake." *Middle East Report* 232 (2004): 32–33.

Al Rawi, Ahmed K. "The US Influence in Shaping Iraq's Sectarian Media." *International Communication Gazette* 75, no. 4 (2013): 374–391.

Anderson, Liam, and Stansfield, Gareth. *The Future of Iraq: Dictatorship, Democracy or Division*. New York: Palgrave Macmillan, 2004.

Brown, Wendy. "American Nightmare: Neoliberalism, Neoconservatism and De-Democratization." *Political Theory* 34, no. 6 (2006): 690–714.

Bush, George W. Full text: George Bush's speech to the American Enterprise Institute. *Guardian*, February 27, 2003. www.theguardian.com/world/2003/feb/27/usa.iraq2.

Campbell, Perri. "'A True Iraqi': Blogging from the Green Zone in Postinvasion Iraq." *International Journal of Contemporary Iraqi Studies* 6, no. 3 (2012): 327–340.

Charrad, Mounira. *States and Women's Rights: The Making of Postcolonial Tunisia, Algeria and Morocco*. Berkeley: University of California Press, 2001.

Cockburn, Patrick. "Iraq's 50,000 'Ghost Soldiers' Analysis: This Is Further Proof of Army Corruption." *Independent*, December 1, 2014. http://www.independent.co.uk/news/world/americas/iraqs-50000-ghost-soldiersanalysis-this-is-further-proof-of-army-corruption-9896611.html.

Danforth, Nick. "Stop Blaming Colonial Borders for the Middle East's Problems." *Atlantic*, September 11, 2013. http://www.theatlantic.com/international/archive/2013/09/stop-blaming-colonial-borders-for-the-middle-easts-problems/279561/2/.

Derluguian, Georgi M. *Bourdieu's Secret Admirer in the Caucasus: A World-System Biography.* Chicago: University of Chicago Press, 2005.

Dodge, Toby. "Coming Face to Face with Bloody Reality: Liberal Common Sense and the Ideological Failure of the Bush Doctrine in Iraq." *International Politics* 46, no. 2/3 (2009): 253–275.

———. "Iraq: The Contradictions of Exogenous State-Building in Historical Perspective." *Third World Quarterly* 27, no. 1 (2006): 187–200.

———. "Iraqi Transitions: From Regime Change to State Collapse." *Third World Quarterly* 26, no. 4–5 (2005): 705–721.

———. "State and Society in Iraq Ten Years after Regime Change: The Rise of a New Authoritarianism." *International Affairs* 89, no. 2 (2013): 241–257.

Fisk, Robert. *The Great War for Civilisation: The Conquest of the Middle East.* London: Harper Perennial, 2006.

Flora, Peter, Stein Kuhnle, and Derek Urwin, eds. *State Formation, Nation-Building, and Mass Politics in Europe: The Theory of Stein Rokkan Based on His Collected Works.* Oxford: Oxford University Press, 1999.

Gökalp, Deniz. "Institutional Restructuring, Social Change and Gender in Iraqi Kurdistan: Notes from the Field." *Middle East Center Blog*, London School of Economics, June 27, 2014. http://blogs.lse.ac.uk/mec/2014/06/27/institutional-restructuring-social-change-and-gender-in-iraqi-kurdistan-notes-from-the-field/.

———. "The New War in Iraq: No Safe Place for the Arabs and the Kurds." *Allegra: A Virtual Lab of Legal Anthropology*, October 22, 2014. http://allegralaboratory.net/the-new-war-in-iraq-no-place-safe-for-the-arabs-and-the-kurds-kurdistan-and-the-kurdish-diaspora.

Haddad, Fanar. "Iraq in 2012." *Hurst*, January 12, 2012. http://www.hurstpublishers.com/iraq-in-2012.

Hadid, Foulath. *Iraq's Democratic Moment.* London: C. Hurst & Company, 2012.

Hussein, Fuad, and Falah Mustafa Bakir. "Iraq's Crisis and the KRG." *Policy Watch* 2282, Washington Institute, July 11, 2014. http://www.washingtoninstitute.org/policy-analysis/view/iraqs-crisis-and-the-krg.

Ismael, Tareq Y., and Jacqueline S. Ismael. "Whither Iraq? Beyond Saddam, Sanctions and Occupation." *Third World Quarterly* 26, no. 4–5 (2005): 609–629.

Jones, Adam. "Humiliation and Masculine Crisis in Iraq." *Al-Raida* 21, no. 104–105 (2004): 70–73.

Katz, William Loren. "A Time to Look over President Wilson's Shoulder." January 28, 2006. http://williamlkatz.com/president-wilson-shoulder.

Krajeski, Jenna, and Sebastian Meyer. "From 'the Other Iraq' to Kurdistan." *Pulitzer Center on Crisis Reporting*, May 2, 2014. http://pulitzercenter.org/projects/middle-east-iraq-fallujah-kurdistan-al-qaeda-civil-unrest.

———. "ISIS Tests Kurdish Bid for Independence." *Pulitzer Center on Crisis Reporting*, September 30, 2014. http://pulitzercenter.org/reporting/middle-east-iraq-kurdistan-peshmerga-isis-independence.

Marr, Phebe. *The Modern History of Iraq.* Boulder, CO: Westview Press, 2012.

Medani, Khalid Mustafa. "State Building in Reverse: The Neo-Liberal 'Reconstruction' of Iraq." *Middle East Report* 232 (2004): 28–35.

Mojab, Shahrzad. "Women's NGOs under Conditions of Occupation and War." *Against the Current*, July–August 2007. http://www.solidarity-us.org/node/576.

Moore, Barrington Jr. *Social Origins of Dictatorship and Democracy: Lord and Peasant in the Making of the Modern World.* Boston: Beacon Press, 1966.

O'Donnell, Guillermo. *On the State, Democratization and Some Conceptual Problems: A Latin American View with Glances at Some Post-Communist Countries.* Working paper #192.

Kellogg Institute, April 1993. http://www.nd.edu/~kellogg/publications/workingpapers /WPS/192.pdf.

Ottaway, Marina, and Carothers, Thomas. *The Greater Middle East Initiative: Off to a False Start.* Carnegie Endowment Policy Brief. May 29, 2004. http://carnegieendowment.org/files /policybrief29.pdf.

Pilger, John. *Paying the Price: Killing the Children of Iraq.* 2000. http://johnpilger.com/videos /paying-the-price-killing-the-children-of-iraq.

Pison-Hindawi, Coralie. *Vingt ans dans l'ombre du Chapitre VII. Eclairage sur deux décennies de Coercition à l'encontre de l'Iraq (Twenty Years in the Shadow of Chapter VII).* Paris: L'Harmattan, 2013.

Polk, William R. *Understanding Iraq.* London: Harper Perennial, 2006.

Relly, Jeannine E., Margaret Zanger, and Shahira Fahmy. "News Media Landscape in a Fragile State: Professional Ethics Perceptions in a Post-Ba'athist Iraq." *Mass Communication and Society* 18, no. 4 (2015): 471–497.

Roberts, Dan. "Obama Confident US Troop Surge in Iraq Will Put Coalition on Offensive." *Guardian*, November 9, 2014. http://www.theguardian.com/world/2014/nov/09/obama-troops -iraq-coalition-isis.

Said, Edward. *Imperial Continuity—Palestine, Iraq, and US Policy.* Walker-Ames Lecture Series, University of Washington, May 8, 2003. http://www.israeli-occupation.org/2003-05-08 /edward-said-imperial-continuity-palestine-iraq-and-us-policy/#sthash.g563KRTR.dpuf.

Scahill, Jeremy. "We Created the Very Threat That We Claim to be Fighting." *Democracy Now*, March 10, 2014. http://www.democracynow.org/2014/10/3/jeremy_scahill_on_obamas _orwellian_war.

Skocpol, Theda. *States and Social Revolutions.* Cambridge: Cambridge University Press, 1979.

Susskind, Yifat. "Promising Democracy, Imposing Theocracy: Gender-Based Violence and the US War on Iraq." Madre, New York: March 6, 2007. http://www.peacewomen.org/assets/file /vaw_promisingdemocracyimposingtheocracy_madre_march2008.pdf.

Tilly, Charles. *Coercion, Capital, and European States, AD 990–1992.* Oxford: Blackwell, 1992.

———. *European Revolutions, 1492–1992.* Oxford: Blackwell, 1993.

Toal, Gerard. "A Conversation with Peter Galbraith about Iraq and State Building." *Geopolitics* 10 (2005): 167–183.

Tripp, Charles. *A History of Iraq.* Cambridge: Cambridge University Press, 2007.

———. "The United States and State-Building in Iraq." *Review of International Studies* 30 (2004): 545–558.

United Nations American Mothers Incorporated. *Mandate.* http://unami.unmissions.org/Default .aspx?tabid=2832&language=en-US.

United Nations Iraq. *New Cooperation Policy between Public Authorities and NGOs Adopted in Kurdistan Region of Iraq.* September 4, 2013. http://www.uniraq.org/index.php?option =com_k2&view=item&id=1117:new-cooperation-policy-between-public-authorities-and -ngos-adopted-in-kurdistan-region-of-iraq&Itemid=605&lang=en.

United Nations Office of the Coordination of Humanitarian Affairs. "Iraq Strategic Response Plan." 2014/2015. https://docs.unocha.org/sites/dms/CAP/SRP_2014-2015_Iraq_Revision .pdf.

United States National Security Council. "The National Security Strategy of the United States of America." 2002. http://www.state.gov/documents/organization/63562.pdf.

Wittes, Tamara Cofman. "The New U.S. Proposal for a Greater Middle East Initiative: An Evaluation." *Middle East Memo Series* 2 of 33. Saban Center for Middle East Policy at the Brookings

Institution, May 10, 2004. http://www.brookings.edu/research/papers/2004/05/10middleeast-wittes.

Zangana, Haifa. "Colonial Feminists from Washington to Baghdad: 'Women for a Free Iraq' as a Case Study." In *Barriers to Reconciliation: Case Studies on Iraq and the Palestine-Israel Conflict*, edited by J. Ismael and W. Haddad, 63–84. Lanham, MD: University Press of America, 2006.

———. "The Three Cyclops of Empire Building: Targeting the Fabric of Iraqi Society." In *Empire's Law: The American Imperial Project and the War to Remake the World*, edited by Amy Bartholomew. London: Pluto Press, 2006.

Zangana, Haifa. "Wailing in Iraq: The Impact on Baghdadi Women." *International Journal of Contemporary Iraqi Studies.* 4, no. 1 and 2 (2010): 41–58.

About the Contributors

Dauda Abubakar is Associate Professor of political science and African studies at University of Michigan-Flint. He taught for several years at University of Maiduguri, Nigeria, where he was the chair of the Political Science Department. He has published numerous scholarly articles in peer-reviewed journals and book chapters. His most recent work, *Violent Non-State Actors in Africa*, is forthcoming.

Eva van Baarle is Assistant Professor of military ethics and philosophy at the Netherlands Defense Academy. She is currently conducting doctoral research on the effects of education on moral competency. Some of her works have been published in the *Journal of Moral Education* and the *Journal for Military Ethics*.

Abu Bakarr Bah is Associate Professor of sociology at Northern Illinois University and editor-in-chief of *African Conflict and Peacebuilding Review*. He is also the author of *Breakdown and Reconstitution: Democracy, the Nation-State, and Ethnicity in Nigeria* and is a 2014 and 2016 Carnegie Foundation African Diaspora Fellow. His most recent works have been published in journals such as *Critical Sociology, African Affairs, Journal of International Peacekeeping, African Today*, and *International Journal of Politics, Culture and Society*.

Ufuk Basar (DBA candidate, MSc, Ret. Capt., Baskent University) is a doctoral student in business administration at Baskent University in Turkey. His areas of research have been focused on management, strategy, organizational behavior and leadership. Some of his works have been published in *The Korean Journal of Defense Analysis, Educational Sciences: Theory & Practice*, and *Journal of Advanced Nursing*.

Deniz Gökalp is Assistant Professor of social sciences at the American University in Dubai. She obtained her PhD in sociology from the University of Texas at Austin. She was also a postdoctoral research fellow in the Middle Eastern Studies Program at the Moynihan Institute of Global Affairs at Syracuse University in New York. She has published at *The Middle East Journal* and *Women's Studies International Forum*.

Rebecca Gulowski is a lecturer at the UNESCO Chair for Peace Studies at the University of Innsbruck, Austria, and a research associate at the Department of

Peace and Conflict Studies, Faculty of Political Science, at the University of Augsburg, Germany. Her research focuses on the sociology of violence, particularly with respect to contemporary warfare and civil wars, transnational conflicts, and social conflict dynamics.

Amy Niang is Assistant Professor in international relations at the University of the Witwatersrand in Johannesburg and a visiting research fellow at the Princeton Institute for International and Regional Studies (PIIRS). Her research is a theoretical investigation into notions of statehood, sovereignty, order, and community and an empirical and historical investigation in state and social processes in the West African region, particularly in the Sahel. Some of her works have been published in *Alternatives: Global, Local, Political*; *African Economic History*; *Politics*; and *Afrique Contemporaine*.

Michelle Schut conducted her doctoral research at Radboud University Nijmegen and the Netherlands Defence Academy. The title of her dissertation is *Soldiers as Strangers: Morally and Culturally Critical Situations during Military Missions*. Some of her works have been published in *Armed Forces & Society*.

Unsal Sigri (PhD, MSc, MA, Ret. Col., Baskent University) is Professor of management at Baskent University, Ankara, Turkey. He has also been working as a lecturer at the Turkish Military Academy since 1998. His areas of research include management, leadership, group dynamics, and conflict resolution. Some of his works have been published in *Educational Sciences: Theory & Practice*, *The Korean Journal of Defense Analysis, and International Peacekeeping*.

M. Abdulkadir Varoglu (DBA, MSc, Ret. Col., Baskent University) is Professor of management at Baskent University, Ankara, Turkey. His research interests include international peacekeeping operations, military sociology, military education, and management and organizational studies.

Index

www.ingramcontent.com/pod-product-compliance
Lightning Source LLC
Chambersburg PA
CBHW020352270326
41926CB00007B/397